M000164033

WOMEN AND AGEING IN BRITISH SOCIETY SINCE 1500

WOMEN AND MEN IN HISTORY

This series, published for students, scholars and interested general readers, will tackle themes in gender history from the early medieval period through to the present day. Gender issues are now an integral part of all history courses and yet many traditional texts do not reflect this change. Much exciting work is now being done to redress the gender imbalances of the past, and we hope that these books will make their own substantial contribution to that process. We hope that these will both synthesize and shape future developments in gender studies.

The General Editors of the series are *Patricia Skinner* (University of Southampton) for the medieval period; *Pamela Sharpe* (University of Bristol) for the early modern period; and *Penny Summerfield* (University of Lancaster) for the modern period. *Margaret Walsh* (University of Nottingham) was the Founding Editor of the series.

Published books:

Imperial Women in Byzantium, 1025–1204: Power, Patronage and Ideology
Barbara Hill

Masculinity in Medieval Europe
D.M. Hadley (ed.)

Gender and Society in Renaissance Italy
Judith C. Brown and Robert C. Davis (eds)

Widowhood in Medieval and Early Modern Europe
Sandra Cavallo and Lyndan Warner (eds)

Gender, Church and State in Early Modern Germany: Essays by Merry E. Wiesner
Merry E. Wiesner

Manhood in Early Modern England: Honour, Sex and Marriage
Elizabeth W. Foyster

English Masculinities, 1600–1800
Tim Hitchcock and Michele Cohen (eds)

Disorderly Women in Eighteenth-Century London: Prostitution in the Metropolis, 1730–1830
Tony Henderson

Gender, Power and the Unitarians in England, 1760–1860
Ruth Watts

Practical Visionaries: Women, Education and Social Progress, 1790–1930
Mary Hilton and Pam Hirsch (eds)

Women and Work in Russia, 1880–1930: A Study in Continuity through Change
Jane McDermid and Anna Hillyar

More than Munitions: Women, Work and the Engineering Industries 1900–1950
Clare Wightman

Women in British Public Life, 1914–1950: Gender, Power and Social Policy
Helen Jones

The Family Story: Blood, Contract and Intimacy, 1830–1960
Leonore Davidoff, Megan Doolittle, Janet Fink and Katherine Holden

Women and the Second World War in France, 1939–1948: Choices and Constraints
Hanna Diamond

WOMEN AND AGEING IN BRITISH SOCIETY SINCE 1500

Edited by
LYNN BOTELHO *and* PAT THANE

Longman

An imprint of **Pearson Education**

Harlow, England · London · New York · Reading, Massachusetts · San Francisco ·
Toronto · Don Mills, Ontario · Sydney · Tokyo · Singapore · Hong Kong · Seoul
Taipei · Cape Town · Madrid · Mexico City · Amsterdam · Munich · Paris · Milan

Pearson Education Limited
Edinburgh Gate
Harlow
Essex CM20 2JE
England

and Associated Companies throughout the world

Visit us on the World Wide Web at:
http://www.pearsoneduc.com

First published 2001

© Pearson Education Limited 2001

All rights reserved; no part of this publication may be reproduced, stored
in a retrieval system, or transmitted in any form or by any means, electronic,
mechanical, photocopying, recording, or otherwise without either the prior
written permission of the Publishers or a licence permitting restricted copying
in the United Kingdom issued by the Copyright Licensing Agency Ltd,
90 Tottenham Court Road, London W1P 0LP.

ISBN 0 582 32901 9 (csd);   0 582 32902 7 (ppr)

British Library Cataloguing-in-Publication Data
A catalogue record for this book is available from the British Library

Library of Congress Cataloging-in-Publication Data
Women and ageing in British society since 1500 / edited by Lynn Botelho and Pat Thane.
        p.   cm.—(Women and men in history)
    Includes bibliographical references and index.
    ISBN 0–582–32901–9—ISBN 0–582–32902–7 (pbk.)
        1. Aged women—Great Britain—History.   2. Old age—Great Britain—History.   3.
    Aging—Social aspects—Great Britain—History.   I. Botelho, L. A. (Lynn A.)   II. Thane,
    Pat.   III. Series.

    HQ1064.G7W66   2000
    305.26'0941—dc21   00–057992

10 9 8 7 6 5 4 3 2 1
05 04 03 02 01

Typeset by 35 in 11/13pt Baskerville MT
Produced by Pearson Education Asia Pte Ltd.
Printed in Singapore

CONTENTS

List of Figures and Tables vii

List of Contributors ix

Acknowledgements xiii

Introduction
Lynn Botelho and Pat Thane 1

1. Strategies of poor aged women and widows in
sixteenth-century London
Claire S. Schen 13

2. Who most needs to marry? Ageing and inequality
among women and men in early modern Norwich
Margaret Pelling 31

3. Old age and menopause in rural women of
early modern Suffolk
Lynn Botelho 43

4. 'I feel myself decay apace': Old age in the diary of
Lady Sarah Cowper (1644–1720)
Anne Kugler 66

5. Old maids: the lifecycle of single women in
early modern England
Amy M. Froide 89

6. The old woman's home in eighteenth-century England
Susannah Ottaway 111

7. The residence patterns of elderly English women in
comparative perspective
Richard Wall 139

8. Old and incapable? Louisa Twining and elderly women
   in Victorian Britain
   Theresa Deane 166

9. 'An inheritance of fear': older women in the
   twentieth-century countryside
   Stephen Hussey 186

10. Old women in twentieth-century Britain
    Pat Thane 207

    Bibliographical essay: Older women in Britain since 1500
    Lynn Botelho and Pat Thane 232

    Index 239

LIST OF FIGURES AND TABLES

FIGURES

Figure 3.1   Female honorific titles in sixteenth- and seventeenth-century Cratfield, Suffolk   50

Figure 3.2   Male honorific titles in sixteenth- and seventeenth-century Cratfield, Suffolk   50

Figure 3.3   Title page of *Mother Shiptons Prophesie* (London, 1685)   57

Figure 6.1   Percentage of women heading a household   117

Figure 6.2   Late seventeenth- and early eighteenth-century urban IRS   128

Figure 6.3   Late eighteenth-century rural IRS   128

Figure 6.4   Early nineteenth-century rural IRS   129

Figure 6.5   Eighteenth-century IRS by class   130

TABLES

Table 6.1   Household heads in eighteenth-century parishes, aggregated by date and economic type   118

Table 6.2   Household position of individuals aged 60+ by period and type of parish   123

Table 6.3   Co-residents of women aged 60+, parishes aggregated by period and economic type   125

Table 7.1   Percentage of elderly persons living alone or with non-relatives only in England over four centuries   142

Table 7.2   Percentage of elderly persons living with spouse or child in England over four centuries   144

Table 7.3   Percentage of elderly persons living with never-married or ever-married child in England over four centuries   146

Table 7.4   Percentage of elderly persons living alone or with
             non-relatives only in rural and urban areas in
             western Europe, 17th C. to 19th C.   148–9

Table 7.5   Percentage of elderly persons living with spouse
             or child in rural and urban areas in western Europe,
             17th C. to 19th C.   150–1

Table 7.6   Percentage of elderly persons living with
             never-married or ever-married child in rural and
             urban areas in western Europe, 17th C. to 19th C.   152–3

Table 7.7   Relative number of elderly widowers and widows
             resident with a son or daughter   155–6

Table 7.8   Percentage of elderly males and females resident
             with a son or daughter, by occupational status   158

Table 9.1   Percentage of the aged population of England and
             Wales in poor law institutions, 1901–31   193

Table 10.1   Expectation of life at birth for generations born
             1841 to 1991, United Kingdom   208

Table 10.2   Ratio of females to males in elderly population,
             Great Britain, 1881–1981   208

Table 10.3   Percentage of population aged 65 and over,
             Great Britain, 1851–1991   209

Table 10.4   Percentage of elderly men and women reported
             as living alone, United Kingdom, 1684–1985   215

LYNN BOTELHO is assistant professor of history at Indiana University of Pennsylvania. She is editing (with Susannah Ottaway and Katharine Kittredge) *Aging in Pre-industrial Societies* (Westport, CT, forthcoming), and is the editor of *The Churchwardens' Accounts of Cratfield, Suffolk, during the 1640s and 1650s* (Bury St Edmunds, 1999). She also has published articles on issues of ageing in early modern England. She is currently completing a manuscript on provisions for the elderly in early modern England.

THERESA DEANE is a DPhil student at the University of Sussex where she is completing her thesis, 'The professionalisation of philanthropy: the case of Louisa Twining 1820–1912'. She has contributed to *Gender, Health and Welfare* (London, 1996, eds Anne Digby and John Stewart) and the *New Dictionary of National Biography* (Oxford, forthcoming). She is also a trained nurse and is experienced in caring for older people both in institutions and in the community.

AMY M. FROIDE is assistant professor of history at University of Tennessee at Chattanooga. She recently co-edited with Judith M. Bennett *Singlewomen in the European Past* (Philadelphia, 1998). Froide is currently a Rockefeller Foundation fellow in residence at the Newberry Library in Chicago where she is working on a manuscript entitled *Singlewomen and the Meanings of Singleness in Early Modern England*.

STEPHEN HUSSEY is Research Associate, School of Education, University of Cambridge. He has published articles on popular custom, women's agricultural employment, work and unemployment, and the use of oral history in television. He has also co-edited a collection of essays with Anthony Fletcher, *Childhood in Question: Children, Parents and the State* (Manchester, 1999). His current project is a book on the rural working-class household in the early twentieth century.

ANNE KUGLER is assistant professor of history at John Carroll University. She is the author of *'Errant Plagiary' and its Uses: The Writing Life and Social*

Milieu of Lady Sarah Cowper (1644–1720) (Stanford, CA, forthcoming). She is also editor of the diary of Lady Sarah Cowper and writes on women, religion and self-fashioning in the early eighteenth century.

SUSANNAH OTTAWAY is assistant professor of history at Carleton College. She is currently working on a book manuscript entitled 'The "decline of life": ageing in eighteenth-century England'. She is also editing (with Lynn A. Botelho and Katharine Kittredge) *Aging in Pre-industrial Societies* (Westport, CT, forthcoming). She has also published articles on issues related to the history of social welfare and the history of ageing in *Continuity and Change* and *Archives*.

MARGARET PELLING is a university research lecturer in the Modern History Faculty, University of Oxford. Her research interests focus on health, medicine and social conditions at and below the level of the 'middling sort' in early modern English towns. She has published a number of articles on women and old age, as well as co-editing with Richard Smith *Life, Death and the Elderly: Historical Perspectives* (London, 1991) and, with Hilary Marland, *The Task of Healing: Medicine, Religion and Gender in England and the Netherlands 1450–1800* (Rotterdam, 1996). Other work upon the aged appears in her recent volume of essays *The Common Lot: Sickness, Medical Occupations and the Urban Poor in Early Modern England* (London, 1998). She is currently completing a monograph on the College of Physicians of London and unlicensed practitioners, 1550–1640 (Basingstoke, forthcoming) which will include chapters on women patients and practitioners.

CLAIRE S. SCHEN is assistant professor of history at Wake Forest University in Winston-Salem, North Carolina. She is currently revising for publication her manuscript 'Charity and lay piety in Reformation London, 1500–1620'. Her essay, 'Women and the London parishes, 1500–1620', appeared in *The Parish in English Life 1400–1600* (Manchester, 1997, eds Katherine French, Gary Gibbs and Beat Kümin).

PAT THANE has been professor of contemporary history at the University of Sussex since 1994. Her main publications are: *The Foundations of the Welfare State* (London, 1982; 2nd edn 1996); *Women and Gender Policies: Women and the Rise of the European Welfare States* co-edited with Gisela Bock (London, 1990); *Old Age from Antiquity to Post-modernity* co-edited with Paul Johnson (LSE) (London, 1998); *Old Age in England: Past Experiences, Present Issues* (Oxford, 2000); *Labour's First Century: The Labour Party 1900–2000* co-edited with Duncan Tanner and Nick Tiratsoo (Cambridge, 2000). She has also published a number of articles on the history of welfare, of women and of Labour, mainly in twentieth-century Britain.

RICHARD WALL is an honorary senior research associate at the Cambridge Group for the History of Population and Social Structure. He has published extensively on the history of the family, charting the long-term evolution of household patterns in Europe from pre-industrial times to the present day. Major studies include *Household and Family in Past Time* (Cambridge, 1972, with Peter Laslett), *Family Forms in Historic Europe* (Cambridge, 1983, with Jay Winter), and *Poor Women and Children in the European Past* (London, 1994, with John Henderson). Richard Wall is also the co-founder and editor of *Continuity and Change*, a journal of the social structure, law and demography of past societies.

ACKNOWLEDGEMENTS

Lynn Botelho would like to thank the Indiana University of Pennsylvania and the Department of History for their support of this project, and the Huntington Library, San Marino, CA, for permission to reproduce the title page of *Mother Shiptons Prophesie* (London, 1685). Personal thanks belong to Irwin Marcus, Elizabeth Ricketts, A.H. Shissler and Tamara Whited.

Pat Thane wishes to thank the Director, Dorothy Sheridan, and the Trustees of the Mass Observation Archive, University of Sussex.

We are grateful to the following for permission to reproduce copyright material:

Figure 3.3, Title page of *Mother Shiptons Prophesie* (London, 1685), reproduced with permission of the Huntingdon Library, San Marino, CA, USA; Table 9.1, from David Thomson, 'Workhouse to nursing home: residential care of elderly people in England since 1840' *Ageing and Society* 3 (1983), p.49, reproduced with permission of Cambridge University Press; Tables 10.1, 10.2 and 10.4, from P. Johnson and J. Falkingham, *Ageing and Economic Welfare* (London, 1992), pp.23, 27 and 33 respectively, reproduced with permission of Sage Publications; Table 10.3, from Pat Thane, 'Old age: burden or benefit' in H. Joshi, ed., *The Changing Population of Britain* (Oxford, 1989), p.57, reproduced with permission of Blackwell Publishers.

Whilst every effort has been made to trace the owners of copyright material, in a few cases this has proved impossible and we take the opportunity to offer our apologies to any copyright holders whose rights we may have unwittingly infringed.

INTRODUCTION

LYNN BOTELHO AND PAT THANE

Few historical commonplaces are as resilient and persistent as those that address the subject of ageing and the nature of old age. For example, the notion that older people, in a not too distant past, received more respect from the young than they do at present is expressed as forcefully and repeatedly now as it was in 1500, and even earlier. Another 'truth' that has only recently been investigated is the belief that, once again in the not too distant past, older people, but particularly older women, lived out their final years in the homes of their adult children. Failing that, old women were believed to live alone, at the margins of society and on the edge of existence. This volume of essays seeks to explode these common stereotypes, and others like them, and to begin to demonstrate the rich and varied reality of five hundred years of female old age.

The historical interest in exploring the verity behind the image of old age is a relatively recent development. Traditionally, history was written about individuals who made an historical impact, those in the prime of life, those whose political decisions shaped the course of events. Elder statesmen who played such roles were not seen as old *per se*, but were viewed only through the prism of politics. The 1960s historiographical shift towards social history, and its increased respect for, and understanding of, the places of class, economics and gender in the shaping of the British past brought scant recognition to the role and place of old age. The elderly were still viewed, if at all, as a homogeneous, insignificant, and in any case, largely historically inaccessible group.

Part of the drive behind the recent interest in the elderly in the past derives from the contemporary debate about the increasing proportion of older people in most late twentieth-century societies. A great deal of attention has centred on the prediction that this increase will place an intolerable strain on the National Health and social services. While such warnings were voiced as early as the 1930s, as pointed out below by Pat Thane, they have yet to come to pass at the start of the new century. Nevertheless, this concern and the debate that it has engendered have done much to raise the public's – and the historical profession's – interest in the issue of ageing.

Another impetus to the study of the elderly in history is derived from the rise and increasing maturity of cultural history. This has stimulated study of age groups and age relations. Starting with the study of children and the cultural construction of childhood, cultural historians have moved with unintended poetic justice through the stages of the lifecycle, before finally engaging with the end stage of life: old age. The time has come, in a sense, for the elderly to take their turn under the historical lens of enquiry. The fact that this coincides with current demographic concerns, and contemporary debate, has added a degree of urgency and present-day relevance to the intrinsic scholarly appeal of the topic.

Significantly, the study of old age manifests a number of the traits characteristic of women's history – and for the same reasons. Until recently the historical profession claimed that little could be learned about the past lives of women. The world was male, the documents it generated were also 'male' in that they reflected male concerns and recorded developments of importance to males. Furthermore, it was assumed that the life experience of women did not differ in any significant way from that of men, or that their actions had no effect on world events. It was not until the 1970s, with the emergence of a sizeable class of professional women, of a women's political identity, and the vocal presence of the Second Wave Feminists, that this paradigm was challenged. With hard and creative work, historians of women have been able to recover vast areas of the female past. Having achieved recognition of the importance and feasibility of women's history, the discipline still suffered growing pains, specifically the tendency in the early years of research to group all women together, as if by sharing the same gender they shared the same experiences, regardless of their social and economic position or their age. This unfortunate clustering of the female sex produced misleading impressions that were exacerbated by another early tendency to concentrate on the powerful and successful women in the past, or to attempt to find a 'golden age' of women that existed in some distant historical past. It has only been within the past fifteen years that historians of women have begun to explore the full range of the female experience and to take account of class, race and ethnicity, as well as other important variables such as age.

In rather striking ways, the historiography of old age has paralleled that of women's history. Scholars of ageing have, like the women's historians before them, had to struggle with fundamental definitions. In this case, when does one become old, and what determines it? Put simply, old age studies have had to overcome the notion that the lives of older people were relatively uniform, homogeneous, insignificant, and lacking in historical interest. The field has had to deconstruct the popular notion that old age was a phase of life characterised only by helplessness and senility. Similarly, it has had to debunk such notions as that religion was nothing more than a salve for aged souls or that old age always led to poverty. It has struggled to overturn the conception that an old age spent in the household of adult children, without independence or authority, was an ideal to be aspired to and a regrettably lost reality. In short, historians of ageing are coming to grips with a set of counter-factual assumptions, and with the fact that old age is a highly nuanced process, one that is culturally embedded and not merely biological.

The historical study of ageing, just as of women, is an exercise which demonstrates how, to echo the language of the Second Wave Feminist, the personal becomes the political. It is only when groups, such as women and the elderly, leave the confines of tradition and the private sphere and become players on the economic and political stage (as was the case with women in the 1970s and the elderly in the 1980s) that they enter into the arena of public debate. Only then does the historical profession seek and find them in the past.

This collection of essays owes an intellectual debt to those early scholars of women and the elderly. We are now finally in a position to explore aspects of both ageing and gender as they converge in the lives of older women. The ten essays gathered below are an important contribution to our understanding of the past, all focused on the history of old age, all centred on understanding the experience of female ageing. This book brings together senior academics and young researchers in a fresh exchange of ideas about the nature of elderly women in Britain's past.

Old age is complex. It is not merely the final stage of life, uncomplicated and universally experienced. It has different meanings for different people, whether one is already older, or whether advanced age is still in one's future, as well as according to social status, economic security, region and, as this book argues, gender. It is with issues such as these that this book engages within the framework of the English past. This collection of essays is not a comprehensive view of old age from 1500 to the present; rather, it focuses on the largest component of the elderly population, yet one that has been ignored, overlooked or subsumed within a more general, and male, narrative of old age – old women.

Ironically, within old age studies the battle for gender analysis has had to be fought once again. The history of older women has been neglected despite the fact that since the beginning of reconstructable demographic information, dating from the sixteenth century, there have always been more old women than old men. Historians such as G. Minois nonetheless contend that few women reached old age because many died in childbirth.[1] Other historians of ageing have made claims reminiscent of an earlier age, such as Joel Rosenthal, an historian of medieval England:

> Matriarchy and the culture of old women, whether on their own or in extended family households, is mostly a lost topic, worth investigation, but hard to treat other than anecdotally . . . The long-lived Margaret Paston and such upper class women as Cecilly, Duchess of York, or Alice Brienne, were not anomalies, but rather have been caught for us by the luck of surviving sources.[2]

As the essays in this collection demonstrate, the history of old age is indeed recoverable, for the poor as well as for the prosperous, for women and for men. The essays that appear below are drawn from each author's ongoing research and are based on archival sources. One of the major strengths of this book has been to illustrate the wide range of sources, both qualitative and quantitative, that can reveal the lives of older women from all classes of society and across many centuries: poor law records, parish registers, household listings, diaries, wills, churchwardens' accounts and the records of non-conformist churches, letters, and the memories and observations of the elderly themselves, to name a few that are utilised below. The history of older people, and of women in particular, no longer remains 'unheeded in the historical literature', but has emerged as a rich field of investigation, which raises fundamental questions about the human experience over time.

The essays suggest, for example, that even the definition of what constitutes old age is far from straightforward and can, as Lynn Botelho and Claire S. Schen point out for the early modern period and as Pat Thane demonstrates for the twentieth century, be defined in a number of ways. Three of the most common ways of framing old age are chronological, functional and cultural. Chronological old age is entered when one reaches a predetermined calendar age. Functional old age is not reached at a set moment, but is entered when an individual can no longer care for herself. Cultural old age combines aspects of these elements (calendar years and functionality) plus other variables, and determines the understanding of old age according to the community's particular value system.

Scholars do not agree as to which definition is the most useful for the study of past societies, for all are useful in different contexts; nor is there a consensus as to what marks the threshold of old age or when that might begin. Botelho takes the question of 'how old is old' as the focal point of her essay and suggests that for poor women in rural seventeenth-century

England, old age was culturally defined and triggered by a host of physical changes associated with menopause at roughly age 50. Others in the volume find that old age began much later in life for women of other social classes and in different historical periods.

The chief outcome of scholarship in this field so far is to destroy 'old age' as a fixed category, unchanging over time, and to assert its relativity and provisionality. 'Comparative anthropological research on the aged in various cultural milieux has revealed relatively few common denominators', writes the sociologist Haim Hazan, a point also made by Rosenthal: 'I now argue against any single "read" on old age as being correct, or all inclusive, or even preferred. We look at the topic from different angles and we see, as we might expect, different images and different hues'.[3] Given that this volume spans five centuries, looks at different social groups, examines a wide range of English localities, and corresponds with the world-altering developments of industrialisation and capitalism, it is not surprising that the contributors offer a stimulating variety of definitions of old age.

The research discussed below is important for the detailed and varied picture it paints of older women, and of the elderly in general. First and foremost it shows that old people are not an undifferentiated, redundant mass. An individual's experience of old age is shaped by her or his class, the period of history lived, and through gender. For some women, the final stage of life is a period of unprecedented freedom and autonomy, while for others it is the rock upon which their physical health founders. It is not necessarily a period of unrelenting helplessness, but rather it has always been a series of stages, each with distinctive characteristics. The young-old, described as 'green old age' by sixteenth-century commentators, now include the active retirees who travel widely, whose vote is sought and whose share of the economic market is being actively pursued. Such individuals clearly have neither entered advanced old age nor joined the ranks of the frail elderly. Significantly, and seemingly without notice, the threshold between the young-old and the old-old has gradually, but steadily, been delayed and moved ever later into life, thanks in part to advances in medicine and in part to rising standards of living. At present, this point in the life-course, which will be crossed by most people living in Britain, occurs at an age past that of the typical lifespan of the sixteenth century. The stages of old age have remained constant throughout the span of time addressed in this volume, but the timing of those stages, as well as their meanings, have changed.

The contributors to this volume pursue a number of new avenues of investigation, explore many of the factors that affect ageing and revisit a number of more familiar ones in a new light. For example, the role of religion and spirituality; poverty, and the elderly's fear of it and the workhouse; their household structures; menopause; independence; and the images of old age, as well as the images that older women have of themselves, are some common themes that can be traced from the sixteenth century to the present.

One of the most promising new areas of research is the place and function of personal piety and organised religion in the lives of older women. These essays offer an initial understanding of the often enigmatic, complex and historical role of religion in the lives of older women. Spirituality and organised religion form part of the continuum of old age, and their contemporary importance is signified by the large number of older people in weekly attendance at church, chapel and temple.

While historians of the early modern period are undoubtedly familiar with the art of the good death, and the need, especially for the elderly for whom death was thought to be just around the corner, to prepare their soul to meet its maker, 'historians have been slow to appreciate religion and spirituality as fundamental aspects' of the lives of many of the elderly.[4] The importance of religion is especially true of the pre-modern world which was viewed as comprising spirits, both good and bad, fighting for a person's soul; where there was little alternative to Christianity and where the hope that Christ's mercy would save an individual from an afterlife in hell was of primary importance. Such beliefs, however, scorned by the elites of the Enlightenment, continue to function among many people to the present day. Given this understanding of the world, religion or personal piety was extremely important in the lives of many. It was of vital importance to know where one stood with God at all times, lest an unexpected accident occur and catch the soul unprepared. Early printed advice books, such as *The Dutifull Advice of a Loving Sonne to his Aged Father* (1636), stressed the need for the elderly, above all others, to ready their souls for death: 'the young man dye quickly, but the old cannot live long . . . therefore if greene yeers should sometimes think of the grave, the thought of old age should continually dwell in the same'.[5]

Religious belief was not merely a means of ensuring a seemly death or an acceptable afterlife; for the elderly it was often an important source of comfort, softening the aches and pains of physical ageing. Anne Kugler's analysis of the writings of Lady Sarah Cowper vividly shows how this noblewoman turned increasingly towards Christianity as she aged. However, Lady Sarah's beliefs not only provided solace in her declining state but also provided a model for proper behaviour in old age, as well as the means that justified her authority within her family and social circle. As Kugler shows, personal piety and religious beliefs formed a large and integral part of Lady Sarah's identity and were fundamental in her understanding of what it meant to be old.

The religious change associated with the Protestant Reformation had a profound impact on the lives of the elderly. In Schen's exploration of the survival strategies employed by older women in sixteenth-century London, England's shift from traditional Christianity to Protestantism had a marked and adverse, if temporary, effect upon the amount of charity available to the poor, a vital ingredient in the survival of both aged women and men. The giving of alms is incumbent on all Christians, be they Catholic or Protestant; yet, in the traditional church, charity was often given in conjunction with religious practices that were later prohibited by Reformed theology, such as purgatory and prayers for the dead. According to Schen's research, elderly women in Reformation London were initially hard pressed to find alternative sources of assistance once these practices, and the charity that accompanied them, were outlawed by the Reformation Parliament. In this case, it was the curtailment of religious expression in others which nevertheless had strong repercussions among the aged.

Amy Froide's essay draws our attention to yet another aspect of the religious life of the elderly: as prominent members of non-conformist congregations of the eighteenth century. Froide speculates that single women may have turned to dissenting forms of Christianity as a comfort in old age, rather as the strictly Anglican and widowed Lady Sarah did at the beginning of the same century. Intriguingly, Froide also suggests that it was only in old age that these women were finally free and independent enough to join a dissenting religious group. Indeed, it may be the weight of their advanced old age, and its perceived wisdom, that overrode their womanhood, thus allowing them some measure of authority and leadership within the intrinsically patriarchal nature of eighteenth-century Christianity.

Religion, however, is strikingly absent from the comments of women in the secular Britain of the late twentieth century, as described by Thane. This may reflect the construction of the sample, which excludes people of Asian, Caribbean or African origins for whom open expression of religion may be a more important feature of identity than for those of white Anglo-Saxon or Celtic origin. Over the twentieth century, religion has played a diminishing part in British public discourse, whatever the strength of private belief.

Despite the very visible presence at all times of the wealthy elderly and the increasingly potentially powerful political position of older people as a group in the twentieth century, financial hardship in old age, especially among old women, stretches from the sixteenth century to the present. The conjunction between old age and poverty is well known, and the elderly poor have been identified as pre-eminent amongst the worthy poor for centuries. As individuals age, their economic viability typically declines, and sometimes their income terminates. In the early modern period, 'retirement' existed only for the select few, leaving the remainder to continue their paid and unpaid work for as long as their strength and abilities allowed. In the western society of the late twentieth century, retirement and a pension until death have become the norm for most people, but that is a very modern development, dating only from the mid-twentieth century. Nonetheless, in both early modern and modern eras, standards of living often decline in old age, and for the economically marginal, poverty ensues shortly thereafter.

Certain phases of the life-course are particularly vulnerable to economic distress; this is known as lifecycle poverty. For most of history, an orphaned childhood was one such time.[6] Another poverty-prone period was middle age, when a couple might be providing not only for their own upkeep but for that of several children as well. As Robert Schwartz has shown for the eighteenth century, young children did not contribute positively to the household economy, but were net consumers until roughly their fifteenth year.[7] Late middle age was a period of reprieve, as the children either left the household or became net producers. The early years of old age continued this relatively stable period; but as the couple aged further they again began to require more income than they could provide for themselves. The structure of the lifecycle often cruelly prohibited the aged individual from turning to their own children for help and support as their needs increased, at least among the lower orders, as this was the point in the lifecycle of the adult offspring when they themselves were over-burdened with children.

A number of the problems faced by the poor over time are explored in this volume. Botelho discusses the effects of poor health and inadequate accommodation on the ageing process of poor rural women. Claire S. Schen and Margaret Pelling explore some of the survival strategies available to older women in the early modern period. Schen builds on Olwen Hufton's famous expression 'the economy of makeshifts', and investigates how women cobbled together a livelihood in sixteenth-century London.[8] For the same century, Pelling uses Norwich's sixteenth-century census of the poor to explore the role of marriage in the lives of aged paupers. Her research suggests that we must rethink the stereotype of the helpless old women in the past, as 'the viability of stereotypes is often held to be inversely related to the amount of concrete evidence available about their objects: the more informed we are, the less valid the stereotype'.[9] Norwich's poor employed a pattern of 'unequal marriages', in other words unions between individuals of dramatically different ages, as a means of stitching together the resources necessary for survivial. Contrary to our expectation, it was not the aged female who proved especially vulnerable in old age, and in need of protection, but rather it was her male counterpart who needed to be married in order to survive. Old women of the lowest orders, it appears, were better equipped for survival in old age than men.

One aspect of the relationship between ageing and poverty that has been little explored for the early modern period is the fear of poverty in old age.

Forming a critical theme of Steve Hussey's essay, this issue is approached from the perspective of sociology, and via oral histories, to expose the fear of becoming poor and dependent in old age. More specifically, Hussey unearths the deep-seated terror of old people in the twentieth century of being sent to the workhouse to live and eventually die in public disgrace. Hussey's essay juxtaposes the fear of destitution and long dependence in this type of public institution with the actual facts of the early twentieth-century workhouse, to conclude that it was 'an inheritance of fear' passed between the generations, and one that had no basis in modern conditions. Instead, this dread was based on the collective memory of the Dickensian-like, Victorian workhouse of the previous century inaugurated with the passage of the poor law of 1834.

The fear of an old age in penury, however, was not confined to those whose middle age was spent on the margins of economic security, but, as Kugler has shown, it was shared by the rich and socially prominent Lady Sarah Cowper during the early eighteenth century. This fear, experienced today by many elderly individuals in Britain, may be one of the major continuities of experience that survives the Industrial Revolution, the development of capitalism and improved standard of living of the late twentieth century.

Theresa Deane's essay is a nicely turned piece that simultaneously explores the fear-inspiring Victorian workhouse, the elderly and elite Louise Twining's efforts to improve the condition of aged poor women, and the nature of privileged and secure old age as experienced by Twining. In this manner, the active and independent old age of the rich and privileged is held up in sharp contrast to the loss of independence and the utter submission experienced by the aged poor. Louise Twining constructed an old age filled with philanthropic work, safe in the comfort of her wealth, but also secure because of her independence as a single woman. Her situation is similar to that of the single women investigated by Froide, women who actively chose to work throughout their later lives, even when there was no economic need to do so; women who gave of themselves to assist others; and women who were free from direct male authority. Single women of even modest means, unlike those among the poor, may have had more independence in old age than all other women.

The question of independence in old age, especially as household heads, was one of the first questions asked by historians and historical demographers. When considering the autonomy of women, the issue was initially conceived in terms of extreme bipolarities: either old women lived alone as outcasts, on the edges of the village and on the margins of society; or they were welcomed immediately upon widowhood into the home of an adult child or niece. This remains one of the most persistent sets of stereotypes and an issue of ongoing debate and study, especially for scholars of the pre-modern world. It would appear that the truth spans these two extremes, and two of the essays presented here are devoted to this question. Susannah Ottaway breaks new and important methodological ground in her handling of the eighteenth-century census-like documents. She concludes that economic conditions did more to determine whether an older woman was able to live up to the cultural ideal of independent living than did her absolute age, except among the very oldest. Therefore, it was the oldest and poorest women of the eighteenth century who were the most isolated, and the least likely to live as society thought they should.

Richard Wall shares Ottaway's focus on household formation but seeks to place the experience of English women between the sixteenth and twentieth centuries within the European context, thereby identifying those features that were shared by women across Europe as well as highlighting those that were particular to England. Wall quickly establishes that most older women in England lived alone, most of the time, rather than with their spouse or children. The household independence of the majority of England's older women compares with their continental counterparts in the same way as English households compare more generally with the European pattern. Elderly women of England and the adjacent areas of the continent share a household composition that favours living alone, while older women in southern Europe are more likely to reside with members of their family. Regional traditions, therefore, are more powerful than old age alone in shaping elderly households.

The most significant changes in household composition, according to Wall, took place in twentieth-century England. After 1921 (1945 for men), the number of older women living alone increased, strengthening this northern European pattern, although the reasons for this intensification are not yet entirely clear. Wall believes that it is the complex interplay of demographic conditions, cultural considerations and rising incomes that ultimately produced this phenomenon. Pat Thane's investigation of late twentieth-century attitudes towards ageing illustrates the intense emotions behind the desire to live alone in old age. Thane, like Wall, suggests that the particular cultural and economic circumstances of the period have permitted more older women than ever to achieve this time-honoured ideal.

Pat Thane's essay is the final chapter of the book. Her analysis of the 1980s Mass Observation responses on ageing highlights a number of themes raised by the other authors and found in other historical periods. Her scholarship pinpoints the desire for independent living, as noted above; the inappropriateness of negative old age stereotypes; the susceptibly of older women to financial hardship, with a forced reliance on an 'economy of makeshifts'; and the difficulty in determining exactly what is meant by old as features or characteristics that are relatively constant in English society.

Thane's work on the images and self-images of these older women is equally revealing in its identification of those areas of old age that we no longer share with the past. The most significant of these is that old age is now an experience that the vast majority of people living in Britain will experience, rather than something limited to a minority of the population. Secondly, retirement and a life-long pension have also become a universal aspect of the old age experience in the late twentieth century. In earlier periods, retirement was available only to the wealthy and, unlike today, it was not a defining feature of later life. The combination of many of the long-term characteristics of old age, such as the desire for independent living, and the distinctively modern features of old age, for example increased longevity and a reliable pension, have resulted in an older population that no longer feels bound by tradition and stereotype. Instead, they tend to define themselves as older, but not old, and to move consciously the entry point into old-old age even later into the life-course.

The aim of this volume is to illustrate the richly textured and varied lives of older women in Britain's past as well as present. The lives discussed below all share certain features and display some similar traits, but in no way are their experiences of old age uniform or homogeneous. These essays have uncovered the diverse nature of female old age over a long span of time and, at any one time, a diversity that shares the experiences of the larger society. Older women are as much a part of society as any other group, and their concerns are as interwoven. Older women are both in this world and *of* it. Clearly, not every aged woman at any time lived out her final years marginalised from society and isolated from the greater world.

This collection of essays has demonstrated, once again, that the life experiences of women – in this case, of older women – are in important respects different from those of men, and are worthy of study on their own merits. Above all, these essays indicate the wealth of evidence for the historical study of two traditionally neglected groups: women and the old. These authors have irrefutably proven that the lives of older women are accessible to historians. Finally, it is hoped that our historical understanding of older women will be of some use to those individuals who turn to the past to address the problems of the present and the future.

Notes

1. G. Minois, *History of Old Age: From Antiquity to the Renaissance* (Cambridge, 1989), p.290.

2. Joel T. Rosenthal, *Old Age in Late Medieval England* (Philadelphia, 1996), p.30.

3. Haim Hazan, *Old Age: Constructions and Deconstructions* (Cambridge, 1994), p.53; Rosenthal, pp.2, 6, 175.

4. Thomas R. Cole, *The Journey of Life: A Cultural History of Aging in America* (Cambridge, 1992), p.xxi.

5. *The Dutifull Advice of a Loving Sonne to his Aged Father* (London, 1636), pp.4–5.

6. Robert Jütte, *Poverty and Deviance in Early Modern Europe* (Cambridge, 1994), pp.36–8; and B.S. Rowntree, *Poverty: A Study of Town Life* (London, 1901), his *Poverty and Progress: A Second Social Survey of York* (London, 1941) and, with G.R. Lavers, *Poverty and the Welfare State* (London, 1951).

7. Robert Schwartz, *Policing the Poor in Eighteenth-century France* (Chapel Hill, NC, 1988), p.106.

8. Olwen H. Hufton, *The Poor of Eighteenth-century France, 1750–1789* (Oxford, 1974), p.69, *passim*.

9. Hazan, *Old Age*, p.28.

CHAPTER ONE

Strategies of poor aged women and widows in sixteenth-century London

CLAIRE S. SCHEN

The Reformation signalled the end of official Catholic practices in England, altering traditional religious practices and disrupting many aspects of parish life. One point where Protestant theology and parochial practice were at odds was in the traditional support for the sick, aged and the poor. Nearly all pre-Reformation gifts to the poor contained the stipulation that the recipient pray for the soul of the benefactor, and often for the benefactor's deceased relatives as well. Protestantism denied the validity of such prayers, and outlawed such practices. Consequently, traditional Catholic charity, with its emphasis on the now heretical prayers for the dead, was curtailed. The civic parish, therefore, was forced to incur additional expenses as it sought to fill this lacuna in poor relief. The result, according to many historians, was the reform of relief and the transformation of medieval ideals of charity into stricter definitions of deserving and undeserving poor, and more parsimonious charitable giving to the indigent.[1] The destitute and aged woman, despite being a traditional figure of the deserving poor, found herself in the midst of these changes, faced with an uncertain future and the damaging possibility of being declared unworthy.[2]

Traditionally, elderly pauper women survived and managed to maintain some independence by utilising networks of kinship, friendship and neighbourhood in their search for charity, employment and poor relief. The reform of poor relief and charity that swept England, and indeed all of Europe, in the late sixteenth century disrupted these strategies for survival. This essay explores how elderly women in London responded to these new conditions and adapted their traditional 'economy of makeshifts', those cobbled together sources of income and support, to fit this new environment.[3]

During the sixteenth century, London perceived or experienced an increase in poverty and withstood waves of religious and cultural change.

Its overcrowded suburbs, in part a product of the attempts of poor people to survive, were condemned by social critics and legislated against by governing elites as fountains of disorder and disease. The city's population grew from an estimated 50,000 in 1500 to 141,000 in 1603, and unlike other cities, its sex ratio was 113 male to 100 female inhabitants.[4] Given its centrality to government, its highly developed civic structure, and its well documented poverty, London is an excellent place to chart the interplay between changing religious practices and the lives of poor, old women. Yet, because of these circumstances, in addition to London's high mortality rates and its urban lifestyle, one must be cautious about generalising from this unique city to the rest of England with its plethora of rural villages and farms.

This study concentrates on four London parishes of varying size and wealth within and without the City walls: St Botolph without Aldersgate, St Mary Woolnoth, St Michael Cornhill and St Stephen Walbrook. As London grew by migration rather than because of a rising birth rate, a demographic study based on 'family reconstitution' would be difficult. Instead, an analysis of the records of the Court of Aldermen and other civic and parochial sources illustrates the erosion of survival strategies of older and poorer women. As Richard Smith has pointed out, religious institutions have often been overlooked in studying the balance between family and collective support for the poor in the past.[5] Similarly, historians of the aged have paid little attention to the impact of the English Reformation on the problems of the aged poor. Therefore, an examination of these parishes' financial and 'business' records, including churchwardens' accounts, vestry minutes and burial registers, as well as literary sources and last wills and testaments, are used to uncover the experience of poor ageing women and widows during the century of England's religious reformation.

Defining age and poverty for women

Old age has been differentiated into chronological, functional and cultural age.[6] Functional old age, or decline in abilities and health, brought many poorer people into contact with sixteenth-century parish officials. Research on the lifecycle of families has shown that as people aged, they dipped further and further into poverty, even if they had not previously been poor.[7] Furthermore, older women were especially likely to suffer from poverty in sixteenth- and early seventeenth-century London. While many of the women on parish poor relief were likely to be chronologically old, others may have been 'old' in 'many social senses', as Peter Stearns has described it, although such women were not old in terms of years.[8] Descriptions of women in personal documents and parish records rarely indicate chronological age, but the nature of women's jobs and households often indicate their physical decline and functional old age. A person's functional age, ultimately, rather than the arrival at a predetermined chronological point, determined both women and men's entry into old age.

Furthermore, the nature of the demographic records of early modern London preclude defining age chronologically. Some sixteenth-century burial registers included information on age at death, but such detail is of dubious value even, or especially, when it seems precise. For instance, the scribe or parish clerk working in St Michael Cornhill recorded remarkable ages: Henry Johnson buried in 1561 at 105; Margery Morgayne buried in 1575, a widow of 100 years. Further, the clerk described eight parishioners over 90 years old between 1561 and 1604 and others he claimed were in their eighties or simply 'very old' or 'ancient'.[9] While some individuals did live to venerable ages, the apparently precise recording of ages, especially since so many were 92 or 94, raises suspicions. Parish officials were likely to exaggerate ages because of the nature of early modern life and the toll it could take on an individual's body. 'Age' had a qualitative dimension that expressed the social or cultural aspects of ageing. Furthermore, parish records, such as these burial registers, also filled a need for spectacle, news or gossip and were read or heard in the church or vestry meeting. They marked and memorialised, and sometimes embroidered on, the significant occasions in the lives of parishioners.

With few reliable chronological markers available, the historian must utilise the vocabulary of the period that describes age and status in order to identify elderly individuals. Parochial records use a variety of terms to delineate the different stages of women's adult lifecycle: mother, mistress, goodwife, widow. These titles identified women in their relationship to other women, to men and to other social groups. Their meaning was also dependent upon the context in which they were used. For example, the word for a parent, 'Mother', served also as a term of address for elderly women of the lower social orders, or could even refer to a 'stout or untidy old woman'.[10] William Gorsuche left a 'poor gown' worth 10s. to Mother Gregory of Hendon, a simple gift for a woman of humble status.[11] The extensive will of Elizabeth Stevyns, written in 1550, illustrates the contrast between mother and mistress. Stevyns left clothing and rent to two women, Mother Gam and Mother Draper.[12] For each, she specified five years' rent money, provided that they lived that long. Later in her will she bequeathed one-time gifts to the widowed Mother More, Mother Katherine in Abchurch Lane, and the widowed Mother Taper.[13] Stevyns considered the first two mothers old, since she suspected they would die within five years, but viewed the other widowed mothers differently. Regardless of their chronological ages, these women were poor and considered worthy recipients of charity.

Alongside these legacies, Stevyns left a number of gold rings inscribed with her initials as a 'token of remembrance' to 'mistresses' and to some well known men, such as Sir Martin Bowes, knight and Lord Mayor of London.[14] 'Mistress' carried a variable meaning, from Falstaff calling the prostitute Doll Tearsheet 'Mistress', to the mistresses hired by the parish to work for low wages, to the wealthy friends identified in wills and testaments like Stevyns's.[15] A mistress had control over servants, households and families, or men's hearts. Mistresses who had worked for low wages may have experienced poverty when grown children left the household or when they felt the effects of ageing. Consequently, this term could also be granted to older women in receipt of poor relief as a token of politeness and respect.[16]

The terms goodwife and widow are more difficult to define in relation to age and status. The goodwife was the female head of a household or establishment, which implied a certain social status and independence, while those goodwives collecting relief through testamentary or parish charity seem to have been considered old by their neighbours.[17] In 1551, Jane Spencer specified a number of goodmen and goodwives (none with shared surnames) to receive gowns, to round out the group of 60 poor men and women in her burial procession, a place reserved (both before and after the Reformation) for the aged, the sick and the poor. Jane Spencer especially remembered her poor neighbours and asked her executors to distribute spice bread at her funeral 'as well among the poor as Rich'. For the relief and refreshment of these neighbours, Spencer provided 40s., while she gave an additional £5 to supply a dinner for her 'other', more prosperous, friends. Her family received linen, silver and other household goods, such as the 'Cain and Abel' coverlet she left her granddaughter.[18] The context of these bequests indicates that these goodwives and goodmen were poor, and probably old. Many needy women were therefore included in the lists of goodwives frequently found in wills.

Goodwives and other ageing women were also hired by the parish officers to perform certain odd jobs, such as washing, examining dead bodies in times of plague and epidemic disease, and nursing the sick, pregnant and orphaned. The 'nuclear-hardship hypothesis' may explain why these female and male independent householders became dependent on relief and parish employment late in their lives.[19] This theory argues that the custom of self-sufficiency for couples or nuclear families in traditional English society meant that the loss of a spouse subjected the survivor to hardship. Kin or the local community, Laslett's 'collectivity' made up of friends, neighbours, parish and city, or more likely a combination of these resources, relieved the survivor. Peter Laslett in particular has stressed the role of the collectivity in supporting ageing or elderly widows.[20] The parish pensions that were distributed for years, even decades, to some older women point to the negative impact of functional old age on women who lacked support from close kin following widowhood. More recently, Laslett and others have acknowledged a greater variability of family formations in England. Nonetheless, this situation may have been especially true in London, a city that grew by migration and was characterised by loose kin ties.

'Widow' could be used to describe any woman whose husband had died and communicated nothing about her chronological age. Widows could and did remarry, but those with few assets had lower rates of remarriage in sixteenth-century London.[21] Some widows had little alternative but to subsist for extended periods on a mixture of relief and parish employment. Irrespective of age, widowhood could occasion conjunctural poverty, but functional old age unquestionably worsened it.

Contextualised reading of parish sources and testaments reveals a number of titles identifying women in need of relief because of sickness or frailty associated with functional old age. Nonetheless, we must exercise caution in our definitions, as other essays in this collection stress. Not all widows were aged or even particularly 'old', but the sources suggest that widows living on pensions from their parishes, searching for dead bodies or nursing the sick were likely, in fact, to be aged.

Survival strategies of ageing poor women

Goodwives, mothers and widows created supportive female networks, worked for parishes and households, sought relief from parishes and collected private charity. All such assistance constituted viable strategies for the poor of the sixteenth century to make a living. The Protestant Reformation dismantled a number of community organisations that had supported the aged and the poor, and arguably strengthened the dichotomy between the deserving and undeserving poor. Studies of Italian confraternities and of religious institutions throughout Europe have shown that this division prevailed across confessional boundaries, but in all cases specific political, social and economic conditions modulated individual responses to poverty.[22]

Demographic strain and economic pressure intersected with these cultural changes to shape the experience of the aged in sixteenth-century London. An analysis of the changing religious climate, of pressing population growth and of sporadic periods of rapid inflation can augment our understanding of the household position of elderly women and the degree of their dependence on the collectivity. Recent debate has centred on whether or not elderly people in past times lived independently or with others.[23] London's rapid population growth initially encouraged individuals to accept lodgers or to prolong their extended family households, although city officials eventually discouraged these practices. Further, historians have debated whether or not the elderly poor, and the elderly more generally, depended on the support of family or the collectivity.[24] Economic downturns may have pushed aged individuals to seek greater collective rather than familial support by diminishing the capacity of kin to provide adequate assistance. London's parochial records cannot show unequivocally the norms of an aged lifestyle. Instead, they illustrate the variety of strategies available to the elderly poor, suggesting that no single 'rule' governed living arrangements.[25]

The traditional Catholic institutions of the late medieval period supplemented individual or family support for the sick, elderly and poor, whether based on religious houses or parishes. Pre-Reformation religious fraternities and guilds not only prayed for their deceased members but also supported living members who had fallen on hard times. The fraternities dedicated to St Katherine and to Sts Fabian and Sebastian in St Botolph's Aldersgate promised 14d. each week to those members experiencing poverty, old age, or loss by fire or flood.[26] Fraternities and religious guilds, however, rarely mentioned the distribution of money to poor members, although guild statutes often mandated such practices. This has led some historians to question whether fraternities really fulfilled these goals.[27] The London and Middlesex Chantry Certificate of 1548, however, offers some evidence of fraternity support for poor brothers and sisters and in particular of aid to the elderly poor. In 1548, royal commissioners evaluated parish church and guild property in response to the 1547 Act of Parliament that demanded the survey and confiscation of endowments intended to support prayers for the dead. Parliament, however, reserved to parishes any property intended for poor relief.[28] Endowments of a Roman Catholic nature, specifically those linked to purgatory and prayers for the dead, reverted to the Crown. Parishes, therefore, struggled to prove that particular bequests were in fact a source of charity and poor relief, despite their original association with Catholic practices.

Proof of charity became an important and successful tactic to keep property away from Crown and Parliament. Many London fraternities in 1548 recorded gifts to the poor from the same funds that supported prayers for souls. The Brotherhood of Our Lady and St Dunstan in St Dunstan's in west London produced a list of named parish poor in receipt of £17 1s. 4d. in fraternity alms that included four 'mothers' among the eight women mentioned, in addition to one couple, one man and one individual without a recorded first name.[29] In St Magnus the fraternity of Salve Regina relieved a sister 'fallen in decay and sick of the palsy', at 1s. per week for her lifetime and to four other women 'fallen in poverty and making their suit to them'.[30] The certificate distinguished between the 'decayed' sister and the others 'fallen' into poverty, suggesting that the first was aged, while the others were poor or beset by tragedy. The fraternity of Our Lady in St Bride Fleet Street supported two widows, three other women and two men to the total of £8 per annum. The men received £2 per annum, perhaps because they also had families or wives, while the women received no more than £1 per annum.[31] The disparity may indicate a difference in the household structures of these men and women or signal a low estimation of the need, or even worth, of women.

The eradication of these Catholic societies and charitable organisations as a direct result of the Protestant Reformation left a significant number of elderly, impotent and sick poor to their own devices, and to the initially under-prepared local authorities. Protestant reformers, including the prominent Simon Fish and Henry Brinkelow, had previously criticised the Catholic Church and its monasteries for misusing money, property and other income given to them in trust and intended for the relief of the poor. Reforming commentators demanded that Protestants perform their Christian duty by distributing alms to the truly worthy poor, and that they should do so without any lingering Catholic hopes that such charity would be repaid by prayers on their behalf or that these gifts brought them closer to salvation. Fundamental to this new understanding of Christian giving to the poor was the emphasis on 'discriminating' poor relief, the careful division of the poor into the worthy and the unworthy: one suitable for relief, the other for punishment.[32]

Petitions from certain London citizens accused the former monasteries of indiscriminate giving and misappropriation of funds. They urged that the former monastic lands be used for the public good, and in relief of the worthy poor, by the construction of new hospitals and other public institutions.[33] Greater London, and the bulk of its citizens, however, had been staunch benefactors of the pre-Reformation religious institutions and their charitable work. For a complex, and not entirely clear, set of reasons, the bulk of London's testators did not immediately transfer their loyalties, and monies, to these fledgling public hospitals. Only slowly did civic institutions earn the charitable and philanthropic support enjoyed by the dissolved or confiscated Catholic institutions; only gradually did this form of relief resume its place in the range of relief available to London's aged women.[34]

Funeral doles and burial processions comprised another part of the economy of makeshifts for pre-Reformation men and women. As we have seen, the members of burial processions and mourners around a dead body in a home or church were often the aged, impotent or sick poor. In 1512, Dame Percivale, for instance, provided money and two meals, of fish or flesh depending on the season, to poor men and women praying about her body. Percivale asked for the most impotent and aged of the poor, allowing them to pray within their homes if they could not leave them.[35] In 1524 John Skevyngton asked 'old Agnes Dicar' to pray for him and provided her with 6s. 8d.[36]

The Reformation prohibited prayers for the dead, but 'hiring' poor and aged mourners persisted, although testators refrained from asking attendants to pray. Simon Smythe provided 2s. 6d. to one woman called Mistress Bees and another named Mother Dorst to be paid on his burial day, without asking for any service.[37] Some post-Reformation testators, however, abhorred the 'pomp and vainglory' of the world and limited mourners to close family and friends.[38] A slow and not widespread cultural transformation, the eschewal of elaborate funeral plans and legislative ambivalence about doles and begging lessened opportunities for the aged and impotent poor, who had often been hired as mourners.[39] Yet, despite some change, mourning remained a viable strategy recognised by the poor and the parishes. A note from the vestry of St Michael Cornhill in 1603 admonished the sexton to allow the parish poor, rather than outsiders, to 'earn' money 'at burials'.[40]

In addition to this continuation of 'pious employment', parishes hired the poor for numerous menial tasks, such as those awarded to goodwives to supplement their relief throughout the sixteenth century.[41] Aged women and men were expected to work as long as they were able. Long before workhouses, and indeed before the introduction of a national poor law in 1601, the Edwardian statute For the Punishment of Vagabonds and Relief of the Poor and Impotent Persons (1547) called for setting the aged poor to work.[42] The midwife Goodie Mercom dwelt in the churchyard of St Michael Cornhill, an example of the small houses and simple shops often rented at reduced rates to widows and goodwives to facilitate their continued self-employment.[43] Parishes hired such women to care for the sick and the orphaned. Taken together, the initatives of London's parishes not only predate the late-sixteenth century national poor relief scheme, but actually prefigure it, in that these practices were to become characteristic of England's tax-based statutory relief of the poor and would stand virtually unchanged until the nineteenth century.

The paid work of women employed by the parish was an extension of women's traditional domestic work. It also replicated the prescribed work of rural gentlewomen.[44] The *Widowes Treasure* (1588) claimed that a widow and gentlewoman in the countryside had set down recipes for medicine and cookery, although 'not orderly set down as many of better skill might have done'.[45] This disclaimer distinguished the woman's work from the 'skilled' work of male practitioners, such as barber surgeons or members of the newly founded college of surgeons. In the case of the employable poor, older women who nursed the poor served joint functions for the parish: gainful employment, at low wages, for some of its dependants in order to minister to others.

Another form of employment in the parish was of the poor and sometimes ageing women as moral overseers, as the devotional work of the pre-Reformation period gave way to moral work in the later sixteenth century. St Botolph's hired older women to oversee the maids' gallery in the church and to maintain order during the service by regulating the social interaction of unmarried men and women. The parish began paying Mistress Peirson to oversee the maids in 1583/84. By 1594, she had become blind, so the parish paid Mistress Wilkinson to assist her. The vestry had recognised Wilkinson's 'great necessity and want' the previous year and reduced the rent of her rooms, curiously described as 'under and over', and probably meaning the charnel house.[46] Wilkinson received another rent reduction in 1597/98; by the following year, Widow Bromley had joined the blind Peirson in overseeing the maids.[47] In 1601/2, the parish paid Peirson and Bromley each 20s., but during a gap in the records, Peirson drops from view. In another long gap, Bromley similarly disappears.[48] Each woman spent twenty years in this capacity of moral overseer, and for half of it Peirson was blind.

Employing ageing or blind women to prevent distractions and flirtations during the church service reflected the intent of Elizabeth's 1576 statute For Setting of the Poor on Work, and for the Avoiding of Idleness. This statute lambasted bastardy and the children left 'to the great Burden of the same Parishes and in defrauding of the Relief of the impotent and aged true Poor of the same Parish', all 'to the evil Example and Encouragement of Lewd Life'.[49] In this view, bastardy and similar disorderly behaviour robbed the deserving aged and impotent poor of their rightful relief. This was a widely held view and contemporaries noted the apparent increase in the number of poor and 'disorderly' people throughout Europe. As William Harrison noted in his *Description of England* (1577), 'There is no commonwealth at this day in Europe wherein there is not great store of poor people'. He continued, 'With us the poor is commonly divided into three sorts, so that some are poor by impotency, as the fatherless child, the aged, blind, and lame, and the diseased person that is judged to be incurable; the second are the poor by casualty . . .'. The 'thriftless poor' follow: the rioter, vagabond, rogue, and strumpet.[50]

Parish joined Parliament and the civil government in reforming living arrangements to prevent the birth of 'foreign' children to the idle poor.[51] 'Residence' required the poor to solicit aid from their birth parish, so poor pregnant women were led to, or whipped out of, parishes, and the parents of foundlings were sought. The Elizabethan law, intended to reduce bastardy or at least to prevent children born out of wedlock from drawing on parish relief, also enabled parishes to trim their rolls of other orphans and the undesirable poor. Hence, the parish paid the impotent and aged poor to oversee the women who might bear bastards or lead 'lewd' lives and defraud them of relief. On the one hand, a godly 'mother' or widow might have seen shepherding the young as a moral responsibility. On the other hand, parish elites, often the same local elites who served on vestries or led companies in the City of London, may have co-opted these vulnerable elderly and infirm women, along with other poor women, as agents of social control.

The reform of parish relief and charity, precipitated by fears of disease and disorder, attacked another component of aged women's household economy: taking in kin, or strangers, as lodgers. Just as ageing and poor women stitched together an income, so too they attempted to orchestrate their living arrangements to save and earn money, often extending domestic activities such as cooking and washing to their paying lodgers.[52] Society's fixation on issues of order in late sixteenth-century London disrupted such makeshifts. Parliamentary legislation in the late sixteenth century, driven by London's desire to curb disease, crime and disorder, and even to prevent fire in the crowded and poor neighbourhoods, prohibited housing lodgers or 'inmates' and dividing houses for the same. However, despite prescriptive legislation, the Court of Aldermen continued to be plagued by this practice.[53] The Court, in July 1607, imprisoned a Gloucestershire man who lived as an inmate in Walbrook ward with his 'wife children and family'.[54] Could 'family' have included an elderly parent? Could an older woman have been their keeper? Margaret Pelling has explored such 'domestic functions' as performed by aged women in the service of non-relatives.[55] While the Court of Aldermen punished the male head of the family, whoever kept the inmates lost resources.

Parishes also oversaw the household formation of the poor, including whether the elderly poor lived with married children, lodged, or kept inmates or lodgers. In these London parishes, this surveillance prevented what David Kertzer has called the 'nuclear reincorporation system', whereby married children either moved in with or brought their elderly parents into their own homes.[56] Peter Laslett once called independent living of the elderly the 'rule', but added that the rule was set by 'social and political authority', especially the poor law as written in 1601 and subsequently revised.[57] While population burgeoned through the sixteenth century, city officials attempted to stem the influx of poor into London and onto the poor rolls, which were determined by residence as well as birth. These demographic and economic exigencies may have tipped the scale, at least in places such as London, so that the parish rather than the individual or family provided the bulk, although not all, of the aid for the aged poor.

The vestry of St Botolph's outlined new rules in 1606 that restricted the 'reincorporation' of families or the creation of extended households. 'The same day it was agreed that no poor of the parish receiving pension or alms weekly shall have any pension or alms paid by the churchwardens or overseers for the poor if they be found to entertain inmates, lodgers or keep their children sons or daughters either married or marriageable within their own houses and dwellings'.[58] The vestry in St Michael Cornhill in 1585 allowed Goody Cherry a portion of a deceased widow's pension only if 'she remove away her daughter that is married'.[59] In 1598 the vestry disrupted a combined household comprising two older women and a younger woman with children. 'Further it was agreed that where as Margaret Peacock & mother Payne had taken into their house goodwife Clarke with her children, that they should presently avoid her out of the house with her children, or else they should lose their pensions & be turned out of the house themselves'.[60] In the case of two sons, the parish showed lenience in allowing them to live with their father in a parish house until the father died. After his death, they received 20 nobles and signed an agreement to be no longer chargeable to the parish, despite their great poverty.[61] Contradictorily, the elderly poor who lost additional income or contributions from lodgers had to lean more heavily on the parish when their own economy of makeshifts faltered.[62]

For the elderly, 'residence' also meant that the churchwardens and vestry men knew their character and place in the neighbourhood, beyond their legal right to reside in the parish. Aged, impotent and poor women who had a long residence in, or connection to, a parish tended to garner community support, perhaps by pricking the conscience of neighbours or drawing on shared past experiences. Parish sources demonstrate the importance of residence in receiving relief before the enactment of the Elizabethan poor law of 1601. St Stephen Walbrook sustained Andrew Ludford, a former parson and a churchwarden, from 1574 until his death in 1580, and then relieved his widow Margaret from 1581, paying for her food, shelter, clothing, debts, and even redeeming her daughter's clothes from pawn for 50s.[63] The parish identified Margaret as 'poor' in their list, along with a few other widows and the sexton, and thereby found an appropriate target for the testamentary bequests increasingly funnelled through churchwardens.[64] Margaret received £5 4s. per year, and more when she suffered from what appears to have been mental illness.[65] She was first described as sick in the accounts of 1582/83, and in the accounts of 1587/88 she entered Bedlam Hospital for the insane. Later, her son kept her for twenty weeks, and the parish contributed £4; his efforts kept the local officials from petitioning for another term in Bedlam. Community aid supplemented rather than replaced the help of neighbours, family, or even a liveried company or other charitable sources for the aged poor.[66] Members of the Grocers' Company paid all or part of Margaret's pension for nearly twenty years, a typical example of the multiple resources brought into the management of one poor widow's ageing.[67] In 1604, Ludford's daughter tried to obtain a pension from the parish, but the vestry only gave her 10s. and told her to make no further suit.[68]

London parishes sustained people of a range of ages – widows, goodwives, mothers and fathers – with 'pensions'; they contributed to Christ's Hospital for fatherless children; and paid 'exhibitions' to poor scholars.[69] Out of the annual rates collected for Christ's Hospital, parishes sometimes retained a portion, with the hospital's agreement, to provide pensions, usually for the sick and the aged. St Mary Woolnoth, for example, employed about £5 of its collection yearly to support 'poor pensioners' from within the parish. In the early seventeenth century, the named pensioner was always a woman, such as Widow Pryce, Margaret Ringe or Widow Clark, but accounts often noted an amount distributed to unnamed poor pensioners.[70] Through the 1580s and 1590s, St Michael's vestry made note of widows, mothers and goodwives in receipt of pensions from the parish and from money collected for Christ's Hospital.

Owing to the limited resources of most parishes, some deserving poor people had to await the death of pensioners before being eligible for regular relief. However, they did not wait passively, hoping to be noticed by the overseers. Instead, women and men actively petitioned the parish. Especially in the economically difficult 1590s, St Michael's vestry recorded women's petitions to take over the rooms and pensions of deceased women.[71] The successful petitioner, however, might live for only a few years in receipt of the parish's benevolence. Churchwardens would grant an occasional disbursement to a younger woman with children in preference to the customary elderly and impotent recipients, but only if they were clearly deserving and in particular need. Out of 'charitable consideration' rather than favouritism, in 1595 the vestry granted the empty chamber in the churchyard to Agnes Hewes and her 'many poor children', because they were abandoned by her 'lewd husband'. The parish further assisted her in getting her youngest child into Christ's Hospital, as well as granting her a small sum of money.[72]

Pensioners and the aged agitated to maintain their place within the parish church, as well as to join its relief rolls. Parishes placed widows together in pews and, judging by vestry minutes, widows fought against being moved to 'inferior' places within the church. The vestry of St Stephen Walbrook struggled to keep the peace while assigning men and women to pews.[73] In 1607, the vestry arranged women's seating according to their status, such as whether their husbands had been churchwardens, but claimed to have done so in order not to displease any 'formerly set before their Ancients'.[74] In St Michael Cornhill, people could sometimes sit outside their assigned pews without paying a fine, in order to hear better the sermon and lessons, since the preacher might also worry about the salvation of the aged and wish them to hear the edifying sermon. Concern for the souls of the often hearing-impaired elderly, combined with a public display of honour to the hoary head, and prompted no doubt by the protests of the aged poor, caused the parish to decide not to remove the 'ancients', nor to charge them a first fine of 2d. and a second of 4d. for sitting closer to the pulpit.[75] Many aged poor women, such as those found in St Stephen Walbrook, were active participants in their own social, economic and religious well-being.

Conclusion

Being old and being a woman in early modern London was a particularly dangerous combination, especially in this period of religious reformation and changing charitable practices. For many ageing women, the result was poverty. The marked tendency for old women to be poor women explains in part women's prominence among the poor, especially in a city with a sex ratio favouring men. Furthermore, culturally valued wisdom and public authority in the parish did not necessarily extend to aged women, or to all men, especially if poor, although they did have recognised areas of expertise, such as care-giving. Fixed resources and moral considerations, in the opinion of parish leaders and wealthy testators, necessitated discrimination concerning who would receive relief and charity. Idle youth, the metaphorical 'children' of 'mothers' and 'fathers', might abscond with the rightful relief of the aged. Thus, parishes oversaw the living arrangements even of the elderly poor and regulated their behaviour for fear of encouraging their own and others' idleness, as when Goody Coke gained her deceased husband's pension 'upon her good behaviour'.[76] In the late sixteenth century, as parishes sought to control illegitimacy, or at least what it cost them, older women may have seemed among the least troublesome of the poor in both moral and economic terms.

Even before the advent of the national poor law, the parish pension played an important role in the survival of poor, aged women, although it was never an individual's sole source of support. Indeed, parish leaders expected a combination of other resources to supplement their efforts in providing for the deserving, aged poor. Older poor women were supported by relief, informal testamentary charity, family contributions in money and care, as well as through their own labour. Religious and cultural changes reshaped the range of resources and strategies available to these women, especially the loss of religious fraternities, the end of purgatory and its prayers for the dead, and the slow alteration of funeral practices.[77] Friendly societies would appear later, but in the late sixteenth and early seventeenth century the loss of Roman Catholic institutions left parishes assuming a greater burden of the collective support. These developments meant that poor, aged women were no longer hired to say prayers and had less access to traditional sources of almsgiving. In the reform of charity and poor relief, aspects of the poor's economy of makeshifts became linked in the minds of the social elite to socially destructive trends, like crime and bastardy. Hence, London parishes joined the Lord Mayor and Parliament in attempting to restrict women's, especially aged women's, survival strategies.

Acknowledgements

I would like to thank the RECREAC fund of Wake Forest University for supporting this research. Earlier versions benefited from presentation at the American Historical Association's 1997 meeting, with comments from Professor Marjorie McIntosh, and to the Wake Forest Faculty Forum on Aging, with comments from Professor Gillian Overing and Doctor William Fleeson. Doctor Julie Edelson and the editors of this volume also contributed helpful comments. Jason Phillips provided valuable research assistance and the undergraduates in History 323 at Wake Forest University carefully considered this project. Any errors remain my own.

Notes

1. Robert Jütte, *Poverty and Deviance in Early Modern Europe* (Cambridge, 1994); Miri Rubin, *Charity and Community in Medieval Cambridge* (Cambridge, 1987); Paul Slack, *Poverty and Policy in Tudor and Stuart England* (London, 1988).

2. Amy Erickson, *Women and Property in Early Modern England* (London and New York, 1993); Marjorie McIntosh, 'Networks of care in Elizabethan English towns: the example of Hadleigh, Suffolk', in Peregrine Horden and Richard M. Smith, eds, *The Locus of Care: Families, Communities, and Institutions in History* (London, 1998); Tim Wales, 'Poverty, poor relief and the life-cycle: some evidence from seventeenth-century Norfolk', in Richard M. Smith, ed., *Land, Kinship and Life-cycle* (Cambridge, 1984), pp.351–404.

3. Olwen Hufton, *The Poor of Eighteenth-century France, 1750–1789* (Oxford, 1975), esp. pp.69–127. Cf. Margaret Pelling, 'Old age, poverty and disability in early modern Norwich', in Margaret Pelling and Richard M. Smith, eds, *Life, Death and the Elderly: Historical Perspectives* (London, 1991), p.75.

4. Population figures from Roger Finlay, quoted in Susan Brigden, *London and the Reformation* (Oxford, 1989), p.133.

5. Richard M. Smith, 'The structured dependence of the elderly as a recent development: some sceptical historical thoughts', *Ageing and Society* 4 (1984), pp.409–28, esp. p.423.

6. See Botelho and the Bibliographic Essay in this volume.

7. Jütte, *Poverty and Deviance*, pp.36–40 and graph p.37.

8. Peter Stearns, 'Old women: some historical observations', *Journal of Family History* 5 (1980), p.46.

9. William H. Overall, ed., *The Accounts of the Churchwardens of the Parish of St Michael Cornhill, in the City of London, from 1456 to 1608* (London, 1883), pp.184–223.

10. Definitions from the *Oxford English Dictionary* (OED) 2nd edn (Oxford, 1989).

11. Public Record Office (hereafter PRO), Probate (hereafter PROB) 11/58, f.63R.

12. PRO, PROB 11/34, f.47R.

13. Ibid., f.48L.

14. Ibid., ff.48L–48R.

15. William Shakespeare, *2 Henry IV*, II.iv.41.

16. OED.

17. OED.

18. PRO, PROB 11/35, f.127R; ff.26R–128L.

19. P. Laslett, 'Family, kinship and collectivity as systems of support in pre-industrial Europe: a consideration of the "nuclear-hardship" hypotheses', *Continuity and Change* 3 (1988), pp.153–77. Discussed in John Walter, 'The social economy of dearth in early modern England', in John Walter and Roger Schofield, eds, *Famine, Disease and the Social Order in Early Modern Society* (Cambridge, 1989), p.82.

20. Laslett, 'Family, kinship and collectivity', pp.154, 164, 168.

21. Vivien Brodsky, 'Widows in late Elizabethan London: remarriage, economic opportunity and family orientations', in Lloyd Bonfield, Richard M. Smith and Keith Wrightson, eds, *The World We Have Gained: Histories of Population and Social Structure* (Oxford, 1986), pp.122–54.

22. Christopher Black, *Italian Confraternities in the Sixteenth Century* (Cambridge, 1989); Samuel K. Cohn, Jr, *The Cult of Remembrance and the Black Death: Six Renaissance Cities in Central Italy* (Baltimore, 1992) and *Death and Property in Siena, 1205–1800: Strategies for the Afterlife* (Baltimore, 1988); Robert M. Kingdon, 'Social

welfare in Calvin's Geneva', *American Historical Review* 76 (1971), pp.50–69; Brian Pullan, 'Catholics and the poor in early modern Europe', *Transactions of the Royal Historical Society*, 5th series, 26 (1976), pp.15–34.

23. See Ottaway and the Bibliographic Essay in this volume.

24. See, for example, D. Kertzer, 'Toward a historical demography of aging', in D. Kertzer and P. Laslett, eds, *Aging in the Past: Demography, Society, and Old Age* (Berkeley, CA, 1995), pp.363–83; Wall, 'Elderly persons and members of their households in England and Wales from preindustrial times to the present', in D. Kertzer and P. Laslett, eds, *Aging in the Past: Demography, Society and Old Age* (Berkeley, CA, 1995), pp.81–106.

25. Cf. Ottaway and Pelling in this volume.

26. Joshua Toulmin Smith, *English Gilds* (London, 1870), pp.6, 9.

27. Caroline Barron, 'The parish fraternities of medieval London', Caroline Barron and Christopher Harper-Bill, eds, *The Church in Pre-Reformation Society: Essays in Honour of F.R.H. Du Boulay* (Woodbridge, 1985), p.27; Barry McRee, 'Charity and gild solidarity in late medieval England', *Journal of British Studies* 32 (1993), pp.195–225.

28. For a concise overview, see C.J. Kitching's introduction in *London and Middlesex Chantry Certificate, 1548* (London, 1980), esp. pp.ix–x.

29. Ibid., p.12.

30. Ibid., p.16.

31. Ibid., p.52.

32. For the best discussion of poor relief in England, see Slack, *Poverty and Policy*.

33. Henry Brinkelow, *The Complaint of Roderick Mors* (1545?; New York, 1973); Christopher Haigh, *English Reformations: Religion, Politics, and Society under the Tudors* (Oxford, 1993), p.68; London, Court of Common Council, Committee in Relation to the Royal Hospitals, *Memoranda, Reference, and Documents relating to the Royal Hospitals of the City of London* (London, 1836).

34. Claire Schen, 'Charity in London, 1500–1620: from the "Wealth of Souls" to the "Most Need"', unpublished PhD thesis (Brandeis University, 1995), p.119.

35. PRO, PROB 11/17, f.218R.

36. PRO, PROB 11/21, ff.317L–319R.

37. PRO, PROB 11/47, f.223R.

38. Schen, 'Charity in London', pp.157–8.

39. Paul Slack, *The English Poor Law, 1531–1782* (Cambridge, 1995), pp.51–2.

40. Guildhall Library (hereafter GL), MS 4072/1, Pt 1, ff.89–89v.

41. Claire Schen, 'Women and the London parishes, 1500–1620', in Katherine French, Gary Gibbs and Beat Kümin, eds, *The Parish in English Life, 1400–1600* (Manchester, 1997), p.258.

42. Slack, *English Poor Law*, p.51.

43. Overall, *Accounts*, p.222.

44. Diane Willen, 'Women in the public sphere in early modern England: the case of the urban working poor', *Sixteenth Century Journal* 19 (1988), pp.559–75.

45. John Partridge, *The Widowes Treasure Plentifully Furnished with Sundry Precious and Approued Secretes in Phisicke and Chirurgery for the Health and Pleasure of Mankinde: Hereunto are Adioyned, Sundry Preties Practises and Conclusions of Cookerie: With many Profitable and Holesome Medicines or Sundrie Diseases in Cattell* (London, 1588), f.A.ij–ij v.

46. GL, MS 1454, rolls 86, 93–5. Charnel house mentioned in roll 76 (1573–74).

47. Ibid., rolls 98, 99. Wilkinson may have remarried. The previous year's account mentioned that she could remain in her rooms as long as she remained in her widowhood.

48. Ibid., rolls 100–101, 102–3.

49. 18 Elizabeth I c.3, *The Statutes of the Realm* (*1575–76*). I am grateful to Jessica Sheetz for this reference.

50. William Harrison, *The Description of England*, Georges Edelen, ed. (1587 edn, first printed 1577; Ithaca, NY, 1968), p.180. See also A.L. Beier, *Masterless Men: The Vagrancy Problem in England, 1560–1640* (London and New York, 1985).

51. Contemporaries used the word 'alien' or 'stranger' to describe people from other countries and the word 'foreign' for an English person from another city or town.

52. Hufton, *Poor of Eighteenth-century France*, esp. pp.69–127.

53. See, for example, Corporation of London Record Office (hereafter CLRO), Repertory of the Court of Aldermen (hereafter Rep.) 25, f.6v (1599), Rep. 27, f.84 (1605), Rep. 28, f.60 (1607).

54. CLRO, Rep. 28, f.60.

55. Pelling, 'Old age, poverty and disability', p.84.

56. Kertzer, 'Toward a historical demography', p.376.

57. Laslett, 'The traditional English family and the aged in our society', in David D. Van Tassel, ed., *Aging, Death and the Completion of Being* (Philadelphia, PA, 1979), pp.97–114 (p.105). He has since revised this view, in 'Necessary knowledge: age and aging in the societies of the past', in Kertzer and Laslett, eds, *Aging in the Past*, p.47.

58. GL, MS 1453/1, f.3. Beginning folio numbers scrambled when separate books were bound together out of sequence.

59. GL, MS 4072/1, Pt 1, f.33.

60. Ibid., f.76v.

61. Ibid., f.37v.

62. Pelling, 'Old age, poverty and disability', p.87; Slack, *Poverty and Policy*, p.85. McIntosh has found evidence of the parish placing children with elderly poor for mutual benefit (personal communication).

63. GL, MS 593/2, ff.75, 76v. For Elizabeth Ludford (Allen) and pawned clothing see GL, MS 594/1, f.41.

64. GL, MS 593/2, f.70. See also Schen, 'Charity in London', on the trend towards even greater management of testamentary bequests by churchwardens, pp.144–6.

65. GL, MS 593/2, f.71.

66. McIntosh, 'Networks of care', *passim*; Wales, 'Poverty, poor relief and the life-cycle', p.384.

67. GL, MS 593/2, ff.71, 74v (Grocers), 76v (Bedlam), 78v (son), 106 (41 weeks of pension).

68. GL, MS 594/1, f.54.

69. For examples, see GL, MS 593/2, f.70.

70. For examples, see GL, MS 1002/1A, ff.206, 274, 297, 303v.

71. GL, MS 4072/1, Pt 1, f.38.

72. Ibid., f.63.

73. GL, MS 594/1, ff.68, 75, 88.

74. Ibid., f.64.

75. GL, MS 4072/1, Pt 1, f.1.

76. GL, MS 4072/1, Pt 1, f.34.

77. Matthew Davies, 'The Tailors of London: corporate charity in the late medieval town', in Rowena E. Archer, ed., *Crown, Government and People in the Fifteenth Century* (Herndon, 1996), pp.161–90, and Joseph P. Ward, *Metropolitan Communities: Trade Guilds, Identity, and Change in Early Modern London* (Stanford, CA, 1997), pp.45–69. More research is needed on craft or trade guilds and their charity both before and after the Reformation.

CHAPTER TWO

Who most needs to marry?
Ageing and inequality among women
and men in early modern Norwich

MARGARET PELLING

This essay looks at a perhaps uniquely rich source on poor men and poor women in early modern England: the Norwich Census of the Poor of 1570. This document, which formed the basis for Norwich's famous poor relief scheme of the 1570s, provides details of age, marital status, household structure, occupation, state of health, means of support, housing and length of residence for 2,359 men, women and children defined as poor. This large group constituted around one-quarter of the English-born population of Norwich, the city next in size and importance after London. My text has as background an earlier essay on work, remarriage, and other expedients, first published in 1991, which looked at people aged 50 and over from the census, and to a more recent essay which analyses the occupations and household structure of older women as given in the same source.[1] The census provides an unusual opportunity to compare inequalities among the poor themselves, and in particular the different situations of men and women. This is especially true with respect to ageing. Among the poor, more 'naked' than their better-off contemporaries, age becomes more glaringly an aspect of inequality, especially, perhaps, inequality between the sexes.

From the 1970s, historians have been providing background for the almost obsessive interest of late twentieth-century social commentators in structures of dependency and the fate of the elderly in different social contexts.[2] More recently, the elderly, who appear to lack the biological, developmental, reproductive and legal forms of definition which apply to younger age groups, have been seen as the last focus of cultural relativism.[3] Historical demographers, in searching for 'hard' facts about the elderly, have at least been able to demonstrate that old men and women actually existed in early modern society – Wrigley and Schofield's estimate for late sixteenth-century England for men and women 60 and over is around 7 per cent.[4] According to this estimate, the census population is somewhat skewed, in that the same age group constitutes 15 per cent of the poor, similar to the proportion of those aged 60 and over in Britain in the 1950s.[5] Thus, regardless of the undoubted effects of poverty in heightening mortality, it is necessary on every ground to eliminate the unthinking assumption that widespread poverty in other or earlier societies 'resolved' the issue of old age. The main problem for the historian trying to identify elderly individuals, especially women, is the absence of information on age. Hence, in part, the tendency to concentrate on widows (who may, however, be of any adult age), since for early modern women marital status had greater importance than adult age as a defining characteristic.[6] On age recording the census is again unusually exhaustive, even for women and children.[7]

It would be wrong, however, to represent the census as anything other than the product of a social process. Consciousness of age could be in itself partly a reflection of inequality, in so far as it became a feature of Elizabethan poor law administration.[8] The census-takers, all of whom almost certainly were male, apparently gathered information by house to house visitation, and there was probably some social distance between them and those they were observing. Within a standard format they used qualitative, evaluative and even emotional language; less obviously, their note-taking represents expectations as to family structure, interpersonal relationships, biological probabilities, human behaviour and social status. Thus, certain inequalities are symbolised in the recording itself: in, for example, the tendency not to distinguish younger children by sex, or the habit of approximating a wife's age to that of her husband. Occasionally, first impressions can be glimpsed in information which is recorded and then amended.

Other forms of inequality, however, are not expressed in terms of lack of information. The data on age, marital status, occupation and state of health are ample enough to permit reflections on the debate between social historians and historical demographers on the legitimacy of economic and demographic determinism. In recent decades, attention has shifted to marriage as the main fulcrum of demographic change, representing the decisions of the many in respect of (it is assumed) economic circumstances.[9] This focus has ultimately raised many vexed but neglected issues about the relationship between aggregate appearances, local circumstances and the individual decision. Why people chose to marry when they did has been revived as a major issue. Within this renewed debate, historians such as Bridget Hill and Barbara Todd have played a vital role in drawing attention to underlying assumptions about motives to marry, and in pointing to the neglect of female agency in this context.[10] The decision to marry is thus a significant focus for discussion about inequalities between men and women. Most of the attention is still given to the process of first marriage, and hence to younger age groups. However, the recent debate between Todd and Jeremy Boulton shows the particular interest attached to decisions made by widows: women who by definition had been relieved of any stigma of spinsterhood, who had possibly gained some financial independence, and who had probably also had children. Traditionally, widows also enjoyed the greatest degree of exemption from the legal and other disabilities suffered by early modern women.[11] Hence, the decision of a widow to marry, or her inability to do so, appears to present relations between the sexes in a particularly refined form, which has more to do with 'choice', and less to do with the perceived standard imperatives.

However, economic independence is usually, whether examined or not, an essential feature of such discussions. The debate has also been concerned with the position of poor widows, especially towards the latter part of the seventeenth century, but chiefly as a subset of the better-off or artisanal widows thought able to choose. The census of 1570 has the advantage of being concerned almost entirely with widows and others making decisions in the *absence* of property. As another effect of this, the discussion is able to move firmly away from the stereotype of the merry, lustful and far too knowledgeable widow who was a favourite subject of contemporary satire. Such a widow need not have been rich, but she was not usually very poor. It is also possible to avoid the distraction of the matching stereotype which has an elderly man buying the affections of a younger woman. In addition, the census predates the widespread operation of the Elizabethan poor law which, in the seventeenth century, allegedly exposed the poor old woman to contempt by drawing attention to the burden of her abject dependency. Its date is also too early for the operation of incentives for men to marry which have been attributed to the old poor law.[12] It is thus possible to consider the issue of agency, if not of choice, as represented in an account less affected by settled attitudes about property or its absence. If one of the effects of poverty is to remove opportunities for differentiation between people, in that it removes most of the material grounds of individual distinction, then the census may have the added virtue of allowing us to get close to the bedrock of assumptions about men and women in late sixteenth-century urban society. The main framework does of course remain economic, but it is also social and moral.

Looking first at marriage, it has to be said at the outset that the marriages of poor people in the census are themselves obscure, let alone the motives behind the decision to marry. It is necessary to make inferences from a structural snapshot: the census population is large enough and well enough described to make this legitimate. The size of Norwich's population can only be estimated, and the sex ratio in the town is unknown.[13] It is beginning to look as if London and the provincial cities were the exception among English towns in the late sixteenth century in not being feminised, but the picture is far from clear.[14] Some might regard sex ratios as a determining factor with respect to marriage, although it is clear also that migration was important, and if a population's perception of its own demography is valid in one context, then it presumably must be allowed to be so in another. That is, if there were more women than men in Norwich, then this would have been perceived, however inaccurately; yet it did not deter other women from coming to the town.

Two striking features about marital structure are apparent in the census population of those 50 and over. The first is the almost entire absence of men living on their own, with other men, or as lodgers. Only 5 per cent of the elderly men can be described as men living without women.[15] Most were married: the word 'widower' occurs scarcely at all, as if the category had no stable existence. Poor men after middle age, it appears, made sure they stayed married. If they lost their wives, they married again, even in old age. It does not alter this point that some of the pairings recognised by the census-takers may have been informal. The tendency of men not to be alone in pre-industrial societies has been noted by a number of historians. However, the full implications of this do not seem to have been considered.[16] The underlying assumption would be that it was easier for men to marry than for women. The Norwich case provides an acid test for this stereotype. It would be hard to imagine a less eligible population than the poor, often unemployed, often sick or disabled, elderly men of the Norwich census. It is difficult to envisage such men being able to marry because of their positive qualities. Rather, recourse has to be made to the further assumption that the position for a poor elderly woman was so much worse than that of any man, that marriage even to a man suffering acute disadvantage was preferable to being alone. This is a more credible position, and to it can be added the full weight of post-Reformation attitudes reinforcing patriarchy and the discipline of marriage. It seems legitimate to infer that some such heavy reinforcement would be necessary to produce the uniformity of structure evident in the census.

The second striking feature in the marital structure of the census population may seem at first to undermine part of the above conclusion. A very large minority of marriages or remarriages involving one or more spouses aged 50 and over were between partners very unequal in age.[17] Among the 533 people in this age group, there were 130 unions in which one spouse was ten or more years older than the other. Often the discrepancy is so great that the younger partner is not included among the elderly at all. The older partner was more often a man, although, notably, older women also seemed able to marry younger men. (There were 38 older wives as opposed to 92 older husbands.) This is a remarkable finding in the context of a north European marriage regime in which partners were rarely more than ten years apart in age, and usually less.[18] It could be taken to suggest that the disadvantage of poverty to women of any age was so great that even elderly, disabled poor men had a kind of added value which allowed them to marry women much younger than themselves – as was *not* the case among those above the level of poverty. In the earlier essays mentioned above (see note 1), a different interpretation is suggested, which is that these unequal unions are better seen as symbiotic and as involving a calculus of disadvantage on both sides.[19] Without rejecting this conclusion, I should like to take the argument further by contrasting the position of women with that of men. Could it not be that it was the men, at least as much if not more than the women, who were desperate to marry? Similarly, do we have to accept the idea that the position of all poor women was so bad that even an old man could pick and choose, giving him the opportunity, not shared by his more prosperous brethren, of choosing a much younger woman?

To discuss this, it is first necessary to look at older women. It should be noted that the sex ratio of the older census population was itself skewed, since only 37 per cent of the elderly were men.[20] There was certainly, within the census population, a substantial group of spouseless women who could in conventional terms be described as 'surplus'.[21] Of the total population of men and women aged 50 and over (533), nearly 37 per cent (197) were spouseless women, although for eight of these it was because they had been deserted.[22] If surplus, these women had not always been so, since only 8 of them were identified as never-married, and in only 32 cases was no marital status given: the rest (over 75 per cent) were widows.[23] It might be argued that prevailing conditions would induce some spinsters to say that they were widows when they were not: there is no reliable way of checking this possibility, especially given the extent of mobility even among the elderly poor.[24] Of the whole group of spouseless women, the majority – around 67 per cent – were, by contrast to the elderly men, living entirely alone. Admittedly, there are problems of ambiguity in both recording and in real life when people are crowded together under the same roof: mutual involvement and mutual assistance can vary enormously and it is impossible to know when individuals in such cases are truly alone, especially when such assistance can be more substantial than that offered by kin. The census-takers were required simply to determine means of support and liability for support; they did, however, note on a few occasions when a lone individual was being supported by friends as opposed to relatives. The possibility cannot be ruled out that some of these lone women supported each other, but in any case their apparent situation still contrasts sharply with that of the much-married older men. Are these women then the 'surplus', the real rejects, the non-productive post-menopausal women disadvantaged by universal prejudice, a skewed sex ratio, and by the ability of poor men to marry younger women?

One way to investigate this is to look at the information provided by the census on occupation and employment.[25] The census-takers were fairly exhaustive in that they attempted to record both – that is, the occupation for which the person had been trained, and what that person actually did. In modern terms, they were in effect measuring structural unemployment, loss of investment in training in particular skills, and even parts of the black or informal economy. They sporadically used such phrases as 'longe in pryson for dett', 'baker, & occupi to gather cony skyns', 'capper, butt make pattins', 'no occupacon & uses byrdinge & nettes', 'no occupacion, nor do work but go on purchace', or 'laborer in the contri with his fryndes'.[26] Nonetheless, as might be expected, there are major differences in the way in which men and women were recorded, which reflect the importance of occupational status in giving identity to even the poorest of men, and, correspondingly, the lack of this form of identity for women.[27] For men aged 50 and over, the census-takers produced a dull tolling to the tune of 'joiner, no work'. Of a total of 197 older men, 83 (42 per cent) were out of work or unable to work. This is excluding those who had some kind of by-employment. Although labourers predominated in the group as a whole, making up over 25 per cent of whom half had no work, a wide range of occupations is given. Unemployed or not, these elderly men at least retained an occupational identity. The obverse of this seems to be that if they could not follow their occupation, they could do little else. It is notable that even labourers did not lose their occupational identity if they took up other work. The labourers were more likely than any other occupation to diversify into other forms of work, but even these were exceptions within their own occupational group.

It is, however, difficult to decide whether we are dealing with an absence or a silence. Given what is known about how frequently early modern artisans diversified the occupations they actually used, as a function of both circumstance and lifecycle stage, it might seem unlikely that all the unemployed elderly men entirely lacked any form of work. If this is the case, the census-takers were complicit with the elderly men themselves in overlooking these minor employments. On the other hand, the penalty of occupational identity might be that minor employments were simply less available to men, again on the basis of attitudes in essence shared by men of very varied social standing. This possibility is reinforced by the feminised nature of many of the by-employments which were recorded for the elderly men: turning spits, keeping prisoners, keeping a church, filling pipes in the textile trade, selling ('going with') aqua vitae, keeping a kitchen, and, uniquely, making lace.[28] These were employments which were either shared with women or more characteristic of female than of male employment. To some extent there is an overlap here between what women did and what very poor people did – filling pipes and selling aqua vitae being two examples – which points to the lower status of women's work overall. Some poor men nevertheless followed other, less 'honourable' occupations which were possibly not available to women: the census-takers also noted porters, a limeburner, a tinker, two slaughtermen and three bodgers or pedlars. In general, however, the alternatives to an honourable occupation – a concept apparently applicable only to men – were either unemployment, or feminised forms of work which were either hidden or largely avoided, even by poor, elderly, married men.[29]

The lone women – women not only spouseless but also alone – provide a considerable contrast to this. Of the total of 132, only 23, or under 18 per cent, were described as not in work. Of those not working, most were severely disabled, being bedridden, lame, very sick or blind. Instead of the rich variety of occupational labels identifying the elderly men, even in the absence of employment, the women are described not by what they were occupationally but by what they did, which was mostly spinning. This was the case even if the woman was noted as not currently working because of ill health. The only exceptions were one woman who was said to be a tailor, and another who was a midwife.[30] Of those women working, nearly 78 per cent were spinning, mostly white warp, but also tow, webbing, wool, 'small stuff', and 'mentle warp'. Others knitted, carded, washed, twisted yarn, helped other women, and filled pipes.[31] Women continued to spin even when very aged, one-handed or nearly blind. Norwich was a textile town, and this uniformity of occupation in part reflects what could euphemistically be called employment opportunities specifically available to women.[32] It should also be acknowledged that many of these women were extremely poor, in effect unable to support themselves even with alms, but other notes included by the census-takers indicated that officials ignored work, even spinning, which was carried out purely for domestic purposes. These poor women were seen as working for their living, however inadequate the rewards might be.

To the work of spinning and knitting, which no adult male is recorded as doing in spite of the apparent opportunities for this employment, must be added employments related to health care. Two barbers among those aged 50 and over are the only men numbered in the Norwich census to whom can be attributed any version of the medical or caring role.[33] Given the ubiquity of medical activity at all levels of society in this period, it seems possible, as already suggested, that some activity of this kind among poor men was obscured. However, there is a range of descriptions around the formula 'helping women' which probably indicate forms of work open to women, perhaps especially older women, and closed to men.[34]

In summary, it is worth considering whether appearances might be deceiving. Instead of a population of desperate, dependent women, anxious to marry even the most disadvantaged of poor men, it may be that it is the men who were least able to sustain an independent, albeit marginal, existence in later life. To counteract this, they married and remarried, and were often, in old age and in adverse economic circumstances, unemployed and dependent upon the work of their wives and children. The conventional and rather condescending idea of poor women flocking to towns to take advantage of welfare provisions or to enter the households of their adult children should be modified by the possibility that they came to towns like Norwich to find work. That women migrated to find work has been suggested by a number of historians, but the casual end of the labour market has tended to remain 'crucial' but 'understudied'.[35] It is quite possible that many of these women, who may have called themselves widows, should be included among those who would have rejected marriage or remarriage as likely to add to their burdens. The value of older women is indicated by the surprising number of couples unequal in age in which the man was the younger. It is true that the census shows a population of men able to find partners; however, it probably needed the entire weight of social attitudes, legal and administrative provisions, and religious pressures to create a climate in which this was possible. The census itself records, occasionally, an 'ill husband' or a man who left his wife without help, but only women are described as unruly, as involved in prostitution, or as abroad out of control in the streets. According to this line of interpretation, the fact that a poor old man was able to marry a younger woman becomes not the ultimate demonstration of how easy it was for men to marry, but a reflection of the greater needs of the younger woman of childbearing age whose chances of an independent existence were far more restricted than those of the older woman.

It is necessary, finally, to return to the concept of the calculus of disadvantage. Older women might have been able to work, but their work was almost certainly monotonous, of low status and ill-paid.[36] The older woman who remained alone could pay a terrible price if she lived on into extreme old age and disability. Similarly, the unemployed man who was supported by his wife and children may have benefited in some sense from the inequalities of a patriarchal society, but he was himself also a victim of inequality. The situation of the poor of the Norwich census of 1570 is not without resonances for present-day societies.

Acknowledgements

This essay is a revised form of a paper given at the First ESSH Conference, Leeuwenhorst, in May 1996. I should like to thank those present for their comments, and the editors of this volume for their encouragement.

Notes

1. See respectively 'Old age, poverty and disability in early modern Norwich: work, remarriage and other expedients', and 'Older women: household, caring and other occupations in the late sixteenth-century town', in M. Pelling, *The Common Lot: Sickness, Medical Occupations and the Urban Poor in Early Modern England* (London, 1998), pp.134–54, 155–75. These and other essays in the same volume provide further details and analysis of the census.

2. In general, see M. Pelling and R.M. Smith, eds, *Life, Death and the Elderly: Historical Perspectives* (London, 1991), and sources there cited.

3. Pelling and Smith, *Life, Death and the Elderly*, p.8.

4. E.A. Wrigley and R. Schofield, *The Population History of England 1541–1871: A Reconstruction* (Cambridge, 1989), App. 3, p.528.

5. Pelling, *Common Lot*, pp.69–72.

6. On widows see, most recently, S. Cavallo and L. Warner, eds, *Widowhood in Medieval and Early Modern Europe* (Harlow, 1999), and references there cited.

7. Pelling, *Common Lot*, p.139.

8. Ibid., p.136.

9. R.M. Smith, 'Marriage processes in the English past: some continuities', in L. Bonfield, R.M. Smith and K. Wrightson, eds, *The World We Have Gained: Histories of Population and Social Structure* (Oxford, 1986), p.43.

10. B.J. Todd, 'The remarrying widow: a stereotype reconsidered', in M. Prior, ed., *Women in English Society 1500–1800* (London, 1985), pp.54–92; B. Hill, 'The marriage age of women and the demographers', *History Workshop Journal* 28 (1989), pp.129–47. See also S. Wright, ' "Holding up half the sky": women and their occupations in eighteenth-century Ludlow', *Midland History* 14 (1989), pp.53–74; P.J.P. Goldberg, ' "For better, for worse": marriage and economic opportunity for women in town and country', in P.J.P. Goldberg, ed., *Woman is a Worthy Wight: Women in English Society c. 1200–1500* (Stroud, 1992), pp.108–25; and in general, A. MacKinnon, 'Were women present at the demographic transition? Questions from a feminist historian to historical demographers', *Gender and History* 7 (1995), pp.222–40.

11. J. Boulton, 'London widowhood revisited: the decline of female remarriage in the seventeenth and early eighteenth centuries', *Continuity and Change* 5 (1990), pp.323–55; B.J. Todd, 'Demographic determinism and female agency: the remarrying widow reconsidered . . . again', ibid. 9 (1994), pp.421–50; A.L. Erickson, *Women and Property in Early Modern England* (London, 1993), esp. Pt IV.

12. Hill, 'Marriage age of women', p.141. On contrary tendencies, see S. Hindle, 'The problem of pauper marriage in seventeenth-century England', *Transactions of the Royal Historical Society*, 6th Ser. 8 (1998), pp.71–89. I am grateful to Steve Hindle for allowing me to see an unpublished version of his essay.

13. On Norwich's population see Pelling, *Common Lot*, pp.69, passim.

14. On sex ratios see Todd, 'Demographic determinism', pp.431–6; P. Griffiths, J. Landers, M. Pelling and R. Tyson, 'Population and disease, estrangement and belonging 1540–1700', in P. Clark, ed., *The Cambridge Urban History of Britain. Vol. 2: 1540–1840* (Cambridge, 2000).

15. Pelling, *Common Lot*, p.147. Of all poor men over the age of 20, including the elderly, only 1.2 per cent (twelve men) were spouseless. Only one of the twelve was given an age under 50: M. Pelling, 'Finding widowers: men without women in English towns before 1700', in Cavallo and Warner, *Widowhood*, p.50.

16. For some exploration of this issue, see Pelling, 'Finding widowers'.

17. On what follows, and for further detail, see Pelling, 'Old age, poverty and disability'.

18. R.M. Smith, 'Geographical diversity in the resort to marriage in late medieval Europe: work, reputation, and unmarried females in the household formation systems of northern and southern Europe', in Goldberg, *Woman is a Worthy Wight*, pp.17–18, 22–7, 35. Such 'unequal' marriages have been noted in passing elsewhere, but interpreted differently: see, for example, A. Bideau, 'A demographic and social analysis of remarriage: the example of the Castellany of Thoissey-en-Daubes, 1670–1840', *Family History* 5 (1980), pp.28–43, esp. p.39.

19. See also Schen in this volume.

20. Pelling, *Common Lot*, p.147.

21. For more detailed analysis of the situation of the spouseless older women, see Pelling, 'Older women'. See also Froide in this volume.

22. For more on the deserted wives and absent husbands, see Pelling, 'Finding widowers'.

23. Here the census appears to follow the general rule for early modern records, in that greater detail is associated with a need for differentiation or identification. What the women given no marital status have in common is not that they were transients, but that they were mostly long-resident or born in Norwich.

24. On migration among the elderly poor, see Pelling, *Common Lot*, pp.139–41.

25. For analysis of occupations in general see Pound's edition of the census: J.F. Pound, ed., *The Norwich Census of the Poor 1570*, Norfolk Record Soc., 40 (1971). It is Pound's edition that is used here. On occupations in relation to health and disability, see Pelling, *Common Lot*; idem, 'Thoroughly resented? Older women and the medical role in early modern London', in L. Hunter and S. Hutton, eds, *Women, Science and Medicine 1500–1700* (Stroud, 1997), pp.63–88. On occupations and multi-occupation among older women, see Pelling, 'Older women'.

26. Pound, *Census*, pp.24, 26, 46, 49, 53, 90. Pound transcribes 'Lettes', but 'nets' seems more plausible in the context of Norwich occupations.

27. See, for example, M. Prior, 'Women and the urban economy: Oxford 1500–1800', in Prior, *Women in English Society*, pp.93–117; M. Pelling, 'Compromised by gender: the role of the male medical practitioner in early modern England', in H. Marland and M. Pelling, eds, *The Task of Healing: Medicine, Religion and Gender in England and the Netherlands 1450–1800* (Rotterdam, 1996), pp.101–34, and references there cited.

28. Pound, *Census*, pp.50, 56, 59, 83, 89, 74. The male lace-weaver had been a worsted-weaver. On lace-making see the work of Pamela Sharpe, e.g. 'Lace-making in early modern England: skills, gender and work culture', paper given to Achievement Project conference, London, 4 June 1994.

29. Occupations in English towns were seen in terms of a hierarchy of status, but the notion of a dishonourable trade seems to have been less specifically developed than in continental Europe: M. Jenner, 'Early modern English conceptions of "cleanliness" and "dirt" as reflected in the environmental regulation of London c.1530–c.1700', unpublished DPhil thesis (University of Oxford, 1991), pp.138–41. I am grateful to Mark Jenner for allowing me access to his thesis. For some discussion of artisanal honour in a French town where there were fewer men than women, see J.R. Farr, *Hands of Honor: Artisans and their World in Dijon, 1550–1650* (Ithaca, NY, 1988), esp. pp.177–95. Garthine Walker rightly stresses forms of female honour as opposed to dishonour, but limits her discussion of female occupations to housewifery: 'Expanding the boundaries of female honour in early modern England', *Transactions of the Royal Historical Society*, 6th series, VI (1996), pp.235–45. On gender factors affecting forms of work, see Pelling, 'Compromised by gender', and references there cited.

30. Pound, *Census*, pp.57, 30.

31. For details of the occupations of the married, spouseless, and lone older women, see Pelling, 'Older women', pp.167–70.

32. Glovemaking in Ludlow at a later period provides another example, although the situation of poor women workers can only be inferred from such sources as Easter lists: Wright, 'Holding up half the sky'.

33. Pound, *Census*, p.45 (Robert Stutter, aged 70, his wife aged 50 'that spyn white warp' – 'veri poor') and p.67 (Edmund Smyth, aged 56, 'barbor & porter of Byshops gate', his wife aged 46, 'that spyn white warpe').

34. On this formula see Pelling, 'Older women', pp.168ff.

35. Wright, 'Holding up half the sky', p.70. See also P. Sharpe, *Adapting to Capitalism: Working Women in the English Economy, 1700–1850* (London, 1996), p.8.

36. In general see A. Clark, *Working Life of Women in the Seventeenth Century* (1919; London, 1982); P.J.P. Goldberg, *Women, Work, and Life Cycle in a Medieval Economy: Women in York and Yorkshire c.1300–1520* (Oxford, 1992); O. Hufton, *The Prospect Before Her: A History of Women in Western Europe. Vol 1: 1500–1800* (London, 1995). On ideological issues see C. Jordan, 'Renaissance women and the question of class', in J.G. Turner, ed., *Sexuality and Gender in Early Modern Europe: Institutions, Texts, Images* (Cambridge, 1993), pp.90–106.

CHAPTER THREE

Old age and menopause in rural women of early modern Suffolk

LYNN BOTELHO

Who is an old woman? One who is called old and does not protest.

Maimonides[1]

At the heart of the study of old age lies the question, how old is old? Yet, historians have seldom asked it, and then only inadequately answered it. This essay explores the ageing process in early modern England, looking specifically at the onset of old age among pauper women in rural Suffolk. The analysis falls into three parts: first, a consideration of the methodological problems surrounding the definition of old age; secondly, an exploration of one community's cultural definition of the onset of old age; and thirdly, an examination of the effects of menopause on rural women and its relationship to female ageing. This essay makes four related arguments about the nature and definition of old age. First, it suggests that old age was determined primarily by cultural considerations, considerations which were, in the deeply iconographic world of early modern England, primarily visual in nature.[2] Consequently, the onset of 'old age' could vary according to sex and status, and probably according to region and occupation. Secondly, this work stresses the concept that old age was subdivided into at least two phases, 'green' old age or the 'young' old, and advanced or decrepit old age. Further, women and men did not enter into or experience these stages in the same fashion. Thirdly, this essay argues that the side-effects of menopause, and not the biological end of fertility, produced a large and wide-ranging set of physical changes on the face and body of poor, rural women that made them look, and be considered, old at approximately age 50. Fourthly, these conclusions challenge the assumptions of many historians who place the onset of old age for all at age 60. Instead, it argues for the use of more subtle approaches in the study of old age, ones that are sensitive to social position, historical period and gender.

Methodological problems

Determining the onset of old age in the past is extremely problematic. Unlike the late twentieth century, with its retirements and old age pensions, there was no rite of passage to mark the beginning of old age in the early modern world. For most of history, individuals have slipped over its boundary in secret, without official acknowledgement by the community, or perhaps even by themselves. 'In darkness and silence', warns Petrarch, 'it hits the unwitting man, and when he thinks it is yet far off, there it is upon his threshold'.[3] Defining the onset of old age is further complicated by the lack of agreement on what actually constitutes this stage of life; indeed, it can be evaluated in three separate ways. Chronological old age is achieved upon the attainment of a specific calendar age, regardless of the individual's mental or physical fitness. Functional old age, on the other hand, is achieved when one can no longer support oneself or participate fully in society, whether or not one has obtained a specific chronological age. Finally, cultural old age, which can include aspects of both chronological and functional old age, is defined by the society in which an individual lives, and in early modern England it was typically associated with certain physical characteristics: toothlessness; stooped shoulders; facial hair for women; and physical frailty for men.[4] All three ageing processes can function simultaneously, and yet not be of equal importance or occur at equal speed. Therefore, the relative importance of each definition must be determined carefully and with reference to a particular setting.[5] For early modern society, with its degrees of wealth and status, its orders and hierarchies, a universal threshold of old age may not only be inappropriate but also inaccurate.

In much of the recent scholarship two tendencies are present which obscure the complex nature of early modern old age. First, many historians use a chronological age to mark the onset of old age and typically set this point at age 60.[6] This is perhaps owing to the influence of demographic history. The demographic method constructs long-range statistical models of populations that often span several centuries and anchor themselves in the known values of population data from the modern period. An example of this is E.A. Wrigley and R. Schofield's influential *The Population History of England 1541–1871: A Reconstruction*. Their 'back projection' methodology, used to determine the population structure of England between 1541 and 1871, designated 60 as the onset of old age.[7] While this procedure is obviously necessary for demographers, other types of historians who ask different sets of questions must be careful not to treat this definition of old age, created specifically for population modelling purposes, as an accurate reflection of the attitudes or experiences of the seventeenth century.

The second recurring problem is that many scholars of the pre-modern world, despite their obvious knowledge of the Ages of Man material discussed below, treat the final stage of the lifecycle as comprising an undifferentiated mass of physically exhausted and helpless individuals. Rather, it is more accurate to view ageing as composed of descending stages.[8]

Early modern commentators were aware that old age, like youth and middle age before it, contained subdivisions. Some, like John Smith in his *The Pourtract of Old Age*, wrote of the threefold nature of ageing.

> First, crude, green [old age], and while it is yet in the beginning, while men are able to do business, and so about their employments, and this is but one little remove from manhood and doth immediately border upon it. The second is full mature, or ripe age; when men begin to leave off their employments and betake themselves to retiredness; when God hath no work for them, and they have no strength for him; or lastly, extream sickly decripit, overgrown old age; in which it may be truly said old age is perished; when their breath is corrupt, when their daies are extinct, and the grave is ready for them.[9]

Others, like Henry Cuffe, conceived of a two-staged old age, along the lines of Aristotle's twofold division of old age. The first phase, from 50 to 65, was marked by the commencement of declining strength, 'but there remaineth a will and readinesse to be doing'. Following this state of declining physical ability but ever-present readiness was, in Cuffe's words, 'decrepit old age'. At this point both the body's strength and 'heat' are

> [so] farre decaied, that not onley all abilitie is taken away, but even all willingenesse, to the least strength and motion of our bodie and this is the conclusion and the end of our life, resembling death itselfe, whose harbinger and fore-runner it is.[10]

Whether divided into two or three phases, the early modern view of old age was not an abrupt descent to decrepitude and failing abilities.[11] Yet, Cuffe described male old age. The life experience of women was generally very different from that of men, and so too was their ageing process. While old age for both women and men comprised ever-descending stages, for poor women it was not a gentle curve towards helplessness. Rather, the first step into old age was a long one, only after which did they join men in their gradual decline. This is not to say that women did not experience green old age, but that men and women experienced it differently.

The most recently published work to confront directly the issue of 'how old is old' is Shulamith Shahar's *Growing Old in the Middle Ages*. While specifically and clearly rejecting the use of chronological ageing in favour of a functional definition, in the end she too settles on age 60 as the line of demarcation between middle and old age. While this essay disagrees with Shahar's choice of age 60 as the universal beginning of old age, her work is significant in its careful consideration of a variety of methods one might attempt when defining the onset of old age, such as the study of the Ages of Man, personal papers, and records.

One of the most obvious approaches to defining the culturally determined start of old age, and one that is thoroughly rejected by Shahar, is an analysis of the Ages of Man: the division of man's development from infancy to old age. The following handwritten English example from the mid-eighteenth century is typical of such schemes, whether they originated in popular or elite culture, in England or elsewhere. This example is particularly interesting because of its fourfold construction of old age, commencing with a 'perceivable decline to Age' at age 49.

> It is supposed that a Man has a new Mind, or at least a great variation every 7 years.
>
> 1st 7   Childhood.
> 2.   14 Youth.
> 3.   21 Betwixt Youth and Manhood.
> 4.   28 The most brisk and lively Part of life.
> 5.   35 The most strong, mature and manly Time of Life.
> 6.   42 A Continuence, very little Decay.
> 7.   49 Perceivable Decline to Age.
> 8.   56 More and More.
> 9.   63 Old Age Apparent.
> 10. 70 Very Old.[12]

Structured around magical numbers such as three, seven and twelve, the years in Christ's life, the four humours, astrology, or Aristotelian biology, the exact ages assigned to each stage of life were not necessarily keyed to man's physical state. According to these sources, male old age could begin anywhere between the ages of 35 and 72.[13] The female lifecycle, however, was seldom depicted in this manner. One example, found in Thomas Tusser's *Five Hundred Points of Good Husbandry*, divided the 'ages of woman' into fourteen-year intervals. Yet, for most people, the stages of a woman's life were separated into thirds: maid, wife and widow: divisions that are not necessarily tied to chronological age.[14] As Shahar demonstrates, the lack of agreement among these prescriptive documents means that they cannot be used to discover definitively the onset of old age.[15]

Another avenue of investigation that Shahar shows to be of dubious value is the extrapolation of the beginning of old age from personal documents, papers and memoirs. Her medieval examples demonstrate that individuals were aware of the gradual process of ageing and complained of growing old well before they actually conceived of themselves as truly aged. This self-awareness was equally present in early modern England. Cries of 'old age!' resound as early as 40, but they were often later denied by declarations of vigorous good health. The Essex vicar Ralph Josselin writes at age 40 of 'a very violent yirke of the crampe in my left calfe. The first I perceived, a warning of old age'.[16] This comment reveals the aches of middle age, a foreshadowing of things to come, but not yet the pains of old age.

Coincidentally, Josselin conceptualised his lifecycle in the same ten ages of man quoted above, and he worried about growing old accordingly: 'I was sensible of it [his 64th birthday] and affected with gods goodness, not troubled in 63 as a critical and dangerous year, though I often thought of it'.[17] Josselin also kept a section of 'sayings' in his diary which further illustrates his belief in the ten-stage lifecycle and, indirectly, his understanding of old age as a gradual decline, framed in this instance according to the days of the week: 'If mans age bee 70: then I now being in my 58 and almost at my . . . Friday midnight, lord fitt mee for a blessed Sabath at hand!'[18]

Instead of using either the Ages of Man or personal anecdote to determine the beginning of old age, Shahar applies the aged-linked exemptions found in legislative texts throughout western Europe. Military service, trial by battle, and municipal services such as the town watch, were all forms of obligation from which those over 60 or 70 years of age were excused. As she admits, the documents were just as likely to use 70 as 60 to mark the beginning of such forbearances.[19] However, legal exemptions, release from military service, or the payment of taxes would limit government resources, either in men or money, and consequently, it would best serve the purposes of government to set these exemptions at ages as late as possible. Furthermore, if one were to apply the concept of degrees of old age, one could argue that, while individuals might begin to age and feel old at age 50, they were by no means helpless or worthless. Indeed, Rosenthal has detailed many instances of aged peers, such as Henry Fitzhugh, successfully leading men in war.[20] As Cuffe and Smith both suggest, the early years of old age were still quite product-ive, and therefore legal exemptions, which appear to mark the decline of physical strength, would not be given to the green elderly, but reserved for their more mature, and decayed, counterparts. A refinement of Shahar's argument would be to follow the general pattern found in the Ages of Man literature and set the onset of old age at some earlier point, and use legal exemptions, based on functionality and declining strength, to mark the threshold into mature old age.

Not surprisingly, the study of female old age is not well served in an analysis of governmental, and therefore male, documents. Shahar, for example,
could locate only two legal texts that addressed female old age exemptions:
the English Statute of Labourers and Henry VII's Statute Against Vagabonds.
Both parliamentary Acts set the legal age of exemption at 60. Yet, as Shahar
herself points out, 'it was plainly in their [the government's] interest to set
the highest age possible for releasing workers from their duties'.[21] Therefore,
it is possible that, as with men, age 60 marked advanced old age for women,
and not its onset. She also refers to the custom of the Crusader kingdoms
that allowed widows over the age of 60 to remain unmarried. In both her
examples, it is probable that the age of exemption was set conservatively. In
the case of the employment laws, it was to ensure a full workforce. In the
second case, it was to maximise the probability that the woman was past
menopause and unable to reproduce, and thus ensure against an improper
marriage, as a union without the aim of procreation was viewed as sinful. In
order to examine female ageing, especially the question of 'how old is old',
we can turn away from the male-orientated world of government documents
and towards the smaller-scale, more individualised accounts of parish life.

Towards a cultural definition of old age

Shulamith Shahar's work is extremely valuable in pointing future research
towards a cultural definition of old age. When analysing pre-industrial societies, many anthropologists believe that 'the only reliable criterion for the
onset of old age seems to be the social and cultural one. The simplest and
safest rule to follow was to consider a person as "old" whenever he was so
regarded and treated by his contemporaries'.[22]

Given the many variables that figure into the definition of old age, it
is not surprising that official documents, generated from the seat of government for specific purposes, are to be handled with care, and that alone
they are not sufficient to determine accurately cultural onset of old age.[23]
Microhistory, the careful observation of the minute details that form the
fabric of the lives of 'real people in actual situations', or, to paraphrase
Edward Muir, the observing of trifles, does, however, provide the required
degree of illumination onto both the pattern of ageing and the mindset of a
particular community to determine its definition of old age.[24]

The following analysis of female ageing is based on a family and parish
reconstitution of sixteenth- and seventeenth-century Cratfield, Suffolk, a
thriving cheese and dairying community of roughly 300 inhabitants.[25] The
family reconstitution identified those individuals who lived past 50 years of

age; the parish reconstitution allowed the construction of biographies for these individuals. These biographies contain all the extant recorded material for each person, often spanning baptism to burial. Therefore, the ageing process is placed in the context of each person's full life.[26]

This parish, like many others in early modern England, often used honorific titles when addressing the aged, worthy poor. Terms such as 'mother', 'father' and 'old' were often given to the elderly poor by their social betters and chronological juniors as a sign of respect and as an honour due their longevity.[27] While such terms could be patronising, their use within the context of charity and poor relief was generally deferential. More prosperous individuals, however, would not willingly forgo their status titles that reflected greater social authority, such as master, mistress or sir, in favour of a purely honorary term that would be shared with their social inferiors. One way to discern when Cratfield considered old age to begin for the poor was, using the biographies, to chart the age at which these titles were first conferred.

In Cratfield, 52 individuals, primarily in the seventeenth century, were referred to as 'mother', 'father' or 'old': all of them were on poor relief. Of these people, we can accurately assign ages to 21 men and 15 women. The average age at the onset of old age, for women and men taken as a group, was 56 years. However, the gender difference between Cratfield's aged poor was startling. Women exhibited the signs of ageing significantly sooner than men. Women were considered old, on average, at age 52, while men were not publicly acknowledged as such until a full nine years later, at age 61.[28]

An examination of female ages reveals that the first use of these honorific titles for the fifteen women under observation ranged from age 34 to age 80. And while the average age was in the early fifties, the majority of women were first viewed as old in their late forties, with the bulk of female ageing occurring around their fiftieth year (see Figure 3.1).

Men, as noted above, were identified as old much later than women, at age 61. Certainly the parish of Littledean in the Deanery of the Forest, Gloucestershire, thought 60 was very old indeed: 'the clercke ys a veri olde man of thage of lx yeres'.[29] Again, the age distribution ranges from their thirties to their eighties; however, there is less consensus concerning these 21 individuals as to which quinquennial year represents the bulk of male ageing (see Figure 3.2). Male ageing proceeded at an idiosyncratic pace, suggesting that the use of honorific titles for men recorded something other than initial entry into old age. It is possible that terms such as 'old' and 'father' marked the outward signs of the physical breakdown of the male body and registered male entry into decrepit old age. This dovetails nicely with Shahar's conception of male functional old age as beginning at age 60.

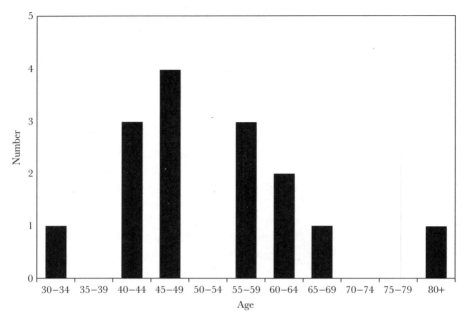

Figure 3.1   Female honorific titles in sixteenth- and seventeenth-century Cratfield, Suffolk

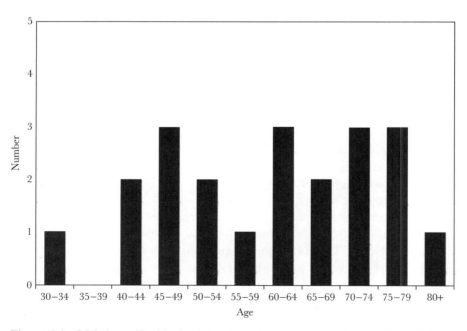

Figure 3.2   Male honorific titles in sixteenth- and seventeenth-century Cratfield, Suffolk

With both men and women, the use of honorific titles was triggered by the same thing: an individual's physical appearance. However, the cultural meanings of these titles differed according to gender; for men it appeared to signal advanced old age, for women its initial onset.

In rural Cratfield, the ageing experience of women was markedly different from that of men. Women's entry into senescence tended to happen to most women near their fiftieth year. It was, possibly dramatically, physically noticeable to their neighbours. This definitive, obvious and somewhat synchronised entry into old age suggests that there was something distinctive about the female experience; something that occurred to all women at roughly the same age; and something that caused women to 'look' old. That something was menopause.[30]

Menopause, when neither treated by modern medicine nor counteracted by a modern diet, can produce physical changes and characteristics associated with ageing. Menopausal women may grow facial hair and develop a stoop. Their skin can become loose and etched with wrinkles. Age spots tend to develop and spread on their faces and hands. The years of poor nutrition and calcium-draining pregnancies could culminate in a toothless mouth. Indeed, many women at menopause went through a 'change', and not just one regarding their reproductive life. For women, old age still comprised stages, from 'young' old to outright helplessness. However, those phases did not always correspond to the evolution expounded by Cuffe and enshrined in the Ages of Man. Many women experienced a marked entry into the first stage of old age, and not men's 'old age creeping on apace'.[31] That is not to say that menopause made women helpless, but that it indicated that the threshold of green old age had definitively and unequivocally been crossed.

Growing old for men was generally a much more gentle and subtle affair, as measured in rural Cratfield by the declining ability of poor men to work and support their households. There was not an abrupt end to male work life, no retirement as experienced in the modern world, except among society's most affluent members. For the poor, whom we study here, only physical disability ended an individual's working life, for unless the parish stepped into the breach, one did not eat if one did not work.[32] Furthermore, men did not experience a collective and biologically triggered entry into green old age, as was the case with female menopause. Male ageing, even among the poor, closely resembled the general observations of Cuffe and Smith.[33] Even the ancients upon whom educated society relied, such as Aristotle and the Hippocratics, confidently stated that men aged more slowly than women.[34] Yet, men too would eventually begin to stoop and lean upon a stick. Their skin would eventually and gradually acquire the looseness and opacity that had manifested itself in women at the menopause. If they were not inclined to baldness in youth and middle age, old age would gradually produce a head of fine and probably grey hair. The attributes of male old age did not develop all at once, or at the same time for all, but proceeded at a much more unpredictable pace, thus explaining the scattered and delayed public acknowledgment of male old age. Eventually, the ageing patterns of elderly women and men would converge and henceforth they would share the same physical characteristics and culturally defined old age attributes. Commentary on the similarities between old men and women dates to classical times. According to Hippocrates, 'menopause signalled the reassimilation of the female body to the male (and hence more tractable) body'.[35]

In rural communities of early modern Suffolk, cultural old age was determined by a number of factors: biology, functionality and appearance. These did not necessarily appear simultaneously, nor were they of equal importance in the community's mind. The visible characteristics associated with old age seem to have been the key variable in Cratfield's identification of a woman or man as old. For women, this occurred significantly sooner than for men. Pauper biographies generated from the parish and family reconstitutions and the language of age have proven one means of addressing the methodological problem of assessing a community's collective beliefs concerning the ageing process. It has revealed distinctive patterns of ageing for both women and men, allowing important distinctions to be drawn about the nature of old age, and consequently to begin to distinguish some of the contours of the final stage of life.

Menopause and rural women

Menopause marks the end of a woman's reproductive ability. It is 'the natural result of age-related changes in ovarian function. It means, literally, the cessation of uterine menstrual cycles', the cessation of her menstrual flow.[36] Despite the misinformed statements of modern scholars who claim that few women in the past lived long enough to experience menopause, Amundsen and Dyers, as well Post, have shown that this biological change occurred in the lives of most women of early modern England, on average, at the age of 50.[37] This same cluster pattern, centred on age 50, was found in the Cratfield data on honorific titles.

It would seem logical, therefore, to conclude that female old age began as a result of infertility, a verdict also reached by many physicians and social commentators from the eighteenth to the early twentieth centuries.[38] More recent scholarship, however, suggests that many societies across time and space, and with differing social organisations, explicitly reject the direct equation of menopause and old age.[39] Indeed, the Cratfield material itself argues against this correlation. The community, even those face-to-face villages of seventeenth-century England, could not know with confidence whether a woman had ceased to be fertile, since marital fertility had typically concluded by age 40, well before the menopausal years.[40] The birth of children, therefore, is not a reliable indicator of fertility and it is unlikely that female old age was equated with the end of reproduction.

Generally, the end of reproduction probably did not signal the beginning of old age to early modern society, but *menopause* did coincide with a host of culturally significant visual changes that resulted in women being labelled old at this stage. The importance and indeed ubiquitous nature of outwardly observable signifiers of status in early modern England can hardly be overestimated, from the sumptuary laws of the Tudors to the beggars' badges of the Stuarts. William Harrison, in his *Description of England* (1577), makes a similar point about the gentry: those who 'bear the port, charge and countenance' associated with the rank of gentlemen, become gentlemen.[41] It is therefore consistent with early modern life to look for and accept the visual indicators of age. A woman became old when she looked old.[42]

Menopause played a critical role in early modern England's cultural definition of old age, but it was its symptoms, rather than its primary biological feature of infertility, which marked women's point of entry into old age. In fact, the biological changes of menopause were little understood by medical writers of the early modern period, with their heavy reliance on the writing of ancient Greece and Rome. It was certainly not clear to the average individual, and menopause remained one of the few bodily functions not discussed in detail by contemporaries and whose treatment was not detailed in housewifery, commonplace and advice books.[43] The body was thought to comprise four humours (blood, bile, black bile and phlegm; or heat, cold, moist and dry). The womb itself was conceived as wandering, moving from place to place within the body. Menopause, known as 'climacteric' to contemporaries, was understood to be the result of the women's body becoming colder and dryer, and closer to death. In fact after menopause, the womb was considered to be lighter and thus more prone to movement.[44]

Since early modern women did not typically write about menopause in surviving documents, or provide remedies in their commonplace books, historians must draw upon modern medical understanding of menopause and read this knowledge backwards into the seventeenth century; or, in the words of David Gentilcore, to make 'unashamed use of the regressive method to shed light on somewhat obscure aspects of the past'.[45] This process is problematic in several ways. First, there is still much that is not understood about menopause in modern women, and the medical profession is not in agreement over its interpretation. Secondly, some of the symptoms of menopause are materially or culturally determined in so far as they are affected by such things as diet and modern child-nursing practice. Despite these serious considerations, a careful reading backwards into the past can shed light on areas that contemporaries did not generally discuss.

We are primarily concerned with the physical, highly visible effects of menopause. Hot flushes, for instance, while unquestionably uncomfortable and among the most commonly mentioned effects of menopause among twentieth-century women, are not of interest here simply because they have no visual manifestation. On the other hand, the hormonal changes of menopause also produce or accelerate many phenomena whose physical symptoms congregate in the face and broad contours of the outward form.

It is the face that registers the physical symptoms of menopause first, and provides many of the culturally defined characteristics of old age. Although most women probably do not have the same violent reaction to the ageing process as Simone de Beauvoir, she was correct about the focal point the face played in publicising the ageing process.[46]

> I often stop, flabbergasted, at the sight of this incredible thing that serves me as a face. I understand La Catiglione, who had every mirror smashed . . . While I was able to look at my face without displeasure I gave it no thought, it could look after itself . . . I loathe my appearance now; the eyebrows slipping down toward the eyes, the bags underneath, the excessive fullness of the cheeks, and that air of sadness around the mouth that wrinkles always bring . . . When I look, I see my face as it was, attacked by the pox of time for which there is no cure.[47]

While a small number of women lose their hair as they age in the same fashion as men, a significant number instead experience the growth of coarse facial hair on the upper lip and chin. William Shakespeare built upon this trait when he questioned the sex of the three witches in *Macbeth*, women obviously of the lower social order: 'you should be women, and yet your beards forbid me to interpret that you are so'.[48] Judging from the numerous references to poor, old women with whiskers, both visually and in print, it appears that plucking or bleaching of facial hair was uncommon for the lower sort in early modern England. Gentlewomen, meanwhile, had a vast array of 'beautifying waters, oyls, oyntments and pounders, to adorn and add loveliness to the face and body', including those for the removal of facial hair.[49]

The face also highlighted another menopausal feature that is universally associated with old age: wrinkled skin. Even Queen Elizabeth I was not able to escape this fate. 'It is said that Queen Elizabeth when young was beautifull, but it declin'd in her middle age; and when old she became deform'd with wrinkles, leanness, and fallen lips'.[50] With the abrupt change in hormone levels in a woman's body at menopause, the skin rapidly loses its thickness and becomes drier.[51] Along with wrinkles, menopause results in skin with a decreased ability to tense up or appear firm. It also begins to lose the ability to tan.[52] Consequently, in early modern Cratfield, a poor, woman's continual exposure to the sun accelerated the skin's ageing process.

A key component of the ageing process hinges on the body's decreased ability to absorb calcium from the digestive tract, something that occurs with ageing and is accentuated by the hormonal changes associated with menopause.[53] Calcium is an essential component of bones, and is constantly being leached away from them. The less calcium that is absorbed from other sources, the more it is drawn from the bones, a process that often results in bone thinning, or osteoporosis, with its bent back, brittle bones, and loss of teeth: symptoms that clearly signal the process of physical decline. One obvious result of thin, weak bones is easily broken limbs and hips, whose successful mending was not always assisted by the practices of early modern medicine. Men also experience bone deterioration as they age, but they also have larger bones to begin with and they are not subject to the sharp hormonal fluctuations of menopause; thus the pernicious combination of calcium loss and declining oestrogen does not occur. Therefore, broken bones tend to occur less frequently and later in life in men. The frequent and easily broken bones experienced by mature women in seventeenth-century England almost certainly identified their owners as 'lame, ympotente, [and] olde'.[54]

The 'dowager's hump', or the hunched and stooped back associated with old women in the past, is one of the most visible symptoms of osteoporosis. This is the result of the orderly breakage of spinal bones. In modern women with osteoporosis, the first set of breaks occurs on average at the age of 60, then again at 65, with the final set of breaks at 70. Starting at roughly the spine's midpoint and following at regular intervals to the base of the spine, these breaks occur at the spine's weakest points. After the bones break, the body produces a layer of fat over these points which only adds to the deformity.[55] 'Such is the feebleness of old age', writes Lady Sarah Cowper, 'made contemptible by crump shoulders, hips and back'.[56]

Certain types of women are more likely to develop this disease than others, and this would have had a direct bearing on ageing women in Cratfield. Slender, small-boned, childless, white women are at greater risk than those who are large-boned, overweight, black, or who have borne children.[57] Early modern England was overwhelmingly white and the physical stature of its inhabitants was significantly smaller than that of their twentieth-century counterparts. And while virtually all of the women in the Cratfield sample were mothers, their grinding poverty ensured that they remained lean. The combination of being white, skinny and small, and without the benefits of modern treatments, suggests that the 'dowager's hump' was found on the backs of Cratfield's rural poor, accompanied by a host of broken and poorly mended bones, and capped by a toothless head.

Teeth, while not themselves bones, are supported on a bed of bones that wither away in the same manner as do those in the spine. The result in this case is periodontal disease and the loss of teeth. The situation in early modern England was far worse than now, as tooth loss was compounded by the lack of modern dental care and increased consumption of sugar, especially in the eighteenth century. In 1715, Lady Sarah Cowper had 'but 3 teeth besides stumps' as of age 71.[58] Complaints of stinking breath and 'teeth of gastful shape' abound in the literature, while advice books of the period are equally full of remedies to disguise bad breath.[59] *A Closet for Ladies and Gentlemen*, first published in 1608, gives explicit instructions involving 'redd sage and ripe croppes of rosemarie', among other ingredients, to distill a remedying water 'for the canker in the mouthe or the rote, or to washe your teath that be hollowe and stinketh'.[60] It would have been the very fortunate menopausal woman indeed who managed to retain even the minority of her teeth.

The general appearance of most elderly poor women would have been very similar to the image projected by contemporary woodcuts and engravings: a bent and broken back, often leaning on a stick to help support her crippled frame, and deeply shrunken mouth clearly without its teeth (Figure 3.3). The old poor woman of woodcut and print was not merely an iconographic device but, in many critical ways, an accurate representation of the poverty-stricken menopausal woman.

One factor that appears to mitigate the physical effects of menopause is diet. A pattern of consumption that is low in fat, high in fibre and calcium, and complemented by regular, weight-bearing exercise is believed to do much to decrease the worst side-effects resulting from the body's declining levels of oestrogen.[61] The diet and lifestyle of rural villagers outwardly seems to match these beneficial requirements. They lived in the open, sweet and healthy air, 'with their "cheering healthy smell of herbs and flowers", their fast-running rivulets, springs and brooks, "pure in taste and smell" and administering both "health and pleaure" to the local inhabitants'.[62] Their diet did not contain much meat, and therefore they were relatively free from the problems associated with its fat content. Fibre from the consumption of fruits and vegetables was just beginning to increase at the close of the seventeenth century, with the use of new crops such as carrots, turnips and potatoes. While it was the poor of the eighteenth century who most clearly benefited from this change in national diet, Cratfield's inhabitants were probably among the earliest inhabitants of the seventeenth century to begin eating such foodstuffs, as this region of England was the first to grow root crops as food for both cattle and the poor.[63] Furthermore, Cratfield's

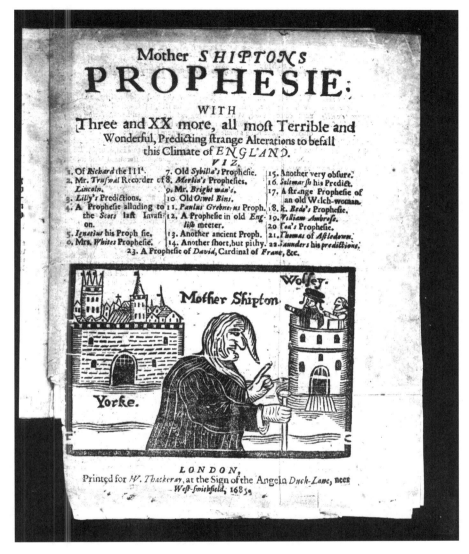

Figure 3.3 Title page of *Mother Shiptons Prophesie* (London, 1685). Reproduced with the permission of the Huntington Library, San Marino, CA, USA

cheese and dairy production meant that its villagers had access to more calcium than most, but this benefit was probably offset by their correspondingly higher consumption of fat from the same source.

Yet, the diet that accompanied a life of poverty did nothing to offset the ill effects of either the unhealthy accommodation or the ageing process associated with menopause. Cratfield's poor subsisted on a diet that was probably familiar to the poor anywhere in England: scant and meagre rations of second- and third-rate bread made from rye and oats, or barley in East Anglia's Cratfield, plus weak beer. Grain was the core of the poor's diet. Andy Appleby explains that 'the groups at the bottom of the economic hierarchy saw a steady deterioration of their diet throughout the sixteenth century, until by the end of the century they suffered malnutrition and, in the 1590s, famine. These were people without a secure "place" in society: the landless labourer, the town worker, the cottager, the vagabond . . . Put simply . . . there were too many people in rural England at the end of the sixteenth century to be fed, given the inequitable distribution of land and the existing agricultural technology'.[64] As noted earlier, Cratfield's poor may have benefited from the introduction of root crops to the region in the mid-seventeenth century. Given Cratfield's overall wealth, they were likely to supplement their staple diet of bread and beer with hard cheese and whey from the dairies of their more prosperous neighbours. Nonetheless, in order to mitigate the worst effects of menopause, women need to maintain a well balanced diet, rich in protein, vitamins, iron and calcium.[65] Even with potential extras, Cratfield's poor seldom achieved a good, nutritional diet: there was seldom enough to eat in times of plenty and virtually nothing in times of trouble.[66]

While the benefits of a good diet and proper exercise may well have contributed to the good health of England's hardy yeoman stock, women of other social sorts had different lifestyles, regimens without the same health-ful benefits. Limiting the physical effects of osteoporosis and menopause requires not only a balanced diet but also the proper amount of exercise: activities that work the body but do not over-tire or exhaust it. Yet the poor woman's physical life was grindingly hard, labouring outdoors with manual tasks and indoors with menial ones. The physicality of such a life was well past the level required to check the process of osteoporosis. Rather, her life was typically at a point of exhaustion, debilitation and physical ruin. Unlike many Suffolk parishes further to the south, Cratfield's economy did not support an underclass of female spinners supplying yarn for the wool trade. Female paid employment in this village consisted predominately of do-mestic help and dairy assistance. Other types of employment were organised by the churchwardens and directed towards the needs of the parish. These tasks were culturally defined as female: the preparation and serving of food for visitors and the town's officers, and the care of the human body in both sickness and death.[67] Regardless of whether she worked indoors or out, a woman's employment was low paid, of little social importance, and so physically wearing as to be ruinous to her health.

The immediate physical surroundings in which these Cratfield women lived, crowded together in almshouse, tenement, cellar and lowly cottage, were widely known for their unhealthy conditions. 'These were the pestilential black spots', writes Mary Dobson, employing the voices of the early modern past, 'the "pest-houses of concentrated contagion", "the foul and loathsome places" where "the air is much corrupted and infected", "the sinister abscesses" of towns, the "close, dirty, stinking and infected" places, the "noisome corners" haunted by plages and fevers'.[68] These conditions were not confined to urban centres: pockets of poverty and corners of contagions existed even in rural settlements. Such circumstances guaranteed that poor women would have already experienced a lifetime of deprivation, poverty and poor health well before they reached menopause. In the minds of this community, the physical changes resulting from menopause shifted most poor women of roughly 50 into the ranks of the active elderly.

An analysis of Cratfield's poor relief payments confirms the negative cumulative effect of poverty on an ageing individual. As they approached their late forties, the poor would begin to collect miscellaneous relief in the form of a few pence or a load of firewood, which helped to offset the decreased income resulting from increased age. Later, as they neared age 60, mature or decrepit old age set in and with it came extended assistance from the parish, typically in the form of a weekly pension, to make up the difference between income lost owing to physical frailty and what was needed for survival. Nonetheless, even for those with poor relief, if one did not work, one did not eat.[69]

Despite their rural environs, their personal habitat, diet and physical exertions conspired against the poor and mature woman to ensure entry into old age near age 50, and to guarantee that the physical changes accompanying menopause were visible to her friends, neighbours and overseers of the poor.[70] Furthermore, not only were such changes visible, but the English of the sixteenth and seventeenth centuries, brought up on a cultural diet of gerontocracy, were trained to notice and acknowledge the 'hoary head'.[71] Thus, their relatively concentrated appearance in a mature woman was commonly viewed as unequivocally announcing her entry into old age. It was not the biological cessation of fertility that made menopause the handmaiden of ageing; rather it was the physical changes, as played out across her face and body, that signified her matriculation into the final stage of life. For rural women, the probable result of a difficult life spent in poverty was early ageing, possibly in advance of more prosperous women. Poverty, with its meagre diet, constant physical demands, and ill health, conspired against poor, rural women to advance the ageing process.[72] In Cratfield, the physical attributes of menopause compounded, magnified and accelerated the effects of poverty to change dramatically a mature woman of 40 to an old one at 50.

Conclusions

Ageing was, and still is, a complex and controversial process. The shift from maturity to old age is a 'moveable feast', predicated on differences in status, gender and historical period. This essay emphasises the importance of cultural considerations in dating the onset of old age and challenges the scholarship that focuses on men and places the beginning of old age for all at age 60. Instead, it looks at poor women in rural Cratfield, Suffolk, during the sixteenth and seventeenth centuries. This village's collective attitudes towards old age may be indicative of other rural societies', especially the view that the ageing experience for women was markedly different from that of men. Nonetheless, not enough is yet known about other rural villages to extrapolate from Cratfield to the larger picture with certainty, and the conclusions reached here extend no further than Cratfield's parish boundaries.

'Social knowledge is formulated and acquired through the structural language of distinctions', explains Haim Hazan. 'Through a complex set of social arrangements, cultural codes are deciphered, negotiated and sustained as conceptual devices for interpreting situations, values and norms'.[73] Honorific titles given to the poor, terms such as 'mother', 'father', and 'old', were explored as cultural markers, and used as a means of identifying when, in this community's view, old age began. As a result, this essay argues that old age for these women began around age 50. Furthermore, old age did not consist of a homogeneous mass of elderly men and women, regardless of the age at which they entered its ranks. Rather, this essay stresses that ageing was, and remains, a process, a series of stages that eventually lead to helplessness and decrepitude, but does not begin there. Women, however, experienced entry into this final stage of life, and the phases within it, very differently from men. While it is true that not all women entered menopause at the same time, with the same range of symptoms, or experienced its hardships to the same degree, it is also true that these women, Cratfield's rural poor, probably shared a similar diet, accommodation and life experience, and they therefore tended to enter menopause and 'green old age' at roughly the same time and within a fairly restricted span of years.

It must also be remembered that the old women described above represent only one type of old age, that of the rural poor. For the poor women of rural, seventeenth-century Suffolk, it was the physical side-effects of menopause, the wrinkled face and gobber tooth,[74] the hairy lip and squinty eye, the stooped back and lamed limbs, that triggered their community's reaction. Ultimately, in the very visual world of early modern Europe, age was assigned, like status, on the basis of visual clues and physical signifiers. In response to Maimonides' question 'Who is an old woman?', for early modern Cratfield we might reply: one who *looks* old'.

Notes

1. Maimonides, *Mishneh Torah, Hilkhot Issurei Bi'ah*, ch. 9 (5). See Michael Signer, 'Honour the hoary head. The aged in the Medieval Jewish community', in Michael Sheehan, ed., *Aging and the Aged in Medieval Europe* (Toronto, 1990), pp.42–3.

2. Modern society is also deeply visually orientated, particularly in North America with its obsession with looking young. Interpreting those visual age markers is perhaps even more problematic than in previous periods, especially when one considers the visually, and deliberately, misleading effects of plastic recon-structive surgery.

3. *Phyisicke Against Fortune by Francis Petrarch. Englished by Thomas Twyne* (London, 1579), f.1v. Also quoted in S. Shahar, *Growing Old in the Middle Ages* (Tel-Aviv, 1995, trans. London, 1997), p.20.

4. For a brief description of the physical characteristics associated with old age, see Mary Abbott, *Life Cycles in England 1560–1700: Cradle to Grave* (London, 1996), p.138.

5. K.M. Weiss, 'Evolutionary perspectives on human aging', in P.T. Amoss and S. Harrell, eds, *Other Ways of Growing Old: Anthropological Perspectives* (Stanford, CA, 1982), p.32.

6. For example: Shahar, *Growing Old*, pp.12–35; R.M. Smith, 'Some issues con-cerning families and their property in rural England 1250–1800' in R.M. Smith, ed., *Land, Kinship and Life-cycle* (Cambridge, 1984), p.84; and Tim Wales, 'Poverty, poor relief and the life-cycle: some evidence from seventeenth-century Norfolk', ibid., p.371.

7. E.A. Wrigley and R. Schofield, *The Population History of England 1541–1871: A Reconstruction* (Cambridge, 1989, 2nd edn).

8. A notable and important exception to these criticisms is Joel Rosenthal's study of medieval England, *Old Age in Late Medieval England*. Yet, his study of ageing is largely an investigation of male old age. He claims that 'matriarchy and the culture of old women, whether on their own or in extended family house-holds, is mostly a lost topic, worth investigation, but hard to treat other than anecdotally'. Joel T. Rosenthal, *Old Age in Late Medieval England* (Philadelphia, 1996), p.30.

9. John Smith, *The Pourtract of Old Age* (London, 1666), p.18. A more recent reiteration of this view is found in Ronald Blythe's *The View in Winter* (London, 1979), p.226, when the aged schoolmaster remarks, 'old age doesn't necessarily mean that one is entirely old – *all* old, if you follow me'.

10. Henry Cuffe, *The Differences of the Ages of Man* (London, 1607), p.120.

11. Haim Hazan, *Old Age: Constructions and Deconstructions* (Cambridge, 1994), pp.63, 68.

12. This was composed on the reverse of the title page to *Extraneous Parochial Antiquities, or An Account of Various Churches with the Funeral Monuments in them in Divers Counties of England*, William Cole Collection, 1746, British Library Additional Manuscripts 5,836, f.1v.

13. Shahar, *Growing Old*, p.17. The literature on this subject is extensive, for examples see Bibliographical Essay, this volume.

14. Sara Mendelson and Patricia Crawford, *Women in Early Modern England 1550–1720* (Oxford, 1998), pp.76–7.

15. Shahar, *Growing Old*, pp.14–18.

16. 4 March 1656/57, *The Diary of Ralph Josselin 1616–1683*, A. Macfarlane, ed., British Academy, Records of Social and Economic History, new series III (London, 1976), p.392; Rosenthal, *Old Age*, pp.5–6.

17. Josselin, p.626.

18. Ibid., p.657.

19. Shahar, *Growing Old*, p.25.

20. Rosenthal, *Old Age*, pp.129–34, esp. p.129.

21. Shahar, *Growing Old*, p.31.

22. L.W. Simmons, *The Role of the Aged in Primitive Society* (New Haven, CT, 1945), p.15; also quoted in J. Roebuck, 'When does old age begin? The evolution of the English definition', *Journal of Social History* 12 (1979), p.426; Rosenthal, *Old Age*, pp.10, 17, 37, *passim*.

23. Cf. Kugler in this volume for the interaction between prescriptive literature and cultural practice.

24. E. Muir, 'Observing trifles', in E. Muir and G. Ruggiero, eds, *Microhistory and the Lost Peoples of Europe*, trans. E. Brandi (London, 1991), p.ix.

25. L.A. Botelho, 'Provisions for the elderly in two early modern Suffolk communities', unpublished PhD thesis (University of Cambridge, 1995), pp.96–123.

26. For a full methodological discussion of this family and parish reconstitution, see Botelho, 'Provisions for the elderly', pp.67–87.

27. M. Biesele and N. Howell, '"The old people give you life": aging among !Kung hunter-gathers', in *Other Ways of Growing Old*, p.79; J. Boulton, *Neighbourhood and Society: A London Suburb in the Seventeenth Century* (Cambridge, 1987), pp.163–4; Hazan, *Old Age*, pp.13–27; M. Pelling, *The Common Lot: Sickness, Medical Occupations and the Urban Poor in Early Modern England* (London, 1998), p.155.

28. The modern world still legislates an 'earlier' female old age, especially in terms of pensions and age-related discounts. Hazan, *Old Age*, p.16; Roebuck, 'When does old age begin?', pp.416–29.

29. Gloucestershire Record Office, Gloucestershire Diocesan Records, Vol. 40, f.226. I would like to thank Caroline Litzenberger for this reference.

30. This idea is raised in Mendelson and Crawford, *Women in Early Modern England*, p.186.

31. As quoted in Abbott, *Life Cycles*, p.141.

32. Abbott, *Life Cycles*, pp.140–1, 143, 145; Mendelson and Crawford, *Women in Early Modern England*, p.261.

33.˙ Peter N. Stearns, 'Old women: some historical observations', *Journal of Family History* 5 (1980), p.44.

34. L.A. Dean-Jones, *Women's Bodies in Classical Greek Science* (Oxford, 1994), pp.103, 105. For early nineteenth-century Britain, see Roebuck, 'When does old age begin?', p.46.

35. Dean-Jones, *Women's Bodies*, p.107; Mendelson and Crawford, *Women in Early Modern England*, p.23.

36. Winnifred B. Culter and Celso-Ramon Garcia, *Menopause: A Guide for Women and Those who Love Them*, rev. edn (London, 1993), p.47.

37. D.W. Amundsen and C.J. Dyers, 'The age of menarche in medieval Europe', *Human Biology* 45 (1973), pp.363–9; J.B. Post, 'Ages of menarche and menopause: some medieval authorities', *Population Studies* 25 (1971), pp.83–7. See also Culter and Garcia, *Menopause*, p.39; Dean-Jones, *Women's Bodies*, p.106; J. Delaney, M.J. Lupton and E. Toth, *The Curse: A Cultural History of Menopause* (New York, 1976), p.178. Mendelson and Crawford, in their *Women in Early Modern England*, p.25, estimate the onset of menopause to be between 45 and 50 years of age. Although controversial, there is some evidence to suggest that 'the length of the reproductive phase of the life course has expanded and contracted during various periods of history'. Jane B. Lancaster and Barbara J. King, 'An evolutionary perspective on menopause' in *In Her Prime: New Views on Middle-aged Women*, 2nd edn, Virginia Kerns and Judith K. Brown, eds (Chicago, 1992), p.11.

38. Germaine Greer, *The Change: Women, Aging and the Menopause* (New York, 1991), pp.140–59; Stearns, 'Old women', p.45.

39. P.T. Amoss with the Salish Native Americans of the Pacific Northwest in 'Coast Salish Elders', in *Other Ways of Growing Old*, p.230; Biesele and Howell, 'The old people', p.79.

40. Wrigley and Schofield, *Population History*, p.254, table 7.25 and pp.452, 479–80; Lancaster and King, 'An evolutionary perspective', pp.7, 9.

41. William Harrison, *The Description of England*, Georges Edelen, ed. (1587 edn, first printed 1577; Ithaca, NY, 1968), p.114.

42. I am grateful to Alison Rowlands for her comments and insights on this point.

43. Lucinda McCray Beier, *Sufferers and Healers: The Experience of Illness in Seventeenth Century England* (London, 1982), p.147.

44. Dean-Jones, *Women's Bodies*, pp.105–9; I. Maclean, *The Renaissance Notion of Women: A Study in The Fortunes of Scholasticism and Medical Science in European Intellectual Life* (Cambridge, 1980), pp.36, 52, 61.

45. David Gentilcore, 'The fear of disease and the disease of fear', in William G. Naphy and Penny Roberts, eds, *Fear in Early Modern Society* (Manchester, 1997), pp.184–208.

46. This is also perhaps why 'facelifts' are perhaps the most common form of cosmetic surgery.

47. S. de Beauvoir, *Force of Circumstance*, trans. R. Howard (New York, 1965), p.656.

48. William Shakespeare, *Macbeth*, I. iii.

49. Sir Hugh Platt, *The Accomplisht Ladys Delight in Preserving, Physick, and Cookery* (London, n.d.), pp.80–98.

50. 25 January 1714. Panshanger MSS, Hertfordshire Public Record Office, D/EP F35, p.38. I would like to thank Anne Kugler for this and all other references in the diary of Lady Sarah Cowper. See Kugler, this volume.

51. Culter and Garcia, *Menopause*, p.74.

52. Ibid., p.84.

53. Ibid., p.99.

54. 39 Elizabeth I c. 3, *The Statutes of the Realm* (1597–98).

55. Culter and Garcia, *Menopause*, pp.102–3.

56. 22 September 1713? Panshanger MSS, Hertfordshire Public Record Office, D/EP F34, p.275.

57. Luoto Riitta, Jaakko Kapro and Antti Uutela, 'Age at natural menopause and sociodemographic status in Finland', *American Journal of Epidemiology* 139 (1994), no.1, pp.64–76, esp. p.65; Culter and Garcia, *Menopause*, p.109.

58. 22 November 1715. Panshanger MSS, Hertfordshire Public Record Office, D/EP F35, p.271.

59. J. Norden, *The Labyrinth of Mans Life. Or Vertues Delight and Envies Opposite* (London, 1609).

60. Anon, *A Closet for Ladies and Gentlewomen, or, The Art of Preserving, Conserving, and Candying* (London, 1608); L.A. Botelho, 'English housewives in theory and in practice, 1500–1640', unpublished MA thesis (Portland State University, 1991), pp.46–8, 59–60.

61. 'Managing menopause: an update', *Harvard Women's Health Watch* 5 (1998), no. 5, pp.2–3; Richard A. Posner, *Aging and Old Age* (London, 1995), p.24.

62. M.J. Dobson, *Contours of Death and Disease in Early Modern England* (Cambridge, 1997), p.17; A. Wear, 'Making sense of health and the environment in early modern England' in Andrew Wear, ed., *Medicine in Society: Historical Essays* (Cambridge, 1992), pp.119–47.

63. Mendelson and Crawford, *Women in Early Modern England*, pp.22, 187; J. Thirsk, *The Agrarian History of England and Wales. Vol. IV: 1500–1640* (Cambridge, 1967), p.47. Cf. Susannah Ottaway, ' "The decline of life": aspects of aging in eighteenth-century England', unpublished PhD thesis (Brown University, 1998), pp.17–81.

64. A.B. Appleby, 'Diet in sixteenth century England: sources, problems, possibilities', in C. Webster, ed., *Health, Medicine and Mortality in the Sixteenth Century* (Cambridge, 1979), pp.105–8.

65. Culter and Garcia, *Menopause*, pp.252–77.

66. Appleby, 'Diet', p.113.

67. Botelho, 'Provisions for the elderly', pp.342–3.

68. Dobson, *Contours*, p.16.

69. Cratfield's poor relief is discussed in detail in Botelho, 'Provisions for the elderly', pp.353–65.

70. According to an eighteenth-century French text, 'bad nourishment' and 'excessive labor' were two of the leading causes of premature ageing. D.G. Troyansky, 'Medical thought on aging in eighteenth-century France', *Proceedings of the Annual Meeting of the Western Society for French History* 13 (1986), p.83.

71. Keith Thomas, *Age and Authority in Early Modern England* (London, 1976).

72. Mendelson and Crawford, *Women in Early Modern England*, pp.187–9; Troyansky, 'Medical thought', p.84; idem, *Old Age in the Old Regime: Image and Experience in Eighteenth-century France* (Ithaca, NY, 1992), pp.116–17.

73. Hazan, *Old Age*, p.1.

74. A 'gobber tooth' is a large tooth that protrudes from the mouth.

CHAPTER FOUR

'I feel myself decay apace': Old age in the diary of Lady Sarah Cowper (1644–1720)

ANNE KUGLER

When Lady Sarah Cowper began her diary in 1700, she was 56 years old, furious with her family, and preparing for death. By 1716, when physical incapacity made it impossible to continue writing, Lady Sarah had produced more than 2,300 pages of commentary on religion, politics, history, society, her family and her own physical decay in a seamless melange of her own words and those of contemporary authors.[1] As with other facets of her life, in taking stock of her ageing process Lady Sarah spoke not only in her own voice from personal experience, but also in the voices of members of her social circle, and of essayists and clergymen who commented on ageing in print. Lady Sarah spoke in those voices self-consciously, selecting her sources to conform with the image of herself she wished to present – an image she used in particular to bolster her claims to authority within her family. In this diary, then, we have both a personal account of old age as experienced in the early eighteenth century, especially valuable for its portrait of a woman's life after childrearing and during widowhood, and a carefully constructed presentation that illustrates uniquely one woman's interaction with the ideology of old age as she encountered it in the literature and conversation of her period.

Using a single diary to investigate the topic of ageing raises the issue of methodology rather forcefully. Why look at one source so closely, and what exactly can be made of such evidence in the larger picture? The first purpose served by the historical examination of Lady Sarah's diary is a cautionary one. More obviously and more thoroughly than most diaries, this remnant of a life, which might initially be taken as the most authentic expression of an early modern English feminine outlook, warns historians of the dangers of thinking of any diary as an unmediated source.[2] Lady Sarah's diary is anything but an unselfconsicous, spontaneous outpouring of a moment's impulse, anything but a veritable rendering of one 'true' moment in time. As are all diaries, it is a self-conscious, selective production with an agenda. Lady Sarah's purpose was to validate her own actions in the face of a bad marriage to an audience consisting of her husband (during his lifetime) and her female descendants. Thus, her experience of ageing, as well as her family life, social interactions and intellectual reflections, are shaped by her effort to maximise authority and look good doing it.

Moreover, Lady Sarah's diary, as any diary, should not be taken as representative of the experiences and outlooks of other women of the period, since its writer, like most diarists, was already unusual in her literacy, high social status and impulse to write. Lady Sarah was even more unusual in the depths of her antipathy to her husband as a driving motivation for self-expression, and most importantly in her wholesale interweaving and appropriation of the literature of the period. This awareness of contemporary writing extends to the very form of the diary, which is a combination of commonplace book (the collection of edifying precepts taken from one's readings, a project advocated by prescriptive authors in the period) and spiritual journal, itself a genre with formal conventions for self-examination drawn from Puritan models. Thus, even as diaries as a category of information are problematical, this diary is even more atypical and complicated than most. Nonetheless, it is that very uniqueness which makes it exceptionally valuable in its explicit link between prescriptive sources and personal practice. If Lady Sarah had not been so self-conscious and so driven, we would not have this extraordinarily integrated record of reading, interacting with and writing about the culture of the day as it pertains to the process of growing older.

The example Lady Sarah offers addresses a number of discussions in the historical scholarship on the elderly in England. In some ways, Lady Sarah's writings support historians' assertions about early modern perceptions of old age, and the messages of prescriptive literature. Specifically, the diary illustrates the variability of the ageing experience, its fluid boundaries, and distinctions between early, vigorous years of old age and later deterioration.[3] But in many respects, Lady Sarah's work serves as warning as well as reinforcement: it speaks especially to the gendered experience of ageing which has not been given serious attention by historians, aside from demographic studies of widowhood.[4] These diary entries remind us that much of the literature of the period took the male example as if it were universal, even though some aspects, such as biological change and retirement, were predicated on gender. Ageing had unique significance for women, whose initial entry into old age was signalled by the end of their reproductive capacity, in the immediate post-menopausal years of the forties and fifties.[5]

For married women, two factors were especially important in their ageing: the shift in identity from mother with children present to mother with adult children, and the presence or absence of a husband. Widowhood without dependent children, and with sufficient financial provision, could be the height of a woman's experience of freedom and autonomy; so while risky, the early post-menopausal years could potentially be the most rewarding of a woman's lifespan.[6] Lady Sarah's adoption of prescriptive texts also makes it clear that interaction with ideology could in some cases at least be explicit and conscious, and that the polarity that historians have observed in prescriptive literature between the view of ageing as decay and of ageing as achieving wisdom, was a dichotomy that people did not necessarily adhere to in their personal outlook.[7] Lady Sarah used both the literature of the period and her own daily experience as a model on which to pattern her own behaviour as an elderly woman: on the one hand acceding to normative values while on the other manipulating ideology as a device for attaining her personal ends.

Lady Sarah began her diary during a particularly difficult period in her life. In her mid-fifties, Lady Sarah had been unhappily married to Sir William Cowper, a lawyer and Whig Member of Parliament for nearly forty years. As she commented on one occasion, 'I have lived with Sir W[illiam] (upon computation) almost 14000 daies, and from the bottom of my soul do beleive I never past one without something to be forgiven him . . .'.[8] At this time, she had two adult sons, also London barristers and politicians, with whom she also had contentious relationships.

In 1700 her situation was especially untenable. As usual, Lady Sarah was spending the summer months in Hertford, a place she found provincial and boring at the best of times. The previous July, her younger son Spencer had been tried for the murder of Sarah Stout, member of an influential Quaker family. Spencer had been advising Sarah Stout financially, and apparently she fell in love with him and committed suicide when he started to avoid her – at any rate, that was the initial verdict. Two months later, however, Sarah Stout's family brought murder charges against Spencer, and although he was acquitted, the Stouts spent the next two years petitioning Parliament for a new trial. When Sir William and Lady Sarah returned to Hertford the next summer, therefore, the scandal was still simmering, and the Cowpers continued to be ostracised. Because of this situation, Lady Sarah seems to have been searching for a way to occupy her days that would afford her comfort and authority in a time of profound personal dissatisfaction:

Most things of this world are to me as tho' I had them not. A hus[band] I have without mutual complaissance or right correspondence. Children without society or kind conversation, a house and servants without authority or command . . . My sattisfaction must arise from the contentment of my own mind, or I shall be totally disconsolate and void of all comfort. A pious life gives power, liberty, ease and peace.[9]

Even early on in the diary it is clear that she had her increasing age and the prospect of death firmly before her, and explicitly related her chosen activities of reading and writing to that which was appropriate for her advanced years:

perhaps some may think my writing so much, a very dull drudgery. But it sufficeth to sattisfy me in the practise, that I find it otherwise. At worst, it may be allow'd an employment as significant as any sort of work I can do, and if for every stitch that others prick in a clout, I with pen set a letter upon paper that, as long may remain a witness to purg me from the scandal of idleness . . . sure then gameing and plays is yet a more wretched amusemt. than unecessary work, for such as are advanc'd in years and draw near the end.[10]

Already in May 1700 Lady Sarah had embarked on the intellectual project of writing her own scriptural commentary, though not without some uneasiness at her presumption at intruding on clerical territory. As her preface demonstrates, she had in mind a future audience to whom she ought to justify her excursion into the province of male authors. Therefore Lady Sarah simultaneously insisted on her originality and disclaimed any pretence to scholarship:

I began to read two chapters a day in the Holy Bible, one out of the Old, and one out of the New Testament, taking notes and observances entirely from my own memory and meditation, without looking into the interpretation of others, or any commentator whatsoever. This I say because the mistakes or errors there found, may be imputed to my own weakness and ignorance, to which indeed they will wholly belong.[11]

Furthermore, Lady Sarah specifically distanced herself from the family duties of earlier stages in her life. Part of this 'vigorous' stage of Lady Sarah's fifties and sixties was a certain degree of freedom from responsibility; in her view: 'I am under no obligation but to live for my self and to spend the remainder of my life as agreeably as I can.'[12] In this new freedom, however, Lady Sarah expected that her children would play a significant part, rewarding her motherly cares now that they were grown and in a position to return favors. This expectation was sorely disappointed, both materially, when anticipated gifts were not received, and emotionally:

This day I made a visit at Cooks' Court, where the neglectfull fashion of my son put me so much out of countenance as perhaps I shall go no more there to meet with him. I seem to be laid by with all imaginable contempt as if I were superannuate at 57 past conversation.[13]

The gap between her expectations and her son's actual behaviour bothered her both on grounds of neglect of filial duty, and because it implied a certain disdain for her age, which was worrisome both in its denial of the very venerability she was claiming, and because she did not identify herself with the picture of the aged that her son's treatment suggested. She still thought of herself as an active participant in the everyday visting that was so important to early modern sociability, and she took her son's lack of receptivity as a troubling categorisation of his mother as socially unfit because of her age.

The tension between retreat and involvement in society as part of the ageing process, and the extent to which retreat was enforced by the attitudes of the young, are issues that recur frequently in Lady Sarah's writings. Ambivalence already marked her attitude towards involvement in the family and social tasks normally allotted to the wife in a gentry family: on the one hand, she discussed and acted upon the possibility of retirement from family duties and visiting duties as if they were attractive options; on the other, Lady Sarah never quite managed to maintain her 'retired' stance. In any case, one might well ask what retirement meant, in the context of a gentlewoman's life. For men, the concept involved cessation of business life, political service or estate management, and the turning over of his financial control of the family property to the next generation of men.[14] For women, unless co-resident with a member of the next generation, there was no real prospect of turning over responsibility for her duties as mistress of the household, and no public, political or economic duties from which to withdraw.[15] Therefore, we must ask if retirement actually existed for women, and if so, in what form? Lady Sarah had already tried withdrawing from her household duties in 1701, not because of her age, but because of her feud with her husband over supervising servants.[16] This tactic had already produced concessions from her husband by the time Lady Sarah spoke of retirement as useful to the practice of religion – a way of elevating her piety and its development to the level of an occupation, and one so important because of its bearing on her soul that it justified rejection of worldly duties if they were a hindrance:

Some endeavor all they can to withdraw from the world and rid their hands of business that they may discharge their duty towards God in their retirment. This is lawfeull, nay commendable if my temper or circumstances be such that my conversation cannot be publick and safe too. ffor then the salvation of my own soul is naturaly the most near concern.[17]

It is unclear, however, whether this retirement is age-based or, like her rejection of household responsibilities, is part of a series of strategies against her husband. In any case, her frequent reports of visits in the subsequent pages of her diary point to sustained ambivalence about the value and practicability of this tactic.

The first significant milestone in the diary in terms of changes in Lady Sarah's experience of ageing was when she fell seriously ill in the winter of 1702. The ailment started as a cold but progressed into a lengthy fever and resulted in permanent blindness in one eye by the end of March.[18] The gravity of her illness and her long recovery also seems to have caused new concentration on the urgency of preparing for death, and its priority as the weightiest business of the ageing:

Are wee grown old, wee have then less time to spare from our most important business. Our forces being diminish'd, our industry shou'd be encreas'd. We shall grow more indispos'd, it will be too late when dotage hath seiz'd upon us . . . There is no care, no employment proper for old age, but to prepare for dissolution . . .[19]

Nonetheless, even in referring to devotional writers to remind herself of the paramount importance of this activity, Lady Sarah still distanced herself from extreme old age, in that the foregoing admonition involved making use of the time left before reaching the degree of decrepitude which would render her incapable of spiritual, as well as physical exercise.[20] This persistent distancing from the infirm stage of old age is notable, since in August 1702 Lady Sarah was having problems reading and feeding herself properly, so that her activity was limited already in some presumably permanent ways.[21] Nonetheless, her actual experience clearly separated her need to prepare for death from the final, infirm stage of life she observed in others:

My Coz: Mas[ters] . . . being a 100 lack 3 . . . hath reduc'd her income to 40[l] yearly paid on May:day to her daughter who keeps her hansomely well. However she ceases not to call for the mony into her own custody and refused meat or drink till she might have it. The daughter no doubt had it not in her power then to produce, but to sattisfy and make her eat she gott 40 quilt counters and put in her purse which serves as well to count ten times a day and lay under the pillow at night . . . Such kind fraud I think commendable . . . A tedious old age is very undesirable, uneasie to our selves and troublesome to others, for the extremity of age, is a declining to the

71

helpless condition of infancy when dotage hath seiz'd us and the body doth survive our soul.[22]

In her own social network, then, Lady Sarah observed both the condition of the incapacitated elderly and the response of the next generation. While commending the young, Lady Sarah in this case adopted the voice of writers who portrayed the profoundly pessimistic side of ageing, focusing on the undesirability of an incapacitated old age.[23] In this same period Lady Sarah began to contemplate more frequently the issue of decline, prompted most often by her social experiences with acquaintances in that condition. While portraying herself as still distant from that situation, she began to see late old age as alarmingly helpless.

As well as expressing her fears of and distaste for the prospect of advancing old age, in these years of remaining vigour Lady Sarah monitored her acquaintance for signs of inappropriate behaviour. She was particularly on the lookout for signs of unbecoming youthfulness in the old, and condemned all comportment which did not conform to the image of a sober old age. Like many prescriptive sources, she especially disapproved of marriage and remarriage for older women, sharply criticising the possibility of continuing sexual activity after menopause:[24]

> Sir T.L. is newly married to a lady old, decrepid with the palsey and other infirmities. Covetousness is thought to be his excuse (if it be one) for 'tis said she is rich; but none can imagine her meaning to be otherwise than to serve a beastly end. The end of marriage (say some) is society and mutual comfort; but they are rather an effect of marriage none of the principle end which is procreation of children and so the continuance of mankind. As for comfort and society they may be betwixt man and man, woman and woman and therfore not proper end of marriage. That conjunction which hath no respect to the right ends for which marriage was ordain'd by God is no lawfull marriage.[25]

In this extended denial of the legitimacy of sexual activity among the no-longer-fertile, and her sharp negation of the validity of mutual comfort as exclusive to, or important for, marriage, she may very well have had her own marriage in mind, not only because it was hardly based on mutual comfort, but also because she and Sir William, by her own report, had ceased having sexual relations after the birth of her fourth son in 1669.[26] For Lady Sarah, justifying her own conjugal relationship, alongside the question of age, required that she view sexual intercourse as entirely propagative in purpose, or else consider herself not virtuous in her celibacy and deficient in her wifely duty. In this case, therefore, the social prescription of sexually inactive old age served for Lady Sarah not as restraint but as validation of her own marital behaviour.

Other related behaviours in women of her age equally incurred her dis-approval – all of them criticised as offensive in their attention to the pleasures and concerns of youth, a preoccupation from which the old ought to be strictly removed. Worst of all were women that still attempted to maintain a young appearance:

> I mett with Lady W____o, of whom it may be said she hath rent her face with painting. She is at least old as I am and hugely infirm yet affects the follys and aires of youth, displayes her breasts and ears adorns both with sparkling gems while her eies look dead, skin rivell'd, cheeks sunk, shaking head, trembling hands, and all things bid shutt up shop and leave to traffick with such vanities or affectation of superfluities which signifys nothing but weakness.[27]

In her consideration of life stages on the occasion of her son's fortieth birthday, Lady Sarah continued this reiteration of prescriptive ideas that femininity belonged to the young, looking back to 40 as the worst age for women.

> Yesterday my son Cooper was full forty year old. In my opinion a man (in respect of good looks) is then att his best; and a woman at the worst stage of life, being neither yong enough to be beautifull, nor old enough to be vener-able. Now att more than threescore (with one eie and no teeth) folks begin to tell me I look well and hansome; I never heard so much in my youth; to fflatter and sooner had been more to the purpose; when it might ha' tickl'd my vanity and made 'em some spark.[28]

In her depiction, while mocking her current impaired appearance, Lady Sarah implied that she had reached an age when, in fact, appearance could garner her respect and veneration, since her face now signified age, and therefore seniority and wisdom, not feminine attractiveness, nor yet the dis-cordance of intermediate years between youthful beauty and venerable old age. Moreover, her amused recounting of clearly insincere flattery suggests that with the loss of femininity came the compensation of 'male' rationality: Lady Sarah implied that in her later years, because of her new de-sexed identity, she was wise enough to recognise insincerity when she heard it, unlike in her emotional, foolish, feminine youth. In this stage of life, she could enjoy the deference implied in such compliments, while dismissing their accuracy or intent.

In most cases having to do with age-inappropriate vanity, Lady Sarah related her social encounters in a condemning tone, and not as if she had anything to learn from the behaviour of others. She instead held herself up as a model of correct deportment, both in outward appearance and proper employment of time. However, Lady Sarah commented on other sorts of faults as if they had the added value of exemplary lessons in how not to conduct herself in old age:

> I went to visit where lives a lady turn'd of fourscore, sees to read gazetts without spectacles, hears very well and dos bragg that all her five senses are perfect as ever. But her mind and understanding 'tis like is fallen into decay for she is undecently obstreperous. It may do well to make her my monitor least I fall into the like loquacity.[29]

If wisdom tended to produce reticence, then a sign of decay of mental faculties was talkativeness, and Lady Sarah might well have wished to maintain her self-prescribed reputation for understanding and correct conversation.

Lady Sarah noted positive, as well as negative models for presenting a decorous public image in vigorous old age:

> . . . This charecter I aim at;
> A firm and equal soul she had engross'd
> Just, even to those that disoblig'd her most
> She grew to love those wrongs she did receive
> ffor, giving her the power to forgive.
> So she in age was mild and grave to all
> Was not morose, but was majestical
> Transcendant things her noble thoughts sublime
> Above the faults and triffles of the time.[30]

This model not only provided an alternative to the pervasive depictions of old women striving foolishly to appear youthful, but also set up the wise aged woman as somehow elevated in her moral and intellectual qualities. Should she be able to overcome melancholy, her thoughts would be not only pious, but majestical, transcendant and sublime – masculine, even, in their profundity and detachment. Here too, then, old age, properly lived, could offer women a level of intellectual credibility not available in their beautiful, but presumably irrational, youth.

Despite all this collecting of experience and planning to emulate models of eminent elderly women, Lady Sarah continued in her ambivalence towards society, repeatedly vowing to retire at least partially from the round of visits. Moreover, in these years of relative vigour, Lady Sarah went one step further in her depiction of retirement, and claimed status for herself and special deference from her family as a result of her attempts at contemplative activity. Repeating her characterisation of retirement as spiritual self-defence, she extended her claim further and demanded that 'the family of the contemplative ought to give him no disturbance but if possible animated to suitable inclinations to his own. But alas! Mine never was such –'.[31] In this elevation of the importance of her spiritual quest, Lady Sarah required privileged space and heightened deference for her activities, bewailing the failures of her family to accord her what she felt was her due at this stage in life.

As before, though, it is clear from her reports of daily activity that Lady Sarah did not significantly reduce her visiting schedule or retire into hermit-like contemplation. By this time, bemoaning worldy engagement may have had specific pertinence, since in October 1705 Lady Sarah's elder son William was named Lord Keeper of the Great Seal, from which post he rapidly advanced to a barony in December 1706 and the Lord Chancellor-ship in May 1707. From late 1705 until the Whig government's fall in 1710, Lady Sarah's family was at the centre of society and politics, and Lady Sarah herself seems to have been the target of a stream of visitors looking for places around her son. As before, Lady Sarah felt that the gratifications of exercising patronage, as well as material and emotional rewards, were due to her as a mother, but again she was disappointed. Thwarted in her attempts to get places for her own clients, neither did she gain financial recompense:

> The Queens birthday is past, and I look'd for the purse and two or tuppence in't. But now my expectation is quite baulk'd and worn out of all date. – To his father he sent after this manner. Ten asses laden with the good things of Egypt –[32]

While she cited the authority of the Bible (Genesis 45:23) to back her vision of the obligations of grown children to their parents, their refusal of this type of reward as part of venerating aged parents serves as a cautionary note. Lady Sarah may have been citing contemporary ideology regarding the respect to be shown to the aged, but she had no way of enforcing her prescription if she encountered resistance.[33]

Also troubling to Lady Sarah in the years of her son William's advance-ment was the broader question of financing her own independent life should her husband die before her. She apparently had little expectation of this happening – Sir William, while slightly older, was in excellent health – but the new shower of wealth that was accompanying the younger William on his political rise may have prompted worries about her own economic prospects as she and her husband aged. About ten days after Sir William's sixty-sixth birthday, the possibility arose that her jointure was insufficient to support her as a widow:

> Visiting Lady Holt we chanc'd to talk about rent charg. Pah, quoth she thats a word devis'd by husbands to cheat their wives. Penny:rent is the thing. I

askt what difference? She answer'd the last was free of all abatements; the other liable to taxes. So home came I with a flea in my ear; and enquir'd of Sir W[illiam] how the matter stood in my case? who told me he cou'd not remember so long; which reply makes it very suspitious that I have been these 20 years under a great mistake.[34]

Her anxiety about her financial solvency as a widow, even when there was no immediate prospect of losing her husband, and the suspicion both she and Lady Holt have of the mechanism of jointure, indicate the perilous nature of widowhood even in the upper ranks of society. If provision were inadequate, and had been made so by the very people who were supposed to protect these women's interests, even elite women might be reduced to straitened circumstances.[35] Lady Sarah took the jointure documents to a legal expert – her son Spencer – who reassured her she was due £400 per year as a pension, plus the house in Hertford for life.[36] Not only is it worth noting Lady Sarah's lack of trust in her husband's benevolence, it is also remarkable that she was both uniquely protected and uniquely vulnerable because of her sons' legal expertise. She might either benefit from excellent advice if her sons were so inclined, or she could be handily deprived of her legal due, should her sons prioritise other family interests, including their own.

The question of solvency in widowhood continued to bother Lady Sarah, especially when Sir William took a lease on a larger house in London and the couple moved there at the end of March 1706. In contemplating the expense, Lady Sarah was again worried that if she should survive Sir William, she would be left in financial straits. Telling Sir William so, he agreed, and promised 'he woud leave order with those to whom he gave his mony that they shou'd pay the rent for my life'[37] – a relief to Lady Sarah, but also extraordinary in that until she brought it up, this possibility had not occurred to Sir William, even though both of them were unlikely to survive the entire length of the lease.

As it turned out, Lady Sarah's concern was only too pertinent: Sir William died suddenly of a stroke on 26 November 1706.[38] After initial expressions of shock (notably, she evinced no grief whatsoever), Lady Sarah's next concern was indeed over the financial provisions made for her widowhood, especially as initially it seemed to her that her sons were planning to go against the terms of her settlement and even to refuse her the cash she needed immediately for bills and rent.[39] In response, Lady Sarah reproduced in her diary the entire text of the jointure settlement.[40] While this was a symbolic act of inscription that validated her interpretation of what was due her as inheritance, it had no legal weight, and would not help her to enforce her rights, especially against sons who were at the top of the legal profession. Shortly thereafter her son William did pay Lady Sarah what was due for the quarter, and even slightly more, but the surplus was evidently intended to offset only part of Lady Sarah's rent, which despite Sir William's assurance, she ended up paying herself.[41]

After this alarming financial start to her widowhood, Lady Sarah's first two years in that state seem to have been the heyday of the diary, and perhaps of her adult life. Unsurprisingly, she rejected all possibility of remarriage. But unlike her treatment of the remarriage of other women, her abhorrence in her own case did not centre on sexual identity, but stemmed from reluctance to give up newly achieved liberty, as can be seen in her contemplation of a long-dead friend, Martin Clifford:

> I then found complaisance in his conversation, and shou'd now be glad of such another companion if I knew how to find him . . . But I meant not for a spouse. Wear not a straight ring. Lead your life in freedom and liberty, and throw not your self into slavery . . .[42]

In her new state, Lady Sarah's relations with her son seem to have improved. It may be that her temperament mellowed with her husband's absence; it also seems as if her new daughter-in-law had much to do with improving the relationship. William announced his marriage to Mary Clavering on 10 February 1707.[43] Mary apparently took a deferential tack with her new mother-in-law, and on her first visit asked Lady Sarah's blessing.[44] Showing Lady Sarah appropriate marks of respect due a parent was perhaps especially easy, since Mary was more than forty years younger than her mother-in-law, unlike William's first wife, Judith, who had entered the family in her late teens, when Lady Sarah was only in her early forties herself. Moreover, Mary continued to observe the proprieties, since in the summer of 1707 Lady Sarah referred to an extended stay at Mary and William's country house with gratification and approval.[45] The relationship improved even further with the birth of a granddaughter in December 1707, for whom Lady Sarah was proud to be named godmother.[46]

In addition, Lady Sarah relished taking over primary responsibility for overseeing the household in her widowhood. Very shortly after Sir William's death, she served notice that she was planning to supervise the servants according to her own vision of order and propriety: 'It is a work well: becoming our elder years to put our families in due order. ffor nothing is more usefull or more beautiful than good order. This by the help of God I intend and purpose.'[47] It is interesting that she cast this reform of the family in terms of the suitability of old age for such a work, rather than explicitly because of her widowhood: here she may have been seizing on a validation for her plans which relied less on the gender component of her new identity and more on the age hierarchy implicit in the identity of widow. In any case, her plans to remedy what she perceived to be her husband's inadequacy extended outside the family as well. In 1708, she donated an investment windfall to charity in a way that both fulfilled the social obligations of her rank and contrasted her understanding of these obligations favorably in comparison with her husband's:

> I have deposited with Sir William Ashurst One 100.[1] to the use of Christs Hospital, since not only charity, but justice requires it shou'd be so, by reason Sir W[illiam] C[owper] was 30 year past chose a governer therof, put in several children as it came to his turn, yet left 'em nothing in return . . .[48]

Lady Sarah explicitly evaluated her new state in terms of the opportunities it presented her with for carrying on the business of her latter years, and in one passage gave an account of herself that displayed the highest degree of contentment to be found over the entire course of the diary:

> Now I have leisure both to examine the errours of my life past, and prepare for that great day wherin all flesh must make an account of their actions. And after a kind of tempestuous life; I have the advantage from my God whom I will daily magnify for this perticuler mercy of an exemption from business, a quiet mind, and a liberal maintainance in this part of my life. When age sounds a retreat from this world and invites mee to contemplation which I take to be the greatest felicity.[49]

Here too she returned to the theme of retirement into a life of contemplation as befitting her age, but this time with the added advantages of financial comfort, autonomy and domestic peace. Furthermore, quoting Montaigne, she asserted her continuing mental activity:

> Altho' I have one foot in the grave yet I desire to learn . . . I toss over books for an honest recreation to please and delight my self. I only endeavor to find out the knowledg which may instruct me how to live and dy well. ffor difficult points I fret not my self about 'em. But after I have given 'em a charg or two I leave 'em as I found them. I seek for good and solid reasons that may instruct me how to sustain the assaults of unruly Passions, and the approaches of death.[50]

While Lady Sarah was following standard social and moral prescription here, this reflection should not be taken as a banal or insincere mouthing of conventional platitudes about the correct activities for living in the last stages of life. The scholarship on prescriptive literature and ageing tends to discount the significance of this religious and moral perception of the duties and nature of old age, devaluing both the force of these ideas and their importance in people's lives in this period.[51] Piety in general, and mental preparation for death with the onset of old age in particular, were sources of comfort, support, authority, and intellectual and moral nourishment for Lady Sarah throughout the volumes of her diary, and are inescapably pervasive themes in her writing. As she said in 1707 about the centrality of reading to her pursuit of a tranquil mind,

> Books every way assist mee, they comfort me in age, and solace me in solitariness. They ease me of the burden of wearisome idleness; they abate the edge of fretting sorrow and divert me from my importunate imagination. They help to bear the provocations of a servant; the importunity of years the unwelcomness of wrinkles and such like mind troubling accidents.[52]

Although the years 1707 and 1708 were a happy time for Lady Sarah, in which she was free to pursue her own pleasures, enjoy her family interactions and exercise the authority of an independent widow of means, by late 1708 there are an increasing number of references to old age in her diary, and a change in the nature of those references. It appears that Lady Sarah's health was slowly declining, and moreover, that her mental condition suffered as well. Rather than achieving a detachment that was sublime, she often experienced depressing listlessness and while she was still keeping a distance between herself and the furthest extent of old age, the gap was narrowing, and she was contemplating increasing debility and decay at the doorstep of such experience, not from a safe remove:

> Since I am Lord Chancellor's mother they feast me about the countryobjects abroad which plainly shew mee I am not yet arriv'd to the worst condition of old age by much. I mett Mr. W.G. who labors under it I beleive with patience; yet sure it must be very tedious if not terrible.[53]

By the next year, Lady Sarah had begun a practice of occasionally cataloguing her physical condition, in all its defects, bewailing especially the possibility of loss of intellectual capability:

> Sixty five years is a great deal of sand in the hour glass. Now I find thro' age, greifs, and infirmitys, my sense is become dull, my memory decay'd, my sight failing, my hearing imperfect, and in all the powers and facultys of my mind and body great debility. My judgment of men and things seems more strong, but whenever that grows weak 'tis like I shall not perceive it.[54]

Despite the beginnings of frequent complaints about her physical, and now more than ever, mental condition, Lady Sarah pointed at this stage to the recompense and comforts of a contemplative life, using her mental faculties to divert her from the pains of physical infirmity:

> Since old age is not only a congregation of diseases but a disease it self and that incurable save by death, the best thing next to a remedy is a diversion of the malady . . . And what is there in the reach of man that can quallify him against the decays that age makes on him, as knowledg and meditation. It abates the tediousness of decrepid age and by contemplation beguiles the weariness of the pillow and chair. He that can read and meditate need not think the evening long, or life tedious.[55]

Here, she used the comfort value of prescriptive literature, which on the one hand characterised age as a disease, but on the other, offered in the absence of remedy, at least the compensation of continued mental activity as particularly appropriate for those in their last days.

Her use of prescriptive material to reflect on old age reached a height in 1710 and 1711, for reasons that may have as much to do with the appearance of new popular periodicals as with her own state. In those years, Lady Sarah read the *Tatler* and then the *Spectator*, and extracted from them items that pertained to social comportment and theological and political issues as well as to her particular stage of life. In these moral essays, Lady Sarah found both cautions against committing stereotypical faults of the aged and an attractive model of old age. As long as she managed to avoid the pitfalls, she had in these essays on sociability a means of claiming a veneration based on not only her age but also the value of her comportment:

> It is pittyable to reflect upon the talkative humor of old people, and the litle figure which that part of life makes in one who cannot employ this natural propensity in discourses which wou'd make 'em venerable . . . The only way of avoiding such a frivolous and triffling old age, is to lay up in our way to it such stores of knowledg and observations as may make us usefull and agreeable in our declining years . . . ffor which reason, as there is nothing more ridiculous than an old triffling story teller; so there is nothing more venerable than one who has turn'd his experience to the entertainment and advantage of mankind.[56]

Equally, Lady Sarah's reading of the periodical press had relevance to her relationship with her elder son. At this point, having ceased to expect material rewards in the form of money or patronage from him, she emphasised instead the benefits of deferential visits. After recording that her son William had come to dinner, she quoted the *Tatler* on the rewards of sociability for the aged:

There is not a greater pleasure to old age than seeing that wee are not quite laid aside in the world; but that we are either used with gratitude for what we were, or honor'd for what wee are . . . Sure old age which is a decay from that vigor which the yonger possess and must certainly (if not prevented against their will) arrive att, shou'd be more forcibly the object of that reverence which honest spirits are enclin'd to from a sense of being themselves liable to what they deserve has overtaken others.[57]

Here, though, the argument for deference from the young, especially children, towards the old is not based on an image of superior wisdom of the elderly, or on filial duty, but on an empathetic awareness that old age will eventually strike everyone, and so deference should be exercised with a self-interested view in the hope of receiving similar reverence in one's own latter years.

Furthermore, by 1710 Lady Sarah saw her son William not just as someone obliged to pay her deference but also as a protector of an increasingly infirm widowed mother:

Some while ago, when my son was seiz'd with a fitt of the strangury; 'tis not to be imagin'd what a dread it cast mee in, least he shou'd dy before me . . . The parting with a beloved son is at any time an affliction; but when they have attain'd prosperity, then it adds weight, by the loss of comfort and assistance to a solitary mother. Such are as the arrows in the hand of the giant; they defend an aged parent, and enable 'em to bear up against adversity, by becoming the stay and support of her age and infirmitys.[58]

In 1712 Lady Sarah contemplated her birthday from the perspective of having achieved full rationality. She may have been echoing Cicero's *On Old Age*, a work reprinted during this period which lauded 'the tranquil and serene old age of a life spent quietly amid pure and refining pursuits',[59] though in her observation there is an ironic tone not present in Cicero's essay:

My Birth:Day. 68. I am arriv'd at a state of tranquility which few people envy. I mean that of an old woman . . . There are few who can grow old with a good grace, and enjoy a pleasing indolent old age, in which passion is subdu'd, and reason exalted . . .[60]

But by that time, Lady Sarah was also apparently beginning to experience a degree of isolation which she had worried about in her fifties and seemed to be coming true in her seventies. She became more and more a living stereotype, and one which presumed an inability to interact well in society. Concrete evidence of the social isolation of very old ladies, and Lady Sarah's keen sense of injury on this count, can be seen in her experience of rejection, even from her own family, when the Cowpers were trying to make a good impression on their social superiors:

> This day Lord C[owper] and Lady dine with D[uke] Roxborough. The Dutchess courteously invited mee, but I forbear to go, saying I am too old to appear in such company from home; which was readily assented to. Love to be conceal'd and litle esteem'd be content to want praise, and never troubl'd when slighted ffor thou canst not undervalue thy self, and if thou thinks't so meanly as there is reason, no contempt will seem unreasonable and therfore it will be very tollerable. Be ever unconcern'd, and secure a good name by living vertuously and humbly.[61]

In this case, Lady Sarah recognised and acceded in her social disability, but was nonetheless hurt when her relatives accepted her offer of self-isolation. She immediately equated this assent with contempt, regardless of having initiated the suggestion herself. Even she recognised some of the reasons why her company might not be welcome, owing to her age, but found it painful nonetheless to experience rejection because of membership of a social category that she even acknowledged as legitimate.

Moreover, she was ready to defend other old women, now without distancing herself, but rather enjoining forbearance among the young, and continued inclusion in the social round:

> I was to visit Lady Falconbridg . . . I beleive she has been esteem'd wise; but alas! The infirmitys of old age, makes her now appear otherwise – yet sure the Bishop of Sarum was to blame when he told mee that he had left off visiting her because she was superanuated. Methinks wee shou'd not be abandon'd for what wee cannot help –[62]

By this time (1713) her complaints not only of physical discomfort, but also of mental stultification increased in their frequency and vehemence. This listlessness eventually degraded her strongest comfort and outlet: religious contemplation. As she had feared and predicted, extreme old age rendered her unfit for the meditative life that was supposed to dignify her later years:

> The same insipid life. To mee the days are come, when I may say I have no pleasure in them. My facultys are broken by the infirmitys of age, fflatt and dull, irksome and tedious, apt to nothing but complaint under the weight of one evil or another that befalls mee. The powers of soul and body are in a languishing condition unfit for the offices of piety, or the acknowledgment of God's benefits which are so slipt out of mind as to have but a dull perception of them.[63]

While in 1714 and 1715 her complaints of physical debility do not cease, the death of Queen Anne and succession of George I were interesting to her both as political developments and as they affected the fortunes of her own family: after having resigned from Queen Anne's ministry in 1710, her son William was appointed again by George as his Lord Chancellor. However, by the summer of 1716, politics were no longer diverting, and as her physical health deteriorated, so did her mental health. For the first time since 1700, her diary seems to have lost its power to comfort and occupy her mind:

> I was wont to supply my diary with what I read, which now is but litle thro' defect of sight. Or with what I heard from others, which now is less than formerly for want of hearing, or by setting down my own thoughts and meditations, which alas now are so very dull and insipid as to afford me no pleasure nor benefit.[64]

At the end of that summer, her illnesses and her mental state combined to ruin completely the diversionary and creative properties of her diary:

> I feel my self decay apace. O Lord! give mee grace to wait patiently till my chang come.
>
> . . . Alas! I can neither hear, read, or think any thing worth setting down. I cannot tell what term to give my pains, whither acute, exquisite, or so forth – But such they are as hinder all enjoyment of life.[65]

In the last days of September, Lady Sarah finally cited physical debility as the reason for abandoning writing altogether, and took leave of her diary:

> The palsey encreases on my hand so that I am forced to leave off my diary, writing is so troublesome to me –
>
> . . . My phrase now is farewell for ever.[66]

Lady Sarah was 72 at this point; she actually died three and a half years later.

On the one hand, then, Lady Sarah's writing displays the negative side of contemporary attitudes to old age – the fear and disgust at its toll on health, mobility and mental capacity, and the contempt felt for the aged, especially the infirm. In that vein, Lady Sarah grimly chronicled her illnesses, the degeneration of her senses, and her attempts to resign herself to her state. On the other hand, however, Lady Sarah appropriated for herself the potential for elevated status in old age which commentators granted to the pious, learned and financially secure. She constructed for herself the image of wise old woman, deserving of veneration for her store of reading and experience, and consequently she claimed special accommodation for her contemplative activity. Moreover, Lady Sarah's age furnished an image of sobriety that counteracted the stereotype of females as frivolous and validated her mental enterprise as befitting one who was near death and therefore concerned with assuring salvation. Thus, Lady Sarah combined two potentially debilitating social identities, the learned woman and the old woman, added the critical ingredient of religious fervour, and created a new role for herself that exploited the potential for respect while attempting to avoid the pitfalls inherent in each role alone. In Lady Sarah's approach, then, the duality of old age is visible as Lady Sarah both assimilated and adapted the contradictions in contemporary perceptions of the elderly. While she echoed her society's fears of death and distaste for decay, her years of elderly vigour (if not her later decline) provided a rewarding role in which to create claims to authority, coupled as they were with her rank, piety, financial security and aptitude for reshaping the ideologies of the period to serve her own agenda.

Notes

1. Hertfordshire Public Record Office Panshanger MSS D/EP F29–F35 Diary of Lady Sarah Cowper, Vols 1–7, 25 July 1700 to 30 September 1716. Diary citations hereafter abbreviated to volume, year and page.

2. On the subject of diarists' construction of a persona and selection of material, see, for example, Margo Culley, ed., *A Day at a Time: The Diary Literature of American Women from 1764 to the Present* (New York, 1985), p.12.

3. Regarding the mutability of age definition, see Botelho, 'Old age and menopause in rural women of early modern Suffolk' in this volume, as well as Margaret Pelling and Richard Smith, eds, *Life, Death and the Elderly: Historical Perspectives* (London, 1991), p.7, and Steven Smith, 'Growing old in an age of transition', in Peter Stearns, ed., *Old Age in Pre-industrial Society* (London, 1982), p.195. For the literary construction of categories of old age see Keith Thomas, 'Age and authority in early modern England', *Proceedings of the British Academy* 62 (1976), p.244; Edward Bever, 'Old age and witchcraft in early modern Europe', in Stearns, ed., *Old Age in Pre-industrial Society*, p.166; and Joel Rosenthal, *Old Age in Late Medieval England* (Philadephia, 1996), p.98.

4. Studies of widowhood include: Margaret Pelling, 'Old age, poverty and disability in early modern Norwich: Work, remarriage and other expedients', in Pelling and Smith, eds, *Life, Death and the Elderly*, pp.74–101; S.J. Wright, 'The elderly and the bereaved in eighteenth-century Ludlow', ibid., pp.102–33;

Barbara Todd, 'The remarrying widow: a stereotype reconsidered', in Mary Prior, ed., *Women in English Society 1500–1800* (New York, 1985), pp.55–81; James Smith, 'Widowhood and ageing in traditional English society', *Ageing and Society* 4 (1984), no.4, pp.429–49.

5. Bever, 'Old age and witchcraft', p.165. Though as Botelho explains in her essay in this volume, many historians consider the age of 60, not 50, to mark the onset of old age, because they use evidence for men's ageing as if it were the universal experience. See also Botelho's argument in this volume that the identification of a woman as elderly may have had more to do with the visible physical signs of menopause than with the end of reproductive capacity *per se*.

6. Regarding autonomy for prosperous widows, and the possibility that this new status helps explain low remarriage rates, see Thomas, 'Age and authority', p.286; Peter Laslett, *A Fresh Map of Life: The Emergence of the Third Age* (London, 1989), p.137; and Barbara Todd, 'The remarrying widow', p.81; though note Rosemary O'Day's caution in *The Family and Family Relationships 1500–1900: England, France, and the United States of America* (New York, 1994), pp.97–9, that this situation applies only to a small stratum of society.

7. Rosenthal, *Old Age in Late Medieval England*, p.94, argues that the prescriptive literature is abstract, normative, and moreover ignores this gap between theoretical schemes and the reality of life experience.

8. Vol. 1 (1702), p.185.

9. Vol. 1 (1700), p.33.

10. Vol. 1 (1701), p.67.

11. D/EP F44 'Collections from the Bible' and Lady Sarah's Own Biblical Commentary. 1700. Preface.

12. Vol. 1 (1701), p.95.

13. Vol. 1 (1701), p.51.

14. See Thomas, 'Age and authority', pp.236–40 and Rosenthal, *Old Age in Late Medieval England*, pp.100–8 regarding retirement for men. For widows turning over control of household to adult sons, see Wright, 'The elderly and the bereaved', p.125.

15. Historians generally agree that co-residency was not the typical experience of elderly women in early modern England, even when widowed. See Richard Smith, 'The structured dependence of the elderly as a recent development: some sceptical historical thought', *Ageing and Society* 4 (1984), no.4, p.419; James Smith, 'Widowhood and ageing in traditional English society', pp.433, 437; and P. Laslett, 'The traditional English family and the aged in our society', in David Van Tassel, ed., *Aging, Death, and the Completion of Being* (Philadephia, 1979), pp.99–103.

16. Vol. 1 (1701), p.168.

17. Vol. 1 (1702), p.181.

18. Vol. 1 (March 1702), pp.196–202.

19. Vol. 1 (1702), p.229.

20. While not in direct quotation, this passage in the diary strongly echoes Pierre Charron, *Of Wisdom* (1697), p.308; Robert Parsons, *Christian Directory* (1660), pp.184–9; and Nathaniel Ranew, *Practical Discourses Concerning Death and Heaven* (1694), pp.43–4. Warnings about the dangers of waiting to prepare for death were standard in many devotional works of the period.

21. Vol. 1 (1702), p.265.

22. Vol. 2 (1703), p.81.

23. See Georges Minois' extensive survey of the pessimistic literature in *History of Old Age: From Antiquity to the Renaissance*, trans. S. Hanbury Tenison (Chicago, 1989), pp.264–70, as well as David Fowler, Lois Fowler and Lois Lamdin, 'Themes of old age in preindustrial western literature', in Stearns, ed., *Old Age in Pre-industrial Society*, pp.19–38. Note, though, that Rosenthal (*Old Age in Late Medieval England*, pp.176–80) rightly points out the opposite position was often taken as well, as for example in new editions of Cicero's *De Senectute*.

24. See Keith Thomas's comment that the aged of both genders were to 'refrain from sexual competition with their youngers' ('Age and authority', p.243). See also Laslett, *A Fresh Map of Life*, p.136; and David Fowler, *et al.*, 'Themes of old age in preindustrial western literature', p.32.

25. Vol. 2 (1704), pp.272–3.

26. Vol. 1 (1701), p.61.

27. Vol. 2 (1704), p.227.

28. Vol. 3 (1705), p.92.

29. Vol. 3 (1705), p.7.

30. Vol. 3 (1705), p.112.

31. Vol. 3 (1705), pp.98–9.

32. Vol. 3 (1706), p.193.

33. See Smith, 'Growing old in an age of transition', in Stearns, *Old Age in Pre-industrial Society*, p.202.

34. Vol. 3 (1705), p.173.

35. See Susan Staves, *Married Women's Separate Property in England 1660–1833* (Cambridge, MA, 1990), pp.27–37, 116–18, for an extended discussion of the process of the replacement of dower rights by jointures in this period. Staves

points out the risks for widows as smaller settlements, usually in the form of a cash pension, took the place of customary rights to one-third of a husband's land.

36. Vol. 3 (1706), p.183.

37. Vol. 3 (1706), p.206.

38. Vol. 4 (1706), p.1.

39. Vol. 4 (1707), pp.16–18.

40. The original document Lady Sarah copied is D/EP T1217 Marriage Settlement of William Cowper and Judith Booth (1686) in which Lady Sarah surrendered her jointure lands to her son William for a cash annuity, a deal typical of the trend Susan Staves observed (*Married Women's Separate Property*, p.115) towards women accepting financial settlements that were not necessarily in their own economic interest, in order to help their sons.

41. Vol. 4 (1707), p.22.

42. Vol. 4 (1707), pp.26–7.

43. Vol. 4 (1707), p.28.

44. Vol. 4 (1707), p.34.

45. Vol. 4 (1707), p.78.

46. Vol. 4 (1708), p.146.

47. Vol. 4 (1706), p.3.

48. Vol. 4 (1708), pp.174–5.

49. Vol. 4 (1707), p.110.

50. Vol. 4 (1707), pp.129–30; quoting Montaigne, *Essays* Vol. 2, ch.10, trans. John Florio (New York, 1980), p.94.

51. Minois consistently refers to a religious life and practices as bigotry (see, for example, *History of Old Age*, p.264); Rosenthal refers to characterisations of old age as a period when one has time for religious contemplation as 'unexceptional pieties' (*Old Age in Late Medieval England*, p.94).

52. Vol. 4 (1707), p.138.

53. Vol. 4 (1708), p.245.

54. Vol. 5 (1709), pp.12–13.

55. Vol. 5 (1709), pp.43–44.

56. Vol. 5 (15 February 1710), pp.112–13; quoting *Tatler* no.132, 11 1710, Donald Bond, ed. (Oxford, 1987), Vol. 2, pp.268–9.

57. Vol. 5 (11 August 1710), p.201; quoting *Tatler* no.207, 5 August 1710, Bond, ed., Vol. 3, pp.97–8.

58. Vol. 5 (1710), pp.221–2.

59. Cicero, *De Senectute* trans. William Falconer, Loeb Library (Cambridge, MA, 1985), p.23. Although there is no explicit mention of this work in the diary, Lady Sarah listed Cicero's *Of the Gods* in her 'Catalogue of Books at London' at the back of commonplace book D/EP F36 in the Panshanger MSS. She may well have read more of Cicero's works; her catalogue is by no means a complete record of her reading, but at least indicates her familiarity with this classical author.

60. Vol. 6 (14 February 1712), p.93.

61. Vol. 6 (1712), p.158.

62. Vol. 6 (1713), p.214.

63. Vol. 6 (1713), p.274.

64. Vol. 7 (1716), p.324.

65. Vol. 7 (4–5 August 1716), p.336.

66. Vol. 7 (29 and 30 September 1716), last page.

CHAPTER FIVE

Old maids: the lifecycle of single women in early modern England

AMY M. FROIDE

Scholars of women in the European past have largely represented female old age as a distressing period of decline. These researchers have emphasised the negative aspects they believe attended women in later life: loss of physical and sexual attractiveness, ill health, mental depression, retirement from economic and social activities, and the consequent lack of a significant social function. For widows they believe the experience was worse: loneliness resulting from the loss of a spouse, poverty attributable to that same loss, and the want of a caregiver. While little work has been done on old women who never married, several historians have assumed that old age for single women would be equally, if not more, depressing than for elderly widows.[1] We could say that if old women in the past laboured under a double burden of gender and age, then old single women experienced a triple burden. An aged single woman was disadvantaged not only by her gender and her age, but also by her marital status. Scholars have presumed that elderly single women would have been scorned for never fulfilling the roles of wife or mother, and that they would have endured a lonely old age without the comfort of a husband (and presumably) children. After all, it was only single women (and not wives and widows) who faced derogatory epithets such as 'old maid' and 'superannuated virgin' that made direct reference to their advanced age.

Nevertheless, we cannot generalise and say that all women in the European past experienced old age as entirely negative. In some ways, old age could be a positive and affirming life-stage for ever-married women (that is, wives and widows).[2] It was in later life that many women experienced increased independence, either as wives who took over the responsibilities of ageing husbands, or as widows who functioned as their husband's deputies. Old age also liberated women from the constraints of childbearing and childrearing, perhaps freeing up more time for themselves. And it was in later life that women began to exercise more authority and engender more respect within both their families and their communities. Nevertheless, because single women have been less studied in their own right (and elderly single women in particular), we do not know if old age was at all positive for this group of women.[3]

This essay examines how never-married women, who were primarily members of the middle social and economic tier of society, experienced old age in seventeenth- and eighteenth-century England. In doing so it is necessary to pay attention to the importance of marital status in differentiating the experiences of women in the past. Scholars of women have rightfully criticised studies of old age that have either ignored the experiences of women or have generalised from the experiences of older men to all of the elderly.[4] However, these same scholars have based their ideas about ageing women in the past almost solely on the experiences of ever-married women.[5] Such findings are not representative of all women, however. The emphasis that researchers have placed on widowhood and its emotional and material effects does nothing to help elucidate the lives of old women who never married. Similarly, the end of years of childbearing as a result of menopause was significant to married women, but we cannot necessarily say the same for single women. By focusing on single women this essay shows how never-married and ever-married women experienced old age in differing ways. The greatest difference was that single women, contrary to scholarly belief, were the women best positioned to enjoy a positive old age. We will find that in seventeenth- and eighteenth-century England, old single women of middling status experienced later life as a period of autonomy, activity and authority. As they aged, these women gained more residential and economic independence, increased their economic, religious and civic activity, extended their familial and civic authority, and continued the social relationships that were significant to them.

Some scholars might argue that single women were a small minority in the past, and so it is unnecessary to take into account how their old age differed from that of ever-married women. We can brush aside these arguments, however. Lifelong single women (or women who never married) comprised between 10 and 20 per cent of all women in England between 1550 and 1750.[6] Even more significantly, lifecycle single women (or adult women who had not yet married, including women who might never do so) made up between one-quarter to half of adult women in early modern England. Lifecycle single women comprised at least 28.5 per cent of adult women in the port of Southampton, 32.6 per cent of women in the Warwickshire village of Fenny Compton, and as much as 54.5 per cent of women in the city of London.[7]

The above numbers include both young and old single women. To determine how many single women were elderly, we need first to define old age in the early modern era. Pre-modern Europeans continued to adhere to the classical belief that human life was divided into stages: an individual would pass through three, four, or even seven of these stages in a lifetime. Although unable to define the onset of middle age and old age with precision, the works delineating the Ages of Man suggest that middle age usually began between the ages of 35 and 45, and old age most frequently commenced between the ages of 50 and 60. Old age itself was often further divided into various stages of decrepitude and senility.[8] But the Ages of Man did not take into account the stages of a woman's life. Women were believed to mature faster than men, so we can only presume that a woman's middle age began at age 35 or earlier and that female old age began before age 60.[9] While the Ages of Man schema does not help us to clarify when women entered old age, the contemporary belief that menopause signalled the onset of old age does. Since women in this time period could enter menopause any time between the ages of 40 and 50, we can conclude that old age for women in early modern England began as early as age 40 and more certainly by a woman's fiftieth birthday.[10]

How many single women in early modern England were over the age of 40? It is difficult to calculate numbers of single women over the age of 40 since the tax listings upon which early modern demographers depend rarely include the ages of those listed. While we cannot derive exact numbers of elderly single women in early modern England, we can get a sense of the age to which an old single woman could expect to live. For instance, in Southampton many never-married women lived into at least their forties and fifties, but single women also commonly made it into their sixties and seventies, and a few even lived into their eighties. Out of 75 single women who lived in Southampton between 1550 and 1750 (and whom we can trace over at least a 25-year period), 24 (or 32 per cent) lived into at least their forties, 22 (29.3 per cent) lived into at least their fifties, 9 (12 per cent) lived into at least their sixties, 12 (16 per cent) lived into at least their seventies, and 4 (5.3 per cent) lived into their eighties. An additional 4 (5.3 per cent) never-married women were referred to as 'old maids' when they were buried, but their exact ages are unknown.[11] These ages at death are only minima since burial records do not survive for at least half of these single women, so their final age is merely based upon their last appearance in Southampton's records. This means that many of these single women lived even longer than our conservative estimates. Southampton's octogenarians included single women such as Sarah Fryer, a long-time property owner in St Michael's parish, who died at the age of 86; Elizabeth Downer, who died in the workhouse after 85 years of life; Elizabeth Shergold, the manager of Southampton's first boarding school for ladies, who died at age 82; and Mary Bernard, who was baptised in 1677 and buried in the town's new graveyard in 1758, at the ripe old age of 81.[12] Such ages were not unheard of in early modern England, but were still exceptional.[13]

When did single women themselves feel they had entered into old age? The single women of Southampton did not refer to menopause directly, but it is significant how many single women began to plan for their old age in their forties and fifties – the age that contemporaries associated with menopause. Single women may have experienced menopause differently from ever-married women; after all, they were not used to years of childbearing which now came to an end. Nevertheless, along with wives and widows, never-married women experienced the physical effects of menopause and the social and cultural effects of a transition that signalled female old age. For example, it was at the age of 40 that Elizabeth Searle made the decision that she would never marry and entrusted her inheritance to Southampton's Corporation in return for an annuity that would provide her with a fixed income for her remaining years.[14] In 1722, Dorothy Wallistone made her final will, revoking all former wills she had made. Since she was born sometime in the 1670s, Wallistone was in her late forties or early fifties when she put her affairs in order for the last time.[15] Other single women from the middling ranks did not plan for their old age until slightly later. Barbara Richards was 62 when she decided to sign the lease of her house over to a local man in return for a fixed annuity. She died nine years later, although the arrangement had evidently been problematic since she had to take the man to court.[16] While single women who made investments and drew up wills were planning for old age, they did not mention age directly. Only Mildred Arnold, who made her will in 1664, stated that she was doing so because she was weak in body 'by reason of age'. Despite her worries, Arnold lived another three years.[17]

We know that, like today, women in the past lived longer than men. But did women of different marital statuses enjoy the same longevity? In particular, did never-married women enjoy better health and live longer than their ever-married sisters, or were they at a disadvantage? The event most likely to ensure an early death for a pre-modern woman was childbirth, but because most single women did not have children, they escaped this hazard. This could have resulted in a higher proportion of never-married than ever-married women surviving to old age. In mid nineteenth-century France, single women over 60 had a 27 per cent lower mortality rate than widows of the same age. Nevertheless, by the end of that century widows were living as long as never-married women, and in the twentieth century widows surpassed the longevity of single women.[18] Therefore we cannot assume that single women always outlived their ever-married peers. Indeed, a young woman in ill health or with a disability was often discouraged from marrying, and so women who were thought likely to die at a young age may have been more likely to remain single than marry. For instance, the single woman whom Southampton's authorities called 'blind' Jane Chaplin lived only into her thirties, and the single woman Anne Call, whom parish officers described as 'lame', died at the age of 37.[19] Nevertheless, unhealthy single women could also exceed expectations. When the Southampton widow Dorothy Shreckenfox died in 1693 she mentioned in her will that her 33 year old single daughter, also called Dorothy, was both deaf and dumb and she committed her to the care of her other two daughters. Although the younger Dorothy's disabilities contributed to her singleness, they did not mean that she died young, for she was buried in 1737 at the age of 77. Since we have evidence that single women died at both young and rather advanced ages, it is not yet possible to decide whether never-married women were likely to outlive or to die younger than their ever-married counterparts.

We do know, however, that contemporary medical theory suggested that never-married women would suffer more ill health than ever-married women as they aged. Adult women of any age who were not married (and so presumably not engaging in regular sexual activity) came to be diagnosed with greensickness, a disease characterised by a greenish tinge of the skin and a morbid appetite, whose only remedy was marriage.[20] Medical commentators also believed that menopause would be more difficult for single women, and any other women who failed to devote themselves fully to husband and children. (Although we attribute this to different reasons today, some childless women still experience an earlier and more difficult menopause). According to early modern physicians, because never-married women had not 'properly' utilised their reproductive organs they could look forward to a sickly old age. Regular exercise of her sexual and reproductive organs (within marriage only, of course) was considered of benefit to a woman's health, even after menopause. Single women, therefore, were at a medical disadvantage.[21] Nevertheless, the actual experiences of older single women do not reveal women incapacitated by biological changes. For instance, the pauper single woman Anne Chaplin, whom Southampton's overseers of the poor had been describing as infirm for over sixty years, lived to the age of 65 at least, at which time she was the sole person responsible for cleaning and looking after the town's Independent church.[22] Likewise, Elin Stout, the daughter of a Lancashire yeoman, was advised by her family not to marry because of her ill health. Stout kept up a busy schedule for such an 'unhealthy' person: keeping house for her brother William, assisting in his trade, caring for her parents, nursing sick family members and fostering her two nieces. Elin Stout worked and lived to the ripe old age of 64, proving that dire medical predictions about elderly single women were not always true in practice.[23]

While many single women could expect to live into their sixth and seventh decades, if not their eighth, never-married women did not have to view this as cause for consternation or concern. Despite predictions of ill health, for single women of middling status these years could be especially healthy and productive. Many of these single women also found their later years to be a period of residential, economic and social freedom, as well as of liberation from dependant roles. No longer someone's daughter or household dependant, older single women became independent adults. Past what society viewed as marriageable age, never-married women could move beyond the recriminations they had faced for never marrying and producing children. As single women of middling rank grew older they also became more autonomous and active. Below we examine the independent activity of such single women by looking at their residential and economic options, their social, religious and civic activities, and finally their social relationships. What will become apparent is that, while scholars have characterised old age as a period of dependency – a decline into a second childhood, when the elderly become dependent upon their families, communities or the state for practical and material assistance – old age for some single women could be rather different.

One of the primary ways in which an older single woman of even limited financial means could exercise her autonomy was by becoming a head of household. When we identify those households headed by a single woman, we find that it was primarily old single women who established their own residences. In the seventeenth- and eighteenth-century communities of Lichfield, Stoke-on-Trent and Corfe Castle, while only between 4.5 and 5.9 per cent of never-married women below the age of 45 headed their own household, between 36.4 and 40 per cent of single women age 45 and over did so.[24] These figures indicate an eight- to ninefold increase in household headship as single women aged. Likewise, it was primarily older single women who comprised the mere 8 per cent of never-married women who headed their own household in seventeenth-century Southampton.[25] For instance, the never-married sisters Elizabeth and Joanna Shergold lived with their mother until she died in 1714. Seven years later they leased their own house for the first time, at the ages of 47 and 39, respectively. Similarly, Barbara Richards was 37 years old when she took over the lease of the home in which she had lived with her mother before the latter died. One reason why single women like Richards and the Shergolds did not set up house until they were older is that they lived in the households of their parent(s) who retained their headship until they died. Once a single woman no longer had a living parent, she no longer had a family home in which to reside. More importantly, she was no longer someone's daughter, but was now an independent and adult single woman. As such, she could set up her own household.

There were other reasons why older and not younger single women were able to establish their own household. One of the principal reasons why only a minority of never-married women ever managed to head their own household was that civic officers did not want single women, especially younger ones, to live on their own. In the sixteenth and seventeenth centuries, town governors condemned and persecuted never-married women who lived and worked on their own. In 1582, Southampton's Court Leet lodged a complaint against 'maid servants that take chambers and so live by themselves masterless and are called by the name of charwomen, which we think not meet or sufferable'.[26] In Norwich, young single women who lived on their own were not referred to as charmaids but rather as 'living at their own hand'.[27] Despite the differences in terminology, the result was the same: officials in both Southampton and Norwich punished single women who dared to live on their own. In 1609, Southampton's officers told the single woman Elizabeth Green that she had two weeks to move into someone else's household (to work as a servant), or that she would be forced to leave the town.[28] While Southampton and Norwich did not explicitly differentiate between younger and elderly single women, in Coventry there was such a distinction. Here the town's officials stipulated 'no single woman . . . under the age of 50 years, take or keep from henceforth houses or rooms themselves . . . but that they go into service.' After much complaint, this age limit was reduced to age 40 three years later, but a line had been drawn between younger and older single women, nonetheless.[29]

Such laws illustrate that older single women were viewed differently from their younger counterparts. Elderly women were able to set up their own household because of contemporary ideas about female morality and sexuality. Civic officials frowned on single women living in their own lodgings because they believed these women would be mistaken for prostitutes, and these officials themselves often elided independent single women and prostitutes.[30] According to these men, it was necessary for an 'honest' single woman to live under the roof of a male patriarch, who would protect her reputation, and coincidentally deter any immoral behaviour in which she might engage. Once a single woman turned 40 or 50, however, she became less of a concern. This was for multiple reasons. First, were commonplace ideas about the sexuality of older women. While some contemporary stereotypes did present older widows and single women as lascivious and lustful, an equal number characterised older women as asexual beings who would be unlikely to marry or have sex at an advanced age.[31] Evidently, Coventry's governors were persuaded by this latter characterisation, for once a single woman was older these officials believed she posed no sexual threat and would no longer be mistaken for a prostitute. Secondly, once a woman was in her forties or fifties, and had presumably gone through menopause, she was unlikely to get pregnant. This gave the townsmen of Coventry a more practical reason for allowing older single women to establish their own household. Even if an older single woman did use the opportunity of living on her own to engage in illicit sexual activity, such behaviour would not result in a child. Unlike a younger woman, an older single woman could not become an economic drain on the local community by producing a bastard child that the parish might have to support. Thirdly, civic governors may have believed that an old single woman, like all aged persons, enjoyed the benefit of wisdom that came with advancing age. In official eyes such wisdom might well have rendered an elderly single woman capable of establishing her own household and maintaining it in a proper fashion.

Whatever the reason for the social acceptance of old single women, the ability to set up their own household led to a substantial increase in the autonomy of never-married women. They could now make their own decisions about how they wanted to live on a day-to-day basis, how they wanted to run their household, and with whom they wanted to live. Even poor old women who could often not afford to live alone were able to maintain their own household by 'spinster clustering' with other lone women, or by taking in lodgers. Interestingly, even prosperous single women who could afford to head their own household by themselves did not usually choose to live alone. Rather, older single women opted to live with family, extended kin, friends and servants. For example, the single gentlewoman Susannah Shreckenfox lived with her widowed sister Elizabeth Plant for many years. When Mrs Plant died, Shreckenfox hired a female servant named Mary Fleetwood to reside with her. Mary Fleetwood seems to have been more of a companion than a mere servant since Shreckenfox made Fleetwood her executrix and heir when she died in 1741.[32] A single woman's companion was most often her own never-married sister, however. Elizabeth and Joanna Shergold lived together with their mother before she died, and thereafter resided with one another for an additional thirty years until Joanna died in 1745/6. Similarly, Jane and Alice Zains jointly ran a linen drapery business and lived together in All Saints parish, Southampton. Their neighbours included Katherine and Lucy Ridge, single sisters who lived and worked together, and Ann and Katherine Fleming, another pair of single sisters who resided together in All Saints.[33] The fact that older single women who headed their own household usually did not reside on their own may have helped mitigate the concerns harboured by Southampton's officials about single women living alone. Nevertheless, single sisters like the Shergolds,

Zains and Ridges, who had the financial freedom to establish their own household, only did so once they reached middle or old age.

Older single women not only exercised more autonomy over their residential options, but as they aged they also gained more independent control of their finances. Indeed, middling single women usually did not begin to appear as property holders, rentiers and moneylenders until their later years. For example, it was in 1754 that the single sisters Elizabeth and Mary Winter, age 62 and 59 respectively, first paid tax on their property in St Marys parish, Southampton.[34] It was also in their old age that Southampton's single women began to diversify their investments. Single women commonly served as moneylenders to both private individuals and public institutions (such as the Corporation of Southampton) throughout their lives; but it was in old age that single women moved beyond simple bonds to other investments such as annuities and mortgages.[35] This was probably because mortgages required a large amount of money, and only older single women, who could have inherited or amassed a sizeable estate over time, would have been able to invest such a substantial sum. For example, a year after her father's death, Ann Goodridge invested her inheritance in a mortgage of a messuage (or townhouse) in St Michael's parish. In 1747, the single woman Mary Fassett purchased the mortgage of a brewer's house, malthouse, gardens, shops and cellars for £65 8s. In two years she earned £6 1s. interest on her investment, or almost 10 per cent; a decent rate of return for the time.[36] Older single women like Fassett preferred low-risk investments, such as land, mortgages and annuities, but even these assets could provide these women with a comfortable old age.

Scholars have found a high correlation between a person's social class or financial stability and their enjoyment of their later years.[37] If this is true, single women would have been the women most likely to enjoy old age, for, unlike wives (who were *femmes coverts*), single women were able to handle their own finances; and unlike widows with children who had little disposable income to invest, single women were able to use their income for themselves, thereby planning for a comfortable and enjoyable old age.

Older single women also enjoyed the autonomy to choose and practise a trade if they needed to plan for a comfortable old age by working rather than investing. It was in their later years that middling status women who never married were likely to enter independent employment for the first time (just as they set up their own household for the first time at an advanced age). An adult single woman, no matter what her age, was a *femme sole*, and as such, legally able to trade and make contracts in her own name. Nevertheless, in Southampton and other towns the economic reality was that single women faced limited options for autonomous employment.[38] Town governors expected never-married women, especially those who were young, to find work as servants; in other words, to work for someone else who was preferably a married male head of household. Legislation in Southampton aimed at charmaids – 'young women and maidens which keep themselves out of service and work for themselves in divers men's houses contrary to the statute [of artificers]' – kept single women from working independently.[39] The 1609 case of Sara Garrett illustrates how Southampton's officials dealt with charmaids. Garrett, a single female immigrant from Jersey, was questioned and found to be lodging with a local man while knitting stockings to maintain herself. Garrett was ordered out of the town.[40] Similarly, in sixteenth- and seventeenth-century Norwich, officials punished young single women who were 'out of place' or 'out of service' with a period of incarceration in the local House of Correction. Likewise, in 1584, Manchester's Court Leet railed against the competition created by 'single women . . . at their own hands [who] do bake and brew and use other trades to the great hurt of the poor inhabitants having wife and children.'[41] The town forbade such women to trade.

Concerns about single working women waned by the end of the seventeenth century as the economy improved, but, even then, single tradeswomen were primarily older women. We can identify the ages of 20 of the 33 single women who were able to set themselves up as independent tradeswomen in Southampton between the 1680s and 1750s. When they began trading, four of these single women were at least in their twenties; two were at least in their thirties; nine were at least in their forties; four were at least in their fifties; and one was in her sixties.[42] This means that 80 per cent of these single tradeswomen began their careers in middle or old age.

One of the reasons why older and not younger single women began to work independently is that when their parents died they no longer had someone to support them or for whom they could work. They may also have been freed from caring for an aged and dying parent. For example, Mary Rowte did not establish her own ironmongery business until the age of 45. Rowte came from a family of ironmongers. Her widowed mother Elizabeth formally taught Rowte's brother Thomas the family trade through an apprenticeship, while at the same time providing Mary with informal training. When widow Rowte died she left only part of her shop goods to Thomas, but reserved 'all the goods, chattels, wares, and merchandises that are in my shop and warehouse, also in the little shop and in the press in the fore gallery, and all my millstones' to her daughter and executrix Mary Rowte. These goods would have been useless to Mary Rowte unless her mother had also instructed her in the ironmongery trade. This proved to have been the case, for once her mother's death ended her role as dependent daughter and worker in her mother's household, Rowte became recognised in Southampton for the first time as a trader in her own right.[43]

Rowte was not unique in beginning to trade independently when a parent died. In 1734, the single woman Elizabeth Langford served as her widowed mother's executrix. Two years later Langford was paying taxes on a house and shop, and a year after that she paid Stall and Art for the first time – an annual fee that allowed her to trade in Southampton.[44] Similarly, in 1697, Ann Faulkner and her widowed sister Mary Stotes served as their mother's co-executrices and were co-heirs to her estate and trade. The following year, Faulkner and Stotes were trading in their own names.[45]

For women like Rowte, Langford and Faulkner, the death of a parent was significant in that it signalled their transition from dependent daughter and worker to independent single tradeswoman. Moreover, a parent's death usually supplied an older single woman with the capital and goods she needed to set herself up in business. A younger single woman might not have these resources until her parents died. Single women did not obtain the resources to start up in business only from parents; other relatives could also be instrumental in helping older single women to establish themselves. For example, in 1701, Alice Zains, a single woman with a Southampton linen drapery business, died. In her will Zains left a portion of her shop goods to her niece, Elizabeth Wheeler, whose name replaced that of her own in Southampton's 1701 list of traders who paid Stall and Art fees to work in the town.[46] In Wheeler's case, the death of a spinster aunt allowed her to enter into independent trade during her middle age.

Old age also provided some single women with a public occupational identity for the first time. For the most part, early modern recordkeepers referred to women by their marital status – 'Agnes Godwin, singlewoman' – and referred to men by their occupational status – 'William Jollife, brewer'. Nevertheless, a handful of older single women did gain a public work identity in the town of Southampton. In the 1741 court proceedings involving a theft from her shop, Southampton's clerk referred to Jane Martin (who was in her late thirties or forties) not by her marital status of 'spinster' but by her occupational status of 'milliner' (a shopkeeper who sold clothing and accessories). Similarly, in 1733 when the 49 year old single woman Ann Goodridge invested in a mortgage she appeared in the document as 'Ann Goodridge, glover'.[47] Achieving an occupational identity was most likely a positive development for single women like Martin and Goodridge, who might well have desired an alternative identity to the roles of wife and mother which they had never filled. (In fact they may have finally achieved a recognised work identity at the age when it became apparent to all that they would never be a wife or mother.) The psychological benefit of work could explain why wealthy single women decided to begin a trade in their later years and continued to work until their death, even though financially this was not necessary. For example, Ann Goodridge began working on her own at the age of 55, even though she had just recently inherited a considerable estate from her father that included a house and a large sum of money. Women like Goodridge illustrate how financial satisfaction was only one of the benefits that work provided to old single women.[48]

The ageing single women of early modern Southampton, especially those of the middling sort, defy scholarly theories about the elderly since they became more independent in their later years. Similarly, these women also challenge the characterisation of old age as a time of withdrawal from the world and from economic, social and political activity. Scholars note that people in the past retired because their declining physical and mental capacities left them less able to participate in various activities and because contemporaries believed elderly people deserved some rest after an active life. Single women may have experienced something akin to retirement in their early years as household dependants, and so they preferred to become more, instead of less, involved in their communities as they aged. Indeed, many never-married women initially entered the economic sphere at the age we might think of people retiring today. For example, in 1742, the single woman Catherine Woods began trading in Southampton at the age of 52; dying only three or four years later. Mary Sibron did not begin trading until she was well past modern retirement age: she began paying Stall and Art when she was 68 years old.[49] There was no mandatory or common age of retirement in the early modern era (and in fact the poor may not have been able to retire), so the single women who worked in their later years were not anomalous in doing so. Rather, it was these women's late entry into trade that was unique. Some single women worked until their death. Jane and Alice Zains continued to work in their linen drapery business until they died in 1698 and 1701, respectively; and the servant Mary Lemon was in service for fifty years until she died in 1742.[50]

Old single women not only chose to forgo retirement from economic activities, they also elected to continue their religious, civic and social involvements in their later years. Indeed, never-married women became more active as they aged, and such activity may have given them a sense of purpose in their later years. For instance, as they aged, single women increased their participation or took more of a leadership role in their church, especially those never-married women who belonged to a dissenting church. It is significant how many single women first entered into or first became more active in a non-conformist sect at a mature age. Ann Terry and Elizabeth Warner, who in the 1640s had both been poor girls apprenticed out by the parish, were numbered among those attending illegal religious meetings in 1683. Terry was 42 years old and Warner was also in her forties when they were first cited for their illegal religious activities.[51] The single sisters Judith and Mary Fassett did not become members of Southampton's Above Bar

Congregational church until 1735, when they were both at least 57 years of age.[52] Perhaps these women turned to religion for comfort as they aged, or perhaps their advanced age provided them with the freedom to join a dissenting religious group. Other old single women took on both informal and formal leadership roles in their congregations in their later years. In 1723, the single woman Mary Sibron, who was in her forties at the time, took over the administration of poor relief for the town's French Huguenot church.[53] Likewise, Anne Goodridge was not recorded as a member of the local Congregational church until she was 42. Six years later her father, who had been one of the church officers, died, and Goodridge organised and handed over his records to the church. The following year she offered the use of her own home to the church for a special occasion.[54] The advanced age of single women like Sibron and Goodridge may well have invested them with some degree of wisdom and authority that allowed them to emerge suddenly as leaders in their respective churches.

Elderly single women, with some degree of financial security, not only became active in the religious sphere in later life, they also extended their role as urban citizens. Old single women in Southampton figured prominently among those citizens who paid taxes and contributed to poor rates. Over the 1730s and 1740s, single female property-holders such as Elizabeth Richards and Elizabeth and Joanna Shergold made substantial contributions to the Holy Rood parish poor rates.[55] In her later years, Mary Sibron combined service to the Huguenot church with annual payments to trade in Southampton, as well as regular payment of taxes on her land in St Michael's parish. For the 27 years between 1723 and 1750, Sibron proved to be a model citizen: quite impressive for a single woman who in 1696 (when she was in her youth) had been ordered out of the town and back to Jersey.[56] Aged single women were also conspicuous among donors to charity, perhaps because their lack of children and heirs allowed them to be. While it was common for testators to donate a few pounds to their parish church and to the poor, when she died in 1692, single woman Louise Bretin left the sizeable sum of £20 to the Huguenot church.[57]

Most importantly, single women figured prominently among the Southampton citizenry who in 1723 signed an oath of loyalty to George I which denounced the pretender to the throne, James Edward Stuart. Not all of the single women who signed this oath were old since one only had to be 18 to sign a political oath, but what is significant is that the signatories to the oath were limited to Southampton's elite.[58] Those single women who signed their names or made their mark were either members of the town's wealthier and more powerful families, or were influential tradeswomen, moneylenders and property-holders in their own right. As the majority of women who worked, owned property and invested were older single women, we can assume that it was elderly single women who comprised a large portion of the female signatories. I have established the ages of 22 of the 61 identifiable single women who signed the oath. Six of these 22 were at least in their twenties; five were at least in their thirties; seven were at least in their forties; and four were at least in their fifties. Therefore 73 per cent of the single women who signed the oath were in their middle or old age. Old single women held a significant place among the elite citizens who thought it necessary to profess their loyalty to the monarch.

Some historians have surmised that women in the past achieved more authority as they aged.[59] For single women of middling status this seems to have been true. The fact that such women were marginalised and kept from living and working on their own when they were younger, but then allowed more residential and economic autonomy in their later years, illustrates that single women increased their power as they aged. Old single women paid taxes and contributed to parish rates as heads of household, served as important creditors to Southampton's Corporation, held positions of authority in their church and signed political oaths. Their communities relied upon the financial and material assistance of prosperous, aged women who remained single. The necessary functions that elderly single women performed in their churches, neighbourhoods and communities earned these women increased (albeit at times grudging) respect in their later years.

Just as Southampton's single women defy the stereotypes of dependency and retirement that scholars have tied indiscriminately to old age, these women also contradict the characterisation of old age as a time of loneliness and isolation. Scholars have based much of this stereotype on the assumption that older women became widows, and as such lost their primary partner in life. Single women, however, had never had a husband. A never-married woman had not focused her energy and affection on this 'primary relationship'. Instead, by the time she was old, a single woman without a husband and children had spent years developing and nurturing relationships beyond the nuclear family. Her circle of kin, friends and neighbours continued to sustain a never-married woman in her later years.[60] Single women in Southampton forged relationships with parents, siblings, cousins, nieces and nephews, neighbours, servants and fellow church members. Even in old age and near death, these women retained many close ties. For instance, in 1664, when the single woman Mildred Arnold made her will because she was weak owing to 'age', she remembered and left bequests to her three brothers, three sisters, all their children, her landlady and her five children, at least seven female friends and their children, a (single) friend's maidservant, and all the friends who would carry her at her funeral.[61] Arnold was by no means a lonely and bereft old single woman; instead, like economic, religious and civic activity, continued social activity also typified the old age of never-married women like Arnold.

Even though a single woman like Arnold enjoyed a range of relationships, she might suffer the loss of a primary relationship that was just as devastating as the loss of a husband. In particular, losing a mother or a sister could be especially difficult for a single woman. Susanna Shreckenfox was lonely after her sister, business partner and housemate died. In her will she asked to be buried 'as near to her sister Elizabeth Plant as possible'.[62] The devastating loss that a single woman could feel might best be summed up by a famous Southampton single woman named Jane Austen, who, when reflecting on the death of her sister Cassandra, said: 'I have lost a treasure, such a sister, such a friend as never can have been surpassed . . . and it is as if I had lost a part of myself.'[63]

Because single women usually cultivated a number of relationships, one loss at least did not mean the end of all companionship for these women. Women who never married also developed close ties with younger people, who had a good chance of outliving them, and this meant that significant relationships might outlast the single women themselves. Many single women had close ties with their nieces in particular. Elizabeth Whislad owned only two pieces of jewellery in her old age; when she died she left her necklace to her mother and her diamond ring to her niece Mary Rowcliffe. When Mary Smith died in 1705 she left more than a diamond ring to her niece, for she gave her entire estate to her brother's daughter Elizabeth Smith.[64] Nieces often served as the heirs of single women; and in viewing their nieces in this way single women may have felt they were leaving a legacy of themselves.

Elderly single women may in fact have benefited from not focusing all their affection and resources on spouses and children, but rather on those whom they chose. Unlike wives, single women did not have to care for an ailing husband, or care for children and grandchildren (although they were the likely primary caregiver for an ageing parent). Unlike widows, never-married women did not have to go through the anguish of losing a spouse and the uncertainties of new-found financial and familial responsibilities. Old single women differed from widows in that they did not have to adapt to living without a spouse, nor did they have to create a new and more independent identity. Single women had had to do these things when they were young, meaning that their later years were ones of continuity in this respect.

Leading their life as they wished, remaining busy, but able to focus on themselves and any others for whom they chose to care, older single women would have been unlikely candidates for depression, another characterisation of old age. They lacked a husband and children to assist them with physical or material needs as they aged, but it was much more likely that an elderly wife would look after and outlive her husband than that he would look after and outlive her. Such a wife was then left alone with no one to care for her as she aged and with no additional income to assist her. She was no better off than a single woman. Historians of pre-modern Europe have also questioned just how solicitous children in the past were in caring for their aged parents.[65] In reality, wives and widows may not have had much of an advantage over single women when it came to receiving assistance in their old age. Indeed, old single women who controlled their own finances may have been at an advantage because they were able to hire servants or a nurse to care for them.

According to scholars of old age, factors such as retaining one's independence, remaining active, and having friends and family with whom to socialise, all lead to a positive experience of old age. The single women of middling status who lived in early modern Southampton enjoyed all of these advantages. Indeed, not only did these women remain independent, they actually extended their autonomy in their later years. They also increased their public presence in the community and their level of activity in economic, social, religious and civic spheres. Finally, never-married women continued to enjoy the circle of kin, friends, neighbours and fellow church-goers that they had developed over the decades. Single women did not have to spend their old age caring for an elderly spouse or young grandchildren, but instead could care for themselves. All of these factors meant that these single women were in a position to successfully negotiate their later years.[66] For middling status single women at least, old age did not have to be a period of decline, dependency or isolation. On the contrary, it could be a period of growth, autonomy and enjoyment. Freed from the constraints of their youth and the constant focus on their 'failure' to fulfil the roles of wife and mother, single women could look forward to their old age. They now resembled post-menopausal women of any marital status, none of whom were bearing children. The relatively high mortality rate in early modern England resulted in many people, women especially, becoming widowed. Older single women may have finally felt 'normal', since so many older people would have been without a spouse.

Scholars have theorised that women in the past and present cope with old age better than men. It may be that single women in the past were the women able to negotiate old age best of all, since for them old age held various advantages. This realisation is only available to us by distinguishing between women on the basis of marital status. In early modern England, a wife or widow experienced a different old age from a woman who never married. If it is true that feminist scholars have avoided the study of older women because women fear the dependent, functionless, isolated older woman they might become, I would suggest that we need to take a closer look at the past to see the positive, alternative role models for older women that can be found there.[67] The 'old maid', once derided and scorned, can instead provide a positive model of old womanhood that women can reclaim for themselves as they age.

Notes

1. Terri Premo believes that as spinsters aged they faced 'greater potential for economic hardship and loneliness' than did married or widowed women. Peter Stearns echoes this sentiment, saying that a widow enjoyed a better economic and social status than a single woman; having married and probably borne children the widow could 'wear her age with pride'. Terri L. Premo, *Winter Friends: Women Growing Old in the New Republic, 1785–1835* (Urbana, IL, 1990), pp.38, 45; Peter N. Stearns, 'Old women: some historical observations', *Journal of Family History* 5 (1980), no.1, p.51.

2. See, for example, Sara Arber and Jay Ginn, *Gender and Later Life: A Sociological Analysis of Resources and Constraints* (London, 1991); Stearns, 'Old women', pp.48, 52; Lois W. Banner, *In Full Flower: Aging Women, Power, and Sexuality. A History* (New York, 1992). In her 2,000-year survey of western history, Banner shows how women have resisted negative stereotypes about aged females, and illustrates how these stereotypes have been more fluid than we might think.

3. On the historiography of single women, see the Bibliographical Essay in this volume.

4. See the Introduction and the Bibliographical Essay in this volume.

5. The only scholarly works to address old, single women in particular are Rita Braito and Donna Anderson, 'The ever-single elderly woman', in Elizabeth W. Markson, ed., *Older Women: Issues and Prospects* (Lexington, MA, 1983); and Premo, *Winter Friends*, ch. 1: ' "Take care that she performs": the old age of wives, widows, and spinsters'. There has been no historical research on elderly single women in pre-modern England.

6. E.A. Wrigley and Roger Schofield, *The Population History of England 1541–1871: A Reconstruction* (London, 1981), p.260; Roger Schofield, 'English marriage patterns revisited', *Journal of Family History* 10 (1985), p.14.

7. Amy M. Froide, 'Single women, work, and community in Southampton, 1550–1750', unpublished PhD thesis (Duke University, 1996), pp.113–15.

8. Joel Rosenthal, *Old Age in Late Medieval England* (Philadelphia, 1996), p.182; Shulamith Shahar, *Growing Old in the Middle Ages* (London, 1997), pp.14–18; Michael Sheehan, ed., *Aging and the Aged in Medieval England* (Toronto, 1990), pp.8–10.

9. Banner, *In Full Flower*, pp.15, 175–7, 181, 184; Patricia Crawford, 'Menstruation in seventeenth-century England', *Past and Present* 91 (1981), p.67. Steven R. Smith, 'Growing old in 17th century England', *Albion* 8 (1976), p.128; Stearns, 'Old women', pp.44–6.

10. Crawford, 'Menstruation', pp.66–7. See Botelho in this volume for a discussion of the relationship between menopause and old age for women in early modern England.

11. I have identified over 2,300 single women who lived in Southampton between 1550 and 1750; however, most of these women appear in isolated instances and cannot be tracked over any significant period of time.

12. Southampton Record Office [hereafter SRO], transcript of Holy Rood Parish Register (1677); transcript of All Saints Parish Register (1758).

13. Of 234 male nobles living between 1558 and 1641, 103 died in their fifties and sixties, 33 in their seventies, and 15 in their eighties. In Colyton, Devon, the average age of death for 227 married persons who died between the years 1538 and 1837 was 56. Of these 227 people, 54 (or 24 per cent) lived even longer, into their seventies and eighties. Mary Abbott, *Life Cycles in England 1560–1720* (New York, 1996), p.135.

14. SRO, SC 2/1/8, f.148v, 183v, 269v, 283v. Annuities were standard investment practices for older single women and widows. By setting up an annuity for herself, Searle was acknowledging that she would live out her life as a single woman (although ironically this was not to be).

15. Hampshire Record Office (hereafter HRO), 1733 A135; SRO, transcript of St Michael's Parish Register (1672, 1674, 1677, 1733). Dorothy Wallistone's baptism is not listed, but in the 1670s the baptisms of her siblings appear in the registers of St Michael's parish, Southampton. I am assuming that Wallistone was also born in this decade.

16. SRO, SC 4/3/453a, b.

17. HRO, 1667 B1.

18. Stearns, 'Old women', p.51.

19. HRO, 1693 A103; SRO, transcript of Holy Rood Parish Register (1660, 1737); SC 2/1/8, pp.32, 72, 130; transcript of South Stoneham Parish Register (1680, 1712); SC 9/4/137; SC/AG 6/1/238; transcript of St Mary's Parish Register (1743). In a society with a life expectancy at birth of 35–45 years, these single women by no means died in their youth. For example, in the Devonshire community of Colyton between 1538 and 1599 the life expectancy at birth was 45 years; between 1600 and 1649 it fell to 42.5 years; between 1650 and 1699 it dropped further to 34 years; and between 1700 and 1749 it rose back to around 40 years. Peter Laslett, 'The history of aging and the aged', in P. Laslett, ed., *Family Life and Illicit Love in Earlier Generations* (Cambridge, 1977), pp.182–3.

20. Greensickness, an anaemic disease, was recognised from at least the late sixteenth century. Sufferers were believed to crave such things as dirt, chalk and coal. John Dunton, *The Ladies Dictionary* (London, 1694).

21. Carroll Smith-Rosenberg, 'Puberty to menopause: the cycle of femininity in nineteenth-century America', in Mary S. Hartman and Lois Banner, eds, *Clio's Consciousness Raised: New Perspectives on the History of Women* (New York, 1974), p.30; Banner, *In Full Flower*, p.169.

22. SRO, D/ABC 1/1, 3, *passim*.

23. J.D. Marshall, ed., *Autobiography of William Stout of Lancaster, 1665–1752* (New York, 1967), pp.68–9, 87, 90–1, 99, 103, 122, 150, 191.

24. Richard Wall derived these figures from the population listings of the two Staffordshire towns of Lichfield (1695) and Stoke-on-Trent (1701), and the rural community of Corfe Castle, Dorset (1790). While 45 is an arbitrary age chosen by present-day demographers to indicate women who permanently never married, Wall's statistics still show how old age correlated with household headship for single women. Richard Wall, 'Woman alone in English society', *Annales de Demographie Historique* 17 (1981), p.311. Also see Wall and Ottaway in this volume.

25. In Southampton, only 8 per cent of adult single women listed in the Marriage Duty tax assessments for 1696 (or 22 out of 292 possible single women) headed their own household. Unfortunately, Southampton's Marriage Duty assessments do not include the ages of those listed. SRO, SC 14/2/66a–68b, 70a–74c. Historical demographers of Britain consider the Marriage Duty assessments to be among the most complete population listings available before the establishment of the census in the nineteenth century.

26. F.J.C. Hearnshaw and D.M. Hearnshaw, eds, *Southampton Court Leet Records AD 1578–1602*, Southampton Record Society, Vol. 2 (Southampton, 1905–6), p.236.

27. Paul Griffiths, *Youth and Authority: Formative Experiences in England 1560–1640* (Oxford, 1996), pp.358, 381–2.

28. J.W. Horrocks, ed., *Assembly Books of Southampton 1609–10*, Southampton Record Society, Vol. 21 (Southampton, 1920), p.59.

29. M.D. Harris, ed., *The Coventry Leet Book*, Early English Text Society, orig. ser. 135 (Oxford, 1908), pp.545, 552, 568.

30. P.J.P. Goldberg, *Women, Work and Life Cycle in a Medieval Economy: Women in York and Yorkshire c. 1300–1520* (Oxford, 1992), pp.155–6; Ruth M. Karras, 'Sex and the singlewoman', in Judith M. Bennett and Amy M. Froide, eds, *Singlewomen in the European Past* (Philadelphia, 1998).

31. For stereotypes about the sexuality of older women, see Banner, *In Full Flower*, chs 4 and 5, esp. pp.131, 144, 171–5, 248. Interestingly, the idea that single

women would not marry after menopause was sometimes proved wrong. In 1671 Elizabeth Searle of Southampton married for the first time, at the advanced age of 52. Her sister Anne Searle, probably age 50, married the following year. Elizabeth Searle established her annuity in 1559, when she was 40, and Anne Searle set up her annuity in 1662. Assuming that Anne set up her annuity at the same age as her sister had, Anne would have been 50 when she married ten years later. SRO, SC 2/1/8, f.148v, 183v, 269v, 283v.

32. HRO, 1741 A119.

33. Single sisters commonly lived and worked together throughout Europe and the United States until at least the nineteenth century, if not later. See, for example, Stearns, 'Old women', p.54; John Cashmere, 'Sisters together: women without men in seventeenth-century French village culture', *Journal of Family History* 21 (1996), no.1, pp.44–62; Lee Chambers-Schiller, *Liberty, A Better Husband. Single Women in America: The Generations of 1780–1840* (New Haven, CT, 1984), especially chs 4 and 6.

34. SRO, SC 14/2/235.

35. For more on single women as money lenders, see Froide, 'Single women', pp.303–61.

36. SRO, SC 4/4/479/2, 16–19.

37. C. Russell, 'Ageing as a feminist issue,' *Women's Studies International Forum* 10 (1987), no.2, p.126; Arber and Ginn, *Gender and Later Life*, ch. 6, and pp.122, 127.

38. For more on how single women's employment opportunities were limited by their marital status, see Amy M. Froide, 'Marital status as a category of difference: singlewomen and widows in early modern England', in Bennett and Froide, eds, *Singlewomen*, pp.127–45. Single women in early modern Oxford faced similar constraints in finding employment. Mary Prior, 'Women and the urban economy: Oxford 1500–1800', in Mary Prior, ed., *Women in English Society 1500–1800* (London, 1985).

39. *Southampton Court Leet Records*, Vol. 2, p.186.

40. W.J. Conner, ed., *The Southampton Mayor's Book of 1606–08*, Southampton Records Series, Vol. 21 (Southampton, 1978), p.97.

41. See Froide, 'Marital status'; Griffiths, *Youth and Authority*, pp.71, 353; J.P. Earwaker, ed., *The Court Leet Records of the Manor of Manchester. Vol. 1: 1552–1686* (Manchester, 1884), p.241.

42. These figures are based on the number of identifiable single women who paid annual Stall and Art fees to trade in Southampton. SRO, SC 6/1/68–108.

43. HRO, 1701 A108.

44. HRO, 1734 A72; SRO, SC AG 8/6/1, SC 6/1/96.

45. HRO, 1697 A48; SRO, SC 6/1/73.

46. HRO, 1701 A107; SRO, SC 6/1/74; SC 14/2/37b. Elizabeth Wheeler was a servant in 1678, which would have made her at least in her late thirties, if not older, when she began to trade on her own in 1701.

47. SRO, SC 9/4/261–261a; SC 4/4/479/2.

48. See Deane, this volume.

49. SRO, SC 6/1/101, 106; transcript of St Michael's Parish Register (1690, 1745).

50. SRO, SC 6/1/73, 74; SC 14/2/68b, 72; HRO, 1742 B73.

51. SRO, SC 9/1/17; A.J. Willis, compiler, and A.L. Merson, eds, *A Calendar of Southampton Apprenticeship Registers 1609–1740*, Southampton Records Series, Vol. 12 (Southampton, 1968); Kugler, this volume. For more on single women and their relation to dissenting sects, see Froide, 'Single women', pp.162–241.

52. SRO, transcript of Above Bar Independent Chapel registers (1735); SC 14/2/37b, 50a.

53. Edwin Welch, ed., *The Minute Book of the French Church at Southampton 1702– 1939*, Southampton Records Series, Vol. 23 (Southampton, 1980), pp.71, 74.

54. SRO, transcript of Above Bar Independent Chapel registers (1726); D/ABC 1/1, f.56v, 59.

55. SRO, SC AG 8/6/1 (1732–1747).

56. *Minute Book of the French Church*, pp.71, 74; SRO, SC 14/2/127; SC 6/1/106.

57. HRO, 1692 A11.

58. SRO, SC 9/1/24. The 492 signers of the 1723 loyalty oath comprised at most 28 per cent of Southampton's adult population.

59. Keith Thomas, 'Age and authority in early modern England', *Proceedings of the British Academy*, 42 (1976), pp.205–48. Much of the evidence for this theory is based on anthropological studies of pre-modern societies. In these societies, post-menopausal women exercise a large amount of authority and influence. Also see Banner on aged women in matriarchal societies and religions, in Banner, *In Full Flower*, chs 2 and 3.

60. Several scholars of elderly women have noted women's ability to build relationships beyond the nuclear family. See Premo, *Winter Friends*, ch. 2 and pp.47, 130–1; Stearns, 'Old women', p.54; Janet Roebuck, 'Grandma as revolutionary: elderly women and some modern patterns of social change', *International Journal of Aging and Human Development 17 (1983)*, no.4, p.57. My contention is that single women would have had more of a need than wives to forge relationships beyond the nuclear family, and single women would have been forging such relationships longer than widows. For more on the social relationships of single women, see Froide, 'Single women', pp.162–241.

61. HRO, 1667 B1.

62. HRO, 1741 A119.

63. Deirdre Le Faye, ed., *Jane Austen's Letters* (New York, 1995), quoted in Terry Castle 'Sister-sister', *London Review of Books* 17 (3 August 1995), pp.3–6.

64. HRO, 1705 P105; 1723 A119.

65. Andrew Cherlin, 'A sense of history: recent research on aging and the family', in Matilda White Riley, ed., *Aging in Society: Selected Reviews of Recent Research* (Hillsdale, NJ, 1983), pp.6–9; Hans Johansen, 'Growing old in an urban environment', *Continuity and Change* 2 (1987), no.2, p.303; Laslett, *Family Life*, pp.174, 177, 179, 212; Rosenthal, *Old Age in Late Medieval England*, p.6. See also Ottaway, this volume.

66. These findings echo the prediction that Cherry Russell makes about elderly single women in her work on ageing as a feminist issue. See Russell, 'Ageing as a feminist issue', p.172.

67. Banner, *In Full Flower*; Russell 'Ageing as a feminist issue', pp.125–32; Arber and Ginn, *Gender and Later Life*.

CHAPTER SIX

The old woman's home in eighteenth-century England

SUSANNAH OTTAWAY

Elizabeth Freke was an elderly widow in 1706 when she wrote to her errant son chastising him for his inattention to her. She thought that he ought to come and live with her at her estate:

> Wher wee might have Joyned together In the Mangagement of whatt God has blessed me With by the Justness and kindness of my deer Husband; for a three Fold Cord is not easily Broken; but single is subject to all manner of accidents; nor is it below the Carractor of A Christian, or Reflection of A Gentleman, to help support the Infirmityes of A diseased Malloncolly Aged Mother (66 years of Age).[1]

Freke's bitterness at her son's neglect raises several questions about how common her situation was in this period. Were children or other family members generally expected to live with elderly women to help them as the debilities accompanying advanced age challenged their ability to maintain their autonomy? Did children actually abide by such expectations, or did older women in the eighteenth century usually remain independent of their families in their 'declining years'?

This essay examines both the cultural ideals concerning the living situation of the elderly and the lived experience of older women (defined as those aged 60 or more[2]). Today, many people seem to expect that elderly individuals will need to move into 'supported living' in their old age.[3] In eighteenth-century England, on the other hand, there appears to have been a strong assumption that the elderly should remain heads of a household throughout their declining years. We will see below that while old men usually did head their own households, an ageing woman's ability to maintain an independent residence declined sharply in later life. This essay also shows that there were expectations that children should help their parents in time of need. However, familial support for the elderly could be problematic, and older women, especially the poor and the very old, could experience a considerable degree of residential isolation from their families in their last years.[4]

The eighteenth century is a particularly important era in which to consider questions of family history. This was an age that saw dramatic changes in England's economy and demography. As mortality and age of marriage declined in the later eighteenth century, fertility rose, the age structure changed and the population of England increased dramatically. Although there was no single moment of sweeping economic transformation, the later eighteenth century witnessed economic changes that set the stage for rapid industrialisation in the nineteenth century. Such changes inevitably affected the lives of the elderly. For example, historians of the family have suggested that industrialisation may have caused greater co-residence among the generations.[5] This study adds some weight to this theory, but we also conclude that there was a great deal of continuity with regard to the household position of the elderly over the eighteenth century.

To generalise about the living arrangements of older individuals in this period we can turn only to fragmentary, qualitative evidence such as Freke's diary cited above, and to the surviving census-type material.[6] Although we make an effort to explore many of the issues raised in the qualitative evidence, the most important conclusions of this essay are derived from household listings. These listings are usually handwritten, unofficial documents, often created by a local clergyman, recording the inhabitants of each of the houses in the parish or town. Here, the surviving listings from the late seventeenth to the early nineteenth century are used in an effort to gather as much data as possible from what is a limited body of material. Eighteen listings from this period were suitable for this study, containing both the ages of the majority of those enumerated and clear divisions among the households. These listings allow us to isolate and examine the household position of elderly women. Household listings do provide significant methodological challenges to the historian: they are not necessarily taken from 'representative' locations; census enumerators may not have included every individual in the parish, and sometimes the relationship between the inhabitants is unclear.[7] Despite these drawbacks, household listings, when selected carefully and interpreted cautiously, can provide some very useful information to those interested in the history of ageing. Although the study of households does not reveal the nuances of interfamilial relationships, it does provide us with knowledge about some basic facts regarding a woman's domestic situation.

Peter Laslett and Richard Wall have utilised a collection of pre-modern household listings to study various aspects of the history of the family.[8] Here we move beyond the work of Laslett and Wall, using a considerably expanded selection of household listings to explore the censuses in some original ways. This essay thus stands apart from earlier studies in both the breadth of its source base and the depth with which, by focusing only on the aged and only on the long eighteenth century, we are able to explore this material.

The essay first tackles the question of cultural attitudes concerning residential independence for the aged, and then looks at whether or not these ideals were reflected in reality. Next, it examines common ideas about the responsibility of family members to support their elderly relatives. Household listings allow us to see whether or not family support occurred through co-residence between elderly women and their close kin. Finally, the essay proposes a new method for examining household listings, providing a useful way to represent important characteristics of a population's residential patterns.

Elderly women as heads of households: eighteenth-century ideals

Eighteenth-century ideals of individualism and independence decreed that individuals placed a high priority on maintaining household autonomy in later life.[9] One of the most significant aspects of the English family system was its neolocalism: that is, the assumption that when children married they would set up their own homes. The logical corollary to neolocalism was the great importance this society placed on having a home of one's own throughout life. For most elderly people, co-residence with children was regarded as a temporary solution to a particular problem. As Peter Laslett has said, 'parents no longer able to maintain their own households might join the households of their children, but . . . only when invited, never as of right'.[10] Barbara Todd, too, found, in her study of Abingdon, Oxfordshire, that there was 'clear evidence that people in the town believed that it was desirable for a widow to have her own home.'[11]

Many sources suggest that, even where an older woman had to struggle to maintain her autonomy, a premium was placed on staying independent. After her husband's death in 1768, Mary Delany, aged 68, decided to move to Bath. Her friend the Duchess of Portland responded, 'I think it very proper Mrs Delany should have a house of her own . . .'.[12] A navvy (an unskilled worker) in 1820 described his mother's unwillingness to leave her home; her attachment to it ('She will never leave the place until she dies') came from its proximity to the grave of her favourite son. In his travels, Arthur Young came across an old couple by the name of Batty who refused to leave their home despite its misery and squalor. Young commented,

'From this instance . . . it is evident that these people hold the possession of such a wretched hovel and garden free from rent as an object which outweighs other comforts.'[13]

Individuals did sometimes hand over the majority of their property to their children and enter a form of retirement. The Sidbury, Devonshire, census of 1829 lists several individuals who had apparently done this: Mary Hardy and her husband, a Norfolk farmer, turned over their farm and its management to their son in 1797; and Lady Isabella Wentworth gave nearly all of her money into her son's hands in the early years of the eighteenth century. However, in all of these cases, the aged individual maintained control of an independent residence. The inhabitants of Sidbury who were listed as 'retired' were still labelled heads of households. Mary Hardy and her husband kept their farmhouse for their own residence, and Isabella Wentworth's son supplied her with a house of her own.[14] These examples suggest that even in those cases where power was given over to the younger generation, older individuals could keep control over their living space. One reason for this, as we will see below, is that contemporaries viewed the care of the elderly by their children as fraught with potential problems.

The building and endowing of almshouses for the elderly poor – often specifically for older widows – was one way in which the need both to support the aged and to allow them to preserve some sense of residential independence was met. Almshouses were a form of community provision for the elderly, but the nature of this provision was very different from that of large institutions such as French hospitals or English workhouses. A place in an almshouse served to preserve a separate living space for the aged person: one in which she was not subject to a co-resident. Walter Godfrey has described a 'change-over' in England from the medieval hospital, 'where everything was in common, to the [early modern] collegiate groups of separate dwellings for almspeople.'[15] The purpose of most widows' almshouses is reflected in the inscription placed on a group of Colchester almshouses in 1726, which read: 'That such as are admitted into these Tenements may find a comfortable Residence, during the Remainder of their Lives . . .'[16] Where almshouses were not present, similar methods for perpetuating the independence of the aged were sometimes used. In Madeley, Shropshire, the Lord of the Manor in the late eighteenth century had a policy of 'building houses for the old and the distressed.'[17]

The assumption that the aged should be independent seems to have pervaded thinking at all levels of society, but there were those who clearly felt that the need for a private fireside did not extend all the way down the social scale to paupers. The poor who had become dependent upon the parish were often expected to cohabit with other paupers rather than to maintain their own dwelling, and this was particularly true of poor women.[18]

Was the eighteenth-century ideal of household independence for the aged applied to the poor?

Eighteenth-century overseers of the poor accounts demonstrate that parish poor relief officers often dictated the residential position of the poor. In Terling, Essex, for example, from 1694 to 1703 eleven parishioners, many of whom were elderly widows, were 'removed' by the overseers from one home into another, many times moving into shared houses. Widow Birchall, for instance, was 'removed' twice in the space of six months, and from 1694 to 1701 she lived in five different houses, including a year in the house of her son Richard and several years spent living with the impoverished Norris family.[19]

A document from Gillingham, Dorset, provides an insight into the deliberate policy lying behind these actions. In a document made for the use of the overseers of the poor in 1765, parish officers were told that it was lawful to erect cottages for the use of the impotent poor of the parish. In answer to the question 'How many Inmates or Families to be lodgd there', the document asserted, 'More than one notwithstanding [the statute of] 31 Eliz.' In this parish, then, the overseers were told that a statute forbidding multiple-family dwellings should not be applied to paupers. Legal experts such as Richard Burn also asserted that paupers could be forced to live together.[20]

On the other hand, the provision of poor relief, including rent payments, to elderly people who continued to live in their own cottages indicates that there was a powerful assumption that even the poorest of the elderly belonged in homes of their own. Parish poor law accounts from all parts of the country include entries for rent payments to elderly persons. Peter King has pointed out that the policy of taking inventories of paupers' goods and leaving paupers in possession of those goods until death (rather than confiscating the belongings of the poor as the parish was legally entitled to do) was one way in which overseers allowed elderly relief recipients to maintain their own households even after they were completely dependent on the parish.[21] In some locations, poor relief policies deliberately prioritised the residential independence of the aged. In Ellesmere, Shropshire, the corporation for the poor only allowed outdoor relief to those aged 70 or more.[22] Similarly, in 1797, the vestry of Blandford Forum, Dorset, was prepared to relieve only the aged and infirm in their own homes.[23] Eighteenth-century observers were well aware that the elderly would go to great lengths to avoid leaving their homes. A resident of Farnham, Surrey, noted: 'Old people (who decline making applications [for relief], that would oblige them to quit their own habitations and neighbours, for, perhaps, more elegant apartments and profligate associates, in a workhouse) often go unrelieved.'[24]

The increased use of workhouses in the late eighteenth century forced a number of elderly persons into institutions. Even so, no more than a small minority of the country's aged were institutionalised, and many of those who were put into workhouses were probably in the last stages of decrepitude.[25] Moreover, sources indicate that in some workhouses a degree of independence was given to old people so that they were not forced to maintain a wholly institutionalised existence. In Liverpool's workhouse:

> The old people, in particular, are provided with lodgings in a most judicious manner: each apartment consists of three small rooms, in which there are one fire-place and four beds, chairs and other little articles of domestic use, that the inmates may possess; who, being thus detached from the rest of the Poor, may consider themselves as comfortably lodged in a secluded cottage; and thus enjoy, in some degree, even in a workhouse, the comforts of a private fire-side.[26]

Similarly, in Gressinghall, Norfolk's House of Industry, 'Old people, and a few others, are allowed to reside in cottages'.[27] Thus sometimes the desire to treat the elderly differently from the other poor, and the effort to give them at least the illusion of privacy, is evident even when the aged were forced into workhouses.

It appears that the ideal of household independence for the aged did extend to the poor, but it was coupled with the practical realisation that it was cheaper for parishes to maintain paupers who lived in shared housing. Parishes weighed individual needs and preferences with the cost of poor relief in determining the extent to which they supported the residential independence of elderly women. Similarly, elderly women themselves would have had to weigh the advantages and costs of staying in their own homes. Below, we use the evidence available from the household listings to assess the ability of elderly women to remain heads of households in later life.

Old women's homes in the eighteenth-century listings

Eighteen household listings from the late seventeenth to early nineteenth century contain adequate information for the purposes of this study. These censuses indicate whether a woman was living in her own home – as a head of household or as the spouse of a household head – or if she was living as a subordinate member of someone else's home. Thus they help us to gain insight into the degree to which elderly women maintained their autonomy.

Eighteenth-century census-makers almost always made a clear distinction between the head of a household (or 'householder') and the other members of a family: heads of family were either placed in a separate column or listed first within the household. Not only does this indicate that enumerators recognised the importance of the role of a head of household,[28] but it also means that household 'headship' is one of the least ambiguous aspects of pre-modern censuses.[29]

The collection of listings indicates that the majority of the elderly women in the listings (64–66 per cent) either headed their own household or were married to a household head (see Table 6.1, p.118).[30] Still, older women were less likely to have an autonomous household position than elderly men. About 20 per cent fewer women than men were a household head (or a spouse of a head), and elderly women were more often found in positions of dependence than were men. In most places, about twice as many women as men lived in households that were headed by neither themselves nor their spouse.[31] Older women also lived alone more often than men: one in ten women compared with one in twenty men. Still, it was not common for aged individuals to live in isolation, and no more than 5 per cent of the elderly women in any of the listings lived in a workhouse.

Figure 6.1 shows that women's ability to head their own household declined with age, but a sharp decline did not occur until advanced old age. Women aged 65 to 74 headed households at a rate slightly lower than those 45 to 54 years old. Women aged 75 and more were far less likely to be a household head than their younger cohorts. The seventeenth-century urban and nineteenth-century rural populations had headship rates of 50 per cent or less for the oldest women; the other three areas showed headship rates of 60 to 70 per cent for this age group. Figure 6.1 shows that all of the listings used here displayed similar trends in the household position of elderly women,

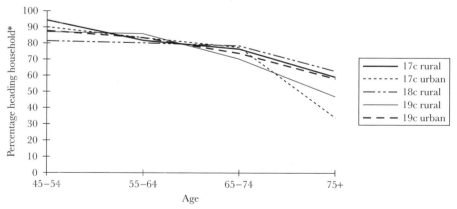

* Figure includes women who were household head, spouse of a household head or who lived alone relative to the total population of women at each age group.

Figure 6.1   Percentage of women heading a household

Table 6.1 Household heads in eighteenth-century parishes, aggregated by date and economic type

	Head/spouse of head		Non-household head		Solitary		In institution		Total
	no.	%	no.	%	no.	%	no.	%	
Females									
Late 17th C. rural[a]	42	66	16	25	6	9	0	0	**64**
Late 18th C. rural[b]	110	64	37	21	23	13	3	2	**173**
Late 19th C. rural[c]	135	66	61	30	7	3	2	1	**205**
Late 17th/early 18th C. urban[d]	141	64	47	21	22	10	12	5	**222**
Early 19th C. urban[e]	160	65	62	25	18	7	8	3	**248**
Total									**912**
Males									
Late 17th C. rural[a]	45	87	7	13	0	0	0	0	**52**
Late 18th C. rural[b]	138	78	28	16	4	2	7	4	**177**
Early 19th C. rural[c]	175	81	30	14	8	4	4	2	**217**
Late 17th/early 18th C. urban[d]	120	81	14	9	4	3	10	7	**148**
Early 19 C. urban[e]	192	84	19	8	11	5	6	3	**228**
Total									**822**

[a] 17th C. rural: Grasmere 1683, Chilvers Coton 1684, Ringmore 1698
[b] Late 18th C. rural: Wetherby 1776, Wembworthy 1779, Corfe Castle 1790, Ardleigh 1796, Winwick 1801
[c] 19th C. rural: Alderley 1811, Thornford 1821, Rostherne 1821, Chiddingly 1821, Whittington 1831, Evenley 1831
[d] 17th/18th C. urban: Lichfield 1692, Stoke 1701
[e] 19th C. urban: Braintree 1821, Tanworth 1821

with all showing a sharp decline in residential independence only after women had reached advanced old age.

Although the headship rates varied only slightly among the populations studied, there were some differences within these populations with regard to socioeconomic status. Four detailed censuses that survive from the late eighteenth century give occupational information for most of the individuals whom they enumerate. These censuses show that, in general, old people from lower down the social scale were less likely to head a household than those from the upper echelons of society. For this exercise, all married women were assigned the occupation of their spouse; where they were living in households headed by a child, they were given that child's occupation (unless the woman's occupation was specified). Individuals living alone were considered household head.

All of the elderly women from the upper and middle classes – those above the level of craftsman – were heads or spouses of heads of households. Among the poorer occupational groups, it appears that an individual's occupation influenced her ability to head a household in later life: 16 per cent of craftswomen (or the wives of craftsmen) and 37 per cent of pauper women were a non-household head.[32] This is not surprising given that we have already seen that many eighteenth-century social commentators felt that poor people ought to live together in order to save money. It would appear that when or where an elderly woman lived in the eighteenth century was less of a determinant of her ability to head a household than what she did for a living. These findings mirror many historians' assertions that household practices varied by economic status. Tom Sokoll, for instance, has shown that pauper women were more likely to live in extended families than were the well-to-do.[33] Our findings here are particularly important because, unlike other analyses of this issue, this study considered only one stage of the life-course. Our focus here solely on elderly women allows us to see that variations in these households were likely to have been due to economic status rather than to life-stage developments.[34]

We have seen that it was considered highly desirable for elderly women in eighteenth-century England to maintain their residential independence. This section has shown that reality often mirrored this assumption: most old women from our household listings were head of household (or the spouse of a head). However, women were less likely than men to maintain residential autonomy (at least partly because of their lower earning potential and their greater likelihood to live as widows), and women's ability to maintain headship declined markedly when they entered advanced old age. We also saw that the poorest women in the censuses were those least likely to be a head of household. The populations studied displayed strikingly similar results, suggesting a considerable continuity across the eighteenth century in terms of both time and location.

Household and family: eighteenth-century ideals

An elderly woman living in this period would have seen most of her contemporaries living as heads of households, but she also must have been aware that many women of her age needed assistance in their daily lives. On whom could an older woman depend for help?

Spouses were certainly obligated to look after one another, and since marriage was the accepted 'natural' state for people at this time, the most important and common co-resident for an elderly person was a spouse. Married couples were expected to reside together, and husbands who deserted their wives were supposed to be caught and punished for doing so. As Richard Burn wrote, 'And further to compel husbands and parents to maintain their own families, the law hath also provided that all persons running away out of the parish, and leaving their families upon the parish, shall be deemed and suffer as incorrigible rogues.'[35] Where a husband was obliged to leave his family, as in the case of military service, the parish was expected to compensate the wife for his absence.

Unfortunately, widowhood was a recurrent feature of the early modern era, and remarriage was comparatively rare among older women.[36] Some literary evidence suggests that, whereas men were encouraged to remarry, older widows who remarried were scorned. This applied particularly to the idea of old widows (those most likely to need assistance) marrying younger men (those most capable of supplying assistance). Widows were told: 'Art thou antient, yet seekest the embraces of a young spouse, he will be the bane of thy latter days; he will bring jealousy to thine heart and misery to thy gray hairs.' And men were warned in even more dire tones of the consequences of marrying an old woman: a man so married soon 'loaths the Embraces, the Conversation, the Presence of his Wife . . .'.[37] Although a spouse's care in old age was important, it is clear that women would often have needed to look beyond their mates for support in their decrepitude.

There is a great deal of evidence to suggest that eighteenth-century cultural norms obliged children to support their aged parents. The law instituting badging of the poor mandated that all residents of a pauper's household wear a badge identifying them as dependent upon the parish, except a 'child . . . permitted to live at home, in order to attend an impotent and helpless parent.'[38] The old poor law also stated that children with sufficient resources had to support necessitous parents.[39] Many texts proclaimed the scriptural obligations of children towards their parents,[40] and prescriptive literature stressed filial responsibilities. One conduct book for women emphasised the worth of unmarried women staying home to care for a 'desolate parent.'[41]

Support beyond shared residence in a household was certainly given to the elderly by their children, but it is hard to find records of such assistance, and the qualitative evidence available suggests that children often gave their parents moral support and caring services rather than money transfers or goods. Among the rich, the elderly usually provided for their own livelihood, and among the poor, children often lacked the resources to assist their ageing parents financially. Thus the sharing of households was one of the most important ways in which the younger generation could assist the older.[42]

On the other hand, co-residence between elderly parents and adult children was recognised as problematical, since the accepted norm was for the aged to maintain residential independence, and for married children to establish their own households. In consequence, where co-residence with adult offspring occurred, these children were usually unmarried, and the parents were most often listed as the heads of the household. This suggests that even where elderly parents lived with their children, and may have relied on their support, the parents were not perceived by census enumerators as subordinate members of their child's household.[43] It also implies that, once children had actually set up independent households they would not usually expect to provide residential support for their parents, even if they helped them in other ways.[44] Such a case was that of Abner Croker, aged 73, a resident of Corfe Castle, Dorset. Although he lived only with his wife, the census enumerator noted that 'He is maintained by his children . . .'.[45] As David Thomson has pointed out, despite the explicit statement within the old poor law that children assume responsibility for their parents, the law as it was actually enacted was very limited. Children were obligated to provide cash payments not shelter, so that a child could not be forced to take an aged parent into his or her home. In fact, the 'family support' section of the old poor law was rarely enforced. The children of the elderly poor seldom had the resources to care for their parents, so parishes frequently supported individuals even when they had children living nearby. In late eighteenth-century Terling, Essex, for instance, almost half of the elderly people living in the workhouse had children living in the parish.[46]

The tension between filial responsibility and the assumption that ageing parents would provide for their own housing is evident in the letters from Lady Isabella Wentworth to her son, the Earl of Strafford. The Earl provided Lady Wentworth with a little house, and she expressed her deep gratitude to him for it: 'Sure I have all the Oblgations, that ever mother had to a son, & I giv you a million thancks for your kynde thought in geving me that hous . . .'. At the same time, she was deeply suspicious that he would take it away from her again and use it for his children, which she clearly felt he had the right to do: 'but now I cannot put the fancy out of my head but that hous will be turned to a better yous then for me. For I know my Lady [Strafford's wife] will Lyke it much better for a Nursery . . .'.[47] A letter from Colonel J.H. Strutt to his father John Strutt, MP, in 1784, also emphasised the problem of cohabitation among the generations.

> I entirely agree with you that the thoughts, opinions, ways and dispositions of old and young (however they may wish to oblige, comfort and make happy each other) are so very different, that it is incompatible and inconsistent with their happiness to live constantly together, unless illness, misfortune or any other particular cause on the one side shou'd render the immediate care and constant attention of the other necessary.[48]

Parents who moved into a child's home were warned by eighteenth-century authors to beware of their position. Daniel Defoe published a scathing attack on the younger generation's failure to respect and support its elders, and similar cautionary tales were published in the eighteenth century.[49] Caleb Trenchfield advised his son and readers that, 'One Father is enough to maintain an hundred Sons, but not an hundred Sons one Father'.[50]

Thus, while filial responsibility for an aged parent was a widely recognised obligation, it is clear that co-residence between the generations was perceived as fraught with difficulties. It will be seen below that many older individuals did reside with their offspring, but our understanding of this situation must be tempered by our knowledge that the obligations of the young towards the old were quite circumscribed. There is also very little evidence to suggest that the obligation to support elderly kin extended beyond the nuclear family.[51]

Household positions and co-residents of elderly women in the household listings

Table 6.2 shows the household position of the aged in thirteen parishes from the late seventeenth to early nineteenth century. These locations all had surviving household listings that allow us to identify the nature of the relationship between co-residents and heads of household. The table shows that most of the elderly women and men listed in our collection of censuses lived with members of their immediate family. This confirms the common assumption of the importance of the nuclear household in early modern England.

Table 6.2 Household position of individuals aged 60+ by period and type of parish

	17th C. rural %	17th C. urban %	18th C. rural %	19th C. rural %	19th C. urban %
Females					
Spouse of household head					
Spouse[a] (w/o children)	14	15	24	20	30
Spouse and children[a]	32	20	16	30	9
Heading household with:					
Children[a]	7	19	14	9	13
Kin[a]	4	2	3	2	3
Only non-relatives	7	7	6	6	7
In household headed by:					
Children[a]	14	4	7	9	8
Parent[a]	0	0	0	1	1
Kin[a]	0	5	3	1	1
Non-relative	7	12	12	19	15
Solitary	14	10	13	2	9
Institutionalised	0	5	2	1	3
Possibly in hh with adult children	7	11	5	14	7
Males					
Heading households with:					
Spouse[a] (w/o children)	29	24	28	21	41
Spouse and children[a]	33	36	28	41	30
Children[a]	25	11	17	15	9
Kin[a]	0	4	2	2	1
Only non-relatives	0	6	5	2	4
In households headed by:					
Children[a]	0	1	3	2	0
Parent[a]	0	0	1	1	0
Kin[a]	0	3	2	2	0
Non-relative	13	6	10	8	6
Solitary	0	3	2	4	6
Institutionalised	0	7	4	2	3
Possibly in hh with adult children	4	3	1	5	3

[a] With or without other (less closely related) co-residents
17th C. rural: Chilvers Coton 1684
17th C. urban: Lichfield 1692, Stoke 1701
18th C. rural: Wetherby 1776, Wembworthy 1779, Corfe Castle 1790, Ardleigh 1796, Winwick 1801
19th C. rural: Alderley 1811, Rostherne 1821, Chiddingly 1821, Whittington 1831
19th C. urban: Braintree 1821

The tendency of older men and women to head households containing their spouse and/or children (the first three categories for women, and the first two for men) shows little traceable change over time and little disparity between economically diverse populations. But Table 6.2 serves to highlight gender differences in residence patterns. Men headed nuclear households (with wife and/or children – the sum of the first three categories) in 71 to 87 per cent of households in this period, while women were in this position in only 52 to 59 per cent of homes. We also see from this table that a substantial proportion of elderly men and women lived in what we today call an 'empty nest' situation, that is residing with a spouse but without children. Between 14 and 30 per cent of the women in our household listings were in this position.[52]

Women were more likely than men to live in homes headed by their children: 4 to 14 per cent of women, compared with 0 to 3 per cent of men. Even in the listings used here, there is a certain amount of ambiguity in the relationship between residents and the heads of their household. It is possible that some elderly inhabitants who appear to be unrelated lodgers were actually parents or in-laws of their co-residents. Table 6.2 includes a category tallying such cases (the 'possibly in household with adult children' category).[53] If all of the individuals in this category actually lived in the houses of their children, then as many as 23 per cent of elderly women, but no more than 7 per cent of elderly men lived in households headed by their children. These figures suggest that a sizeable proportion of those women who had lost their ability to head their own nuclear family spent their last years in the homes of their children. Thus the nuclear family was not less important to women than men, but it did serve a slightly different function in terms of the household. While women quite often lived as subordinate members within their children's homes, elderly men nearly always lived as heads of nuclear family units.

Table 6.2 shows us patterns of both household headship and co-residents, but it does not fully represent the types of resident with whom the elderly co-habited because some co-residents were unreported. Where an individual was living with a spouse and a sister, for example, the individual was recorded in a category that indicated only the presence of the former and not the latter. In Table 6.3 this weakness is remedied through an examination of the percentage of elderly women who lived with various categories of co-resident. Here, if a woman was living with a spouse and a sibling, the presence of both is recorded. Consequently the columns add up to more than 100 per cent because the presence of all types of co-resident are recorded, so households often appear in multiple categories.

As before, the importance of the nuclear family is striking. One-third to one-half of the elderly women lived with their husband and/or children.

Table 6.3 Co-residents of women aged 60+, parishes aggregated by period and economic type

	Chilvers Coton, 1684 %	17th–18th C. urban %	18th C. rural %	Braintree, 1821 %	19th C. rural %
Spouse	46	36	40	40	53
Children	54	51	39	32	50
Non-nuclear kin					
(incl. grandchildren)	18	17	26	11	33
Grandchildren	18	9	20	11	26
Lodgers[a]	7	16	16	15	18
Servants[a]	14	15	12	6	20
Solitary	14	10	13	9	2
Institution	0	5	2	3	1
Possibly living with children	7	7	3	7	14
Total number	**28**	**222**	**173**	**149**	**161**

[a] Lodger and servant categories do not include those who were lodgers or servants themselves.

Historical demographers have used computer modelling (microsimulation) to estimate the proportion of individuals in eighteenth-century England who would have had living kin, given the demographic constraints of this period.[54] These computer models take into account such factors as mortality and fertility rates, migration patterns and so on. According to this model, between 69 and 81 per cent of 66 year old women in pre-industrial England would have had a living child. Our evidence, when combined with the computer model, suggests that between 40 and 78 per cent of elderly women with living children co-habited with them.[55] Thus, in most of the populations studied here, a majority of the elderly women who had surviving children lived with their offspring, but a significant proportion of older women – between 22 and 60 per cent – who could have cohabited with a son or daughter either chose not to do so or somehow lost the opportunity.

Table 6.3 also reveals the importance of non-nuclear kin in the households of aged women, particularly in the rural areas. Most of the kin in Table 6.3 are grandchildren. In the rural areas, 18 to 26 per cent of women lived with grandchildren. Perhaps grandchildren provided useful labour in rural areas. More likely, however, considering that most of these children were very young indeed, the presence of grandchildren suggests the role that grandmothers played in caring for their children's offspring. We have a rare look at the relationship that existed between an elderly woman and her descendants in the case of Sarah Dibben, an elderly pauper from the parish of Puddletown, Dorset. Her settlement examination states that she was brought into her son's home in the late eighteenth century because 'his wife being brought to bed, He desirid her to go and abide with him, and take care of his wife and family'.[56] It is likely that Dibben's case represents a typical situation: grandmothers could provide useful services when they lived with their children's families, and the current of support between generations often flowed downwards from the old to the young.

The proportion of elderly women's households with lodgers is surprisingly consistent over the century in both rural and urban areas.[57] Lodgers appear to have been an important element in a significant minority of elderly homes. Their presence points to a number of possible living situations.[58] These lodgers may have been placed in the house by parish officers, taken in to earn some extra money, or they may have been widowed or unmarried people who needed to band together for economic and social reasons. In any case, taking in lodgers was one way in which the aged could maintain a greater degree of independence from both family members and parish officers.[59] The significant proportion of households that contained servants also suggests that elderly women were not infrequently able to maintain a degree of prosperity as well as independence into their last days.

A new method of representing the household position of the elderly

By comparing the position of older women with that of their younger neighbours we have revealed that old women were less likely than middle-aged women to head their own household. It would be useful to make a similar comparison between the household position of the elderly and the middle-aged in terms of co-residents. Ideally, we would like to know whether the ageing process led to increased co-residence with or isolation from a person's close kin. Unfortunately, because we lack consecutive censuses, we cannot know to what extent women from our listings changed their household situations as they aged. However, we can compare the homes of elderly women with those of their middle-aged neighbours asking: were the aged more or less likely than the younger members of their community to live with co-residents who would have been under an obligation to care for them? In other words, were old people more or less 'residentially secure' than middle-aged individuals. Historians have tried several ways to represent answers to this question, but none of the current methods allows us to note the patterns of co-residence in a single picture.[60] Here we will introduce a new way to answer this question, hoping that this method might also provide a useful means of comparing household data across time and cultures.

The following method is premised on two assumptions: first, that an individual's quality of life could have been significantly affected by the presence of co-residents (hence, their 'residential security' depended on these co-residents); second, that we can create a scale from the most to the least important co-residents in terms of an individual's obligation to assist an elderly co-habitant. Utilising the analysis considered above, and drawing on the work of other family historians and sociologists, we can say with some confidence that the co-residents most likely to feel a responsibility to help an elderly person are, in order of importance: spouses, children, kin beyond the nuclear household, and individuals unrelated to the elderly person.[61]

Because a clear hierarchy exists in the importance of various categories of co-residents, the type of residential position occupied by each individual can be indicated on a numerical scale. This scale forms an 'index of residential security' (IRS). Every individual that appeared in our set of household listings was assigned a number that indicates their position on this scale. Those who lived with both a spouse and children would be nearly guaranteed to have access to assistance from family members; these individuals were given an IRS value of 7 because they were at the highest level of residential security. People living in institutions were already dependent on the parish and separated from their kin, so they were assigned the lowest number on the scale: 1. The other household positions are ranged between these. Individuals living with a spouse but not children were assigned a 6; those with children and no spouse were given a 5. Persons co-resident with only non-nuclear kin were given a 4; those with non-relatives only were assigned a 3. Individuals living alone were given an IRS of 2.[62] The IRS values are shown in Figures 6.2 to 6.4 in 'boxplot' graphs.[63] Boxplots are graphs with boxes which contain the 50 per cent of values falling between the 25th and 75th percentiles, and lines that extend from the box to the highest and lowest values. A horizontal line inside the box indicates the median, and outlying values are indicated by an asterix.

Figures 6.2 to 6.4 show that residential security decreased with age. Middle-aged men and women in all of the census populations were very secure. None of the boxplots for men and women under age 50 falls below the level of 5, so almost all middle-aged people lived within a nuclear family household. (IRS numbers of 5, 6 or 7 indicate a nuclear family household, and a line is drawn on the graphs at the level 5 to emphasise which of the age groups fall beneath this line; these age groups would be those suffering from 'nuclear hardship'.)[64] At the same time, women were much less secure than men at almost every age. Not only is the median value for women

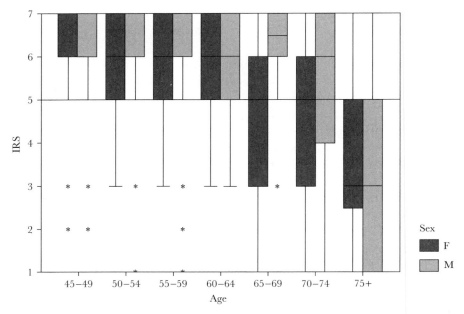

Figure 6.2　Late seventeenth- and early eighteenth-century urban IRS

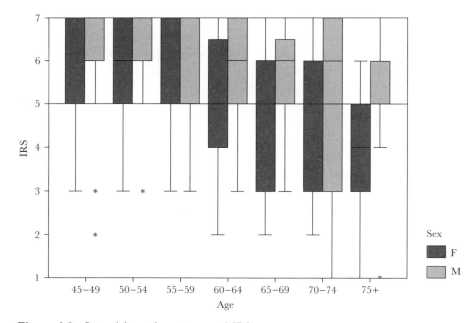

Figure 6.3　Late eighteenth-century rural IRS

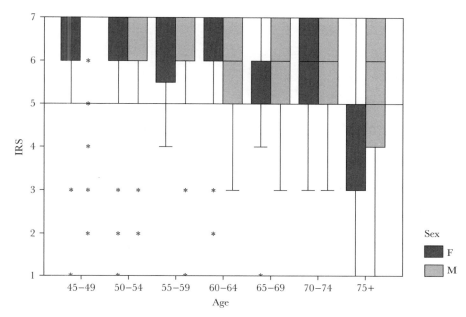

Figure 6.4 Early nineteenth-century rural IRS

lower than that for men, but more women than men lived in total isolation from members of their families.

Although each graph indicates that residential security varied by age and gender, these boxplots also show us some notable disparities among the different sets of listings used here. The boxplot for the late seventeenth- and early eighteenth-century urban populations (Figure 6.2) shows elderly women at their most vulnerable. Many women over 64 lived only with non-relatives, and a significant number lived alone or in an institution; those over the age of 74 were even more isolated from their kin. In the late eighteenth-century rural populations (Figure 6.3), women in 'young-old age' (60 to 64) were slightly less residentially secure, and women in 'decrepit old age' (75 and more) were in slightly better residential positions than their counterparts in Figure 6.2. Old men in the late eighteenth-century censuses were no more isolated than their middle-aged neighbours until the age of 70. Overall, the elderly in late eighteenth-century rural parishes seem to have enjoyed more residential security than those individuals from urban areas a century earlier.

The IRS for the early nineteenth-century rural parishes looks quite different from Figures 6.2 and 6.3. The residential security of the individuals in the early nineteenth-century populations did not change markedly until the very last age category; both the middle-aged and the elderly members of these nineteenth-century parishes were residing with members of their

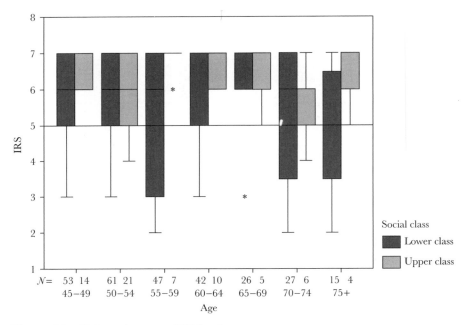

Figure 6.5 Eighteenth-century IRS by class

nuclear families in an overwhelming majority of cases. The IRS graphs thus suggest that there was a change over time in the household listings used in this study. The elderly men and women enumerated in the later censuses were more likely to live with their close kin than were the individuals from the earlier listings. This offers further suggestive evidence for the hypothesis that changes in household structure may be linked to the economic and social changes of the industrial period.[65] The fact that this change was obscured until we looked at the boxplots, where all the data are displayed in one picture, speaks volumes for the utility of this methodological tool.

Figure 6.5 shows that household position was a function of occupation as well as of age. We can see that economically secure elderly women (those classed as tradesmen and above) lived in the most secure household situations. It is not that 'lower class' women necessarily lived in less complex household situations – they were quite likely to live with other widowed women, for example – but they were more isolated from close family members than were their 'upper-class' counterparts.[66] 'Lower-class' women aged 55 to 59 appear to have been particularly isolated from their close kin, perhaps because so many of the women in this group were widows.[67] It is significant that the greatest disparity between the lower classes and the better-off is evident for those aged 70 and more. This was also the point in their life when the elderly were most likely to become fully dependent on the parish for economic support.[68] Once again, the IRS has helped us to see clearly that the most vulnerable members of the population were those least likely to have benefited from co-residence with nuclear family members.[69]

Conclusion

We began this essay with the example of Elizabeth Freke, and the question of how common was her experience. In a sense, we now have a simple answer to this question: no more than 23 per cent (at the very most) of the women in our household listings lived in homes headed by their children. It was more common for elderly women to remain head (or spouse of the head) of household through their declining years than for them to move into a child's home. At the same time, it is clear that this culture had expectations that ageing parents would not isolate themselves from their children, and the household listings demonstrate that children often did figure prominently in the homes of their ageing mothers. In the populations studied here, around four of every ten women aged 60 or more lived with a child. Furthermore, children outside the household clearly played important roles in assisting their parents, economically, physically and emotionally.[70] This would seem to indicate a rather rosy view of the lives of elderly women in this period, but such a view would be inadequate.

Certainly, there were expectations in this period that the elderly should preserve their independence, but ideals of autonomy were compromised by the real difficulties that older women faced in retaining their independence. Many of our sources also revealed a deep scepticism about the dependability of children and the depth of a child's responsibility to assist an ageing parent. In particular, both qualitative and quantitative sources demonstrated that the oldest and poorest women were those most likely to fall into positions of dependence in the homes (or workhouses) of others, and these women were also those least likely to co-reside with their close kin. Despite the cultural ideals of independence and supportive family networks, then, the eighteenth century was no 'golden age of ageing' for elderly women. Old women, especially those in their last days, and those suffering from poverty, remained very vulnerable to isolation and dependence.

Acknowledgements

I am grateful to Richard Wall for his generosity in sharing his many insights on the household listings used in this study. I would also like to thank the editors of this volume as well as Tim Harris, David Kertzer, Peter Laslett, Burr Litchfield, Ingrid Tague and Samantha Williams for their comments on earlier drafts of this essay. The research for this study was assisted by grants from the Joint Committee on Western Europe of the American Council of Learned Societies and the Social Science Research Council, with funds provided from the Ford and Mellon Foundations. Additional support was provided by Brown University, the Friends of Historic Essex, and the Research Institute for the Study of Man.

Notes

1. Mary Carbery, ed., *Mrs. Elizabeth Freke: Her Diary 1671 to 1714* (Cork, 1913), p.65.

2. The reasons for using the age of 60 are set forth in Susannah Ottaway, 'The "decline of life": aspects of aging in eighteenth-century England', unpublished PhD thesis (Brown University, 1998), pp.17–81. Diaries, medical treatises, and legal and poor law sources were used in conjunction with demographic evidence in determining that individuals were generally considered old only after they had reached the age of 60. Cf. Botelho in this volume.

3. See, for example, 'The last nanny', *New York Times Magazine*, 30 November 1997.

4. The importance of co-resident kin in offering support has been emphasised by many family historians including Richard Wall in his Introduction to Richard Wall, Jean Robin and Peter Laslett, eds, *Family Forms in Historic Europe* (Cambridge, 1983), p.6; Peter Laslett, 'The history of aging and the aged', in Peter Laslett, ed., *Family Life and Illicit Love in Earlier Generations* (Cambridge, 1977), pp.174–213.

5. Michael Anderson, *Family Structure in Nineteenth-century Lancashire* (Cambridge, 1971), p.74, *passim*.

6. See Pelling in this volume for an examination of a sixteenth-century census of the poor.

7. For problems related to the study of households in the past see, for example, Daniel Scott Smith, 'Historical changes in the household structure of the elderly in economically developed societies', in Robert Fogel, *et al.*, eds, *Aging: Stability and Change in the Family* (New York, 1981), pp.94–5; David I. Kertzer, 'Household history and sociological theory', *Annual Review of Sociology* 17 (1991), pp.155–79; Barry Reay, 'Kinship and the neighborhood in rural England: the myth of the autonomous nuclear family', *Journal of Family History* 21 (1996), pp.87–104.

8. Laslett and Wall's work on household listings is found in Peter Laslett and Richard Wall, eds, *Household and Family in Past Time* (Cambridge, 1972); Wall,

Laslett and Robin, eds, *Family Forms*, as well as in numerous articles, including Peter Laslett, 'The history of aging and the aged' in his *Family Life and Illicit Love in Earlier Generations* (Cambridge, 1997), pp.179–213, and Wall, 'Elderly persons and members of their households in England and Wales from preindustrial times to the present', in David Kertzer and Peter Laslett, eds, *Aging in the Past: Demography, Society and Old Age* (Berkeley, CA, 1995). Their work has generated much criticism, including Lutz K. Berkner, 'The uses and misuses of census data for the historical analysis of family structure', *Journal of Interdisciplinary History* 4 (1975), pp.721–38.

9. For more details on this, see Ottaway, 'The "decline of life"', pp.17–81, 156–208.

10. P. Laslett, 'Family, kinship and collectivity as systems of support in pre-industrial Europe: a consideration of the "nuclear hardship" hypothesis', *Continuity and Change*, 3 (1988), pp.153–76.

11. P. Laslett, 'Family, kinship and collectivity as systems of support in pre-industrial Europe: a consideration of the "nuclear hardship" hypothesis', *Continuity and Change* 3 (1988), pp.153–76; B.H. Todd, 'Widowhood in a market town: Abingdon 1540–1720', unpublished D.Phil. thesis (Oxford, 1983), p.3; Ottaway, 'The "decline of life"', pp.156–293.

12. C.E. Vulliamy, *Aspasia: The Life and Letters of Mary Granville, Mrs Delany (1700–1788)* (London, 1935), p.179.

13. John Burnett, *Useful Toil: Autobiographies of Working People from the 1820s to the 1920s* (London, 1974), p.56. Arthur Young, 'An inquiry into the propriety of supplying wastes to the better maintenance and support of the poor', *Annals of Agriculture* 36 (1801), pp.581–3. My thanks to Leigh Shaw-Taylor for this reference. Another example is in Margaret Maria Verney, ed., *Verney Letters of the Eighteenth Century from the Manuscripts at Claydon House*, Vol. I (London, 1930), pp.22–3.

14. Devonshire Record Office, 2096 A/PZ1; B. Cozens Hardy, ed., *Mary Hardy's Diary*, Norfolk Record Society, Vol. 37 (Norwich, 1968), pp.3, 81–2. In 1797, William Hardy gave his business and property to his son and in exchange was given an annuity of £300 and retained the house and its contents. Isabella Wentworth to Thomas, Earl of Strafford, British Library (hereafter BL) Add. MS 22,225 [September, 1712?]. I am grateful to Ingrid Tague for the Strafford references.

15. Walter Godfrey, *The English Almshouse* (London, 1955), p.45. Alannah Tomkins has noted that in all of the workhouses she studied, 'there was a distinctly different experience to be had as opposed to charity accommodations for the poor in almshouses and to the accommodation in tenements provided by overseers.' Alannah Tomkins, 'The experience of urban poverty: a comparison of Oxford and Shrewsbury 1740 to 1770', unpublished D.Phil. thesis (Oxford, 1994), pp.127–8.

16. June Beardsley, 'Some Essex almshouses' (University of Cambridge Board of Extra Mural Studies Certificate in English Local History, September 1983). This research paper is held at the Essex Record Office.

17. Joseph Plymley, *General View of the Agriculture of Shropshire* (1803), p.343, quoted in Wall, 'Mean household size in England from printed sources', in Laslett and Wall, *Household and Family*, p.170.

18. For an example of such a view, see Thomas Ruggles, *The History of the Poor: Their Rights, Duties and the Laws Respecting Them: In a Series of Letters* (London, 1797), p.92, and James Shaw, *The Parochial Lawyer: Or, Churchwarden and Overseer's Guide and Assistant Containing the Statute Law*, 3rd edn (London, 1831), p.104.

19. Essex Record Office (hereafter ERO), D/P 299/12/0. Similar policies were evident in Great Leighs, Essex, ERO D/P 137/8/1.

20. Dorset Record Office (hereafter DRO), D/GIM: A3/3/1. The 31 Elizabeth I c. 7 dictated, 'Only one family might live in one house and no house was to be built in the country unless it had four acres of land attached.' E.M. Leonard, *The Early History of English Poor Relief* (Cambridge, 1900), p.73. Richard Burn, *The Justice of the Peace and Parish Officer*, Vol. II (London, 1755), p.265.

21. Peter King, 'Pauper inventories and the material lives of the poor in the eighteenth and early nineteenth centuries', in Tim Hitchcock, Peter King and Pamela Sharpe, eds, *Chronicling Poverty: The Voices and Strategies of the English Poor, 1640–1840* (New York, 1997), p.182.

22. F.M. Eden, *The State of the Poor*, 3 vols (London, 1797), Vol. III, p.723, and also see example on p.712.

23. George Body, 'The administration of the poor laws in Dorset 1760–1834, with special reference to agrarian distress', unpublished PhD thesis (Southampton, 1965), p.167.

24. Eden, *The State of the Poor*, Vol. III, p.718.

25. For examples of the decrepitude of the elderly in workhouses, see, for example, John Cary, *An Account of the Proceedings of the Corporation of Bristol* (London, 1700), pp.16–17, in BL, *Tracts Relating to the Poor* 1027.I.18/3; *Report from the Committee Appointed to Make Inquiries Relating to the Employment, Relief and Maintenance of the Poor*, in Sheila Lambert, ed., *The House of Commons Sessional Papers*, Vol. 31 (Wilmington, DE, 1975), pp.33–4.

26. Eden, *The State of the Poor*, Vol. II, p.329.

27. Ibid., p.460.

28. See the Bibliographical Essay in this volume.

29. The household listings used here are held by the Cambridge Group for the History of Population and Social Structure. An important methodological

decision that I made in determining the degree to which elderly individuals were able to maintain the status of household heads was to count lodgers among those who were considered to have failed in this respect. Cf. Laslett, Introduction, *Household and Family*; Thomas Sokoll, *Household and Family among the Poor* (Bochum, 1993), pp.76–82.

30. Headship rates for men and women tended to follow the same patterns within each census. Richard Wall, examining a more diverse group of censuses, also noted that where headship rates for men were high, so too were those for women. See Wall's Introduction in *Family Forms*, pp.39–40. On widows' likelihood of continuing to reside in their own household, see James E. Smith, 'Widowhood and ageing', *Ageing and Society* 4 (1984), pp.429–49.

31. In these censuses, 8–16 per cent of men and 21–30 per cent of women were non-household heads. Cf. Pelling in this volume. Pelling has reached different conclusions for the sixteenth century for several of the following points.

32. For an extended discussion, see Ottaway, 'The "decline of life" ', pp.82–155.

33. Sokoll, *Household and Family among the Poor*, pp.167–71.

34. For a useful overview of the effect of social/economic status on household composition, see Kertzer, 'Household history', pp.166–8.

35. Burn, *The Justice of the Peace*, Vol. II, p.262.

36. Susan Wright noted that, 'few widows from [eighteenth-century] Ludlow remarried when compared to men.' Wright, 'The elderly and bereaved in eighteenth-century Ludlow', in Margaret Pelling and Richard Smith, eds, *Life, Death and the Elderly: Historical Perspectives* (London, 1991), p.126. See essays in J. Dupaquier, ed., *Marriage and Remarriage in Populations of the Past* (Kristiansand, Norway, 1979). For statistics on remarriage see E.A. Wrigley, R.S. Davies, J.E. Oeppen and R.S. Schofield, eds, *English Population History from Family Reconstitution 1580–1837* (Cambridge, 1997), pp.172–7.

37. William Kenrick, *The Whole Duty of a Woman* (Walpole, 1797), p.66; *The Folly, Sin, and Danger of Marrying Widows and Old Women in General, Demonstrated and Earnestly Addressed to the Batchelors of Great Britain by a True Penitent* (London, 1746), p.9. See also C. Carlton, 'The widow's tale: male myths and female reality in sixteenth- and seventeenth-century England', *Albion* 10 (1978), pp.118–29.

38. Burn, *The Justice of the Peace*, Vol. II, p.267.

39. For an extended discussion of filial responsibility to the elderly, see S. Ottaway, 'Providing for the elderly in eighteenth-century England', *Continuity and Change* 13 (1998), no.3, pp.391–418.

40. See, for example, Edward Hyde, Earl of Clarendon, *Two Dialogues: Of the Want of Respect Due to Age and Concerning Education* (2nd edn, 1756; Los Angeles, 1984), pp.287–8.

41. *The Female Aegis: Or the Duties of Woman from Childhood to Old Age, and in Most Situations of Life, Exemplified* (London, 1798), pp.168, 171. The Eighteenth Century Microfilm Collection 780, no.3.

42. Ottaway, 'Providing for the elderly', *passim*.

43. For example, there are cases in the Corfe Castle census where co-resident children made higher wages than parents who nonetheless maintained nominal headship of the household.

44. For more on the obligation of children to support their parents, see Ralph A. Houlbrooke, *The English Family 1450–1700* (London, 1984), esp. pp.189–95; Laslett, 'The history of ageing and the aged', *passim*; Joel Rosenthal, *Old Age in Late Medieval England* (Philadelphia, 1996), p.174, n.4; Keith Thomas, 'Age and authority in early modern England', *Proceedings of the British Academy* 62 (1976), pp.238–41.

45. Croker's position is also quoted in P. Laslett, *A Fresh Map of Life* (London, 1989), p.127.

46. David Thomson, ' "I am not my father's keeper": families and the elderly in nineteenth-century England', *Law and History Review* 2 (1984), pp.265–86; but cf. Pat Thane, 'Old people and their families in the English past', in Martin Daunton, ed., *Charity, Self-interest and Welfare in the English Past* (New York, 1996), pp.113–38. Ottaway, 'The "decline of life" ', pp.156–208, 375; Idem, 'Providing for the elderly', pp.391–418.

47. Isabella Wentworth to Thomas, Earl of Strafford. BL Add. MS 22,225. 9 September [1712], fos. 170–1. See Kugler, this volume, for the fear of poverty in old age among socially elite women.

48. Hon. Charles Strutt, *The Strutt Family of Terling 1650–1873* (Essex, 1939), p.36.

49. Daniel Defoe, *The Protestant Monastery . . . With a Caution to People in Years; How They Give the Staff Out of Their Hands and Leave Themselves to the Mercy of Others* (London, 1727).

50. Caleb Trenchfield, *A Cap of Gray Hairs for a Green Head, or the Father's Counsel to His Son, an Apprentice in London Concerning Wholsom Instructions for the Management of a Mans Whole Life*, 5th edn (London, 1710), p.147. Pat Thane believes that where co-residence between the generations occurred, 'there was deep awareness of the dangers of such a course'. Thane, 'Old people and their families', p.134.

51. Ottaway, 'The "decline of life" ', pp.82–155.

52. In contrast, Laslett has written that about half of aged women and somewhat fewer elderly men resided in empty nest households, while Wall believed that this household form was 'relatively rare' in the pre-modern period. Laslett, 'History of aging and the aged', pp.203–5; Wall, 'Elderly persons', p.89.

53. Where the surname of the aged individuals was the same as that of a household head or co-resident of appropriate age (at least twenty years younger), it was assumed that there was a parental link. Otherwise, no relationship was assumed, but the individual was recorded in a category ('possibly in households with adult children') indicating that she or he *may* have been the parent of an adult co-resident.

54. Steven Ruggles has demonstrated the importance of considering demographic regimes when studying households in 'The transformation of American family structure', *American Historical Review* 99 (1994), pp.103–28.

55. This is true since 32 to 54 per cent of elderly women's homes contained children. Peter Laslett, 'La parente en chiffres', *Annales ESC* 43 (1988), p.17. Laslett's article lists figures for both favourable and unfavourable demographic regimes. If we used the figure for minimal survival of children, 46 to 78 per cent of elderly women with living children co-resided with them; if we use the figure for maximal survival, the percentages drop to 40 to 67 per cent. These numbers are obviously rough estimates for our purposes: microsimulation produces population models, not historical data, and not all co-resident children helped their parents.

56. DRO, PE/PUD OV3/261–62. My study of overseers' accounts and vestry minutes showed no evidence of grandchildren caring for their grandparents, but grandparents were not infrequently seen to care for their grandchildren. Ottaway, 'Providing for the elderly', pp.391–418; Margaret Pelling found evidence of co-resident grandchildren helping their grandparents in the Norwich census of the poor of 1570. 'Old age, poverty, and disability in early modern Norwich: work, remarriage and other expedients', in Pelling and Smith, *Life, Death and the Elderly*, pp.85–6.

57. Cf. Laslett, 'Mean household size in England since the sixteenth century' in P. Laslett and R. Wall, eds, *Household and Family in Past Times* (Cambridge, 1972), pp.125–58, in particular p.134; Schen, this volume; Sokoll, *Household and Family among the Poor*, pp.79–80.

58. These are discussed in detail in appendix B of Ottaway, 'The "decline of life" '.

59. The low number of households with only non-relatives in the earlier tables indicates that lodgers rarely functioned as kin substitutes in these locations.

60. Richard Wall used a series of graphs for co-residents in his 'Historical development of the household in Europe', in Evert van Imhoff *et al.*, eds, *Household Demography and Household Modelling* (New York, 1995), pp.19–52.

61. On the importance of spouses, see Karen Altergott, 'Marriage, gender, and social relations in later life', in Warren A. Peterson and Jill Quadagno, eds, *Social Bonds in Later Life, Aging and Interdependence* (Beverly Hills, CA, 1985), pp.51–5 *passim*; Nancy F. Mouser, 'Marital status and life satisfaction: a study of older men', ibid., pp.71–90. For more details on the logic behind this scale, see Ottaway, 'The "decline of life" ', pp.209–93.

62. This scheme combines features of those used by social gerontologists and by historians. Where historians have traditionally been interested in household type, 'the typology of the gerontologists depends on a set of priorities in the coding of family structure'. Daniel S. Smith, 'Historical change in the household structure of the elderly in economically developed society', in R.W. Fogel, E. Hatfield, S.B. Kiesler and E. Shanas, eds, *Aging, Stability and Change in the Family* (London, 1981), pp.91–114.

63. I am grateful to Jim Oeppen for suggesting that I use boxplots.

64. See P. Laslett, 'Family, kinship and collectivity as systems of support', pp.153–76.

65. See, for example, Anderson, *Family Structure*.

66. Cf. Sokoll, *Household and Family among the Poor*, pp.167–71, on the likelihood of Ardleigh paupers to form extended family households. A likely reason for the disparity between Sokoll's and my findings is that Sokoll considered paupers separately from the labouring poor and marginal poor, while my data consider all the poor in one class.

67. James Smith has pointed out that more than one-third of brides who lived to old age in traditional English society would expect to be widowed by age 55. James E. Smith, 'Widowhood and ageing', p.430.

68. See Ottaway, 'The "decline of life"', pp.209–93.

69. It should be noted that the significant number of individuals who could not be placed in an occupational group generally had very insecure residential situations (see table 2.7 in Ottaway, 'The "decline of life"'). Many of these individuals were widows or lodgers. Had these individuals been included, the IRS for lower-class individuals would appear even more dramatically insecure.

70. See Ottaway, 'Providing for the elderly', *passim*.

CHAPTER SEVEN

The residence patterns of elderly English women in comparative perspective

RICHARD WALL

The purpose of this essay is to measure the nature and extent of variations between the sixteenth century and the present day in the residence patterns of elderly women in England. Comparisons are also made with the residence patterns of elderly English men and with the household and family patterns of elderly men and women in other parts of Europe. The impact on residence patterns of the elderly of socioeconomic factors is considered by noting the ways in which these patterns varied according to the occupational status of the elderly person and whether they were resident in town or in the country.

The onset of old age has been defined throughout this essay as commencing at 65.[1] There is no particular magic in the choice of 65, but 65 marks the conventional onset of old age in studies of the elderly in contemporary Britain and therefore facilitates a comparative perspective.[2] The earnings of wage-earning men in Corfe Castle in Dorset began to fall from the age of 60, but the decisive decline occurred only after they had reached their seventies.[3]

The justification for a study on these lines is the dearth of comparative studies of the living arrangements of the elderly in Europe despite the pioneering efforts of Peter Laslett.[4] Comparative investigations of residence patterns in the past have focused almost exclusively on household forms using the standard classification of household types into nuclear, extended and multiple and have neglected the situation of particular age groups such as the elderly.[5] In this chapter, comparisons of the residence patterns of the elderly in a set of English communities with those of the elderly in populations from France, Belgium and Hungary will establish whether the experience of the English elderly was as distinctive in a European context as Macfarlane has (without very much evidence) argued was characteristic of the English social system.[6] The analysis of the residence patterns of the elderly also enables us to explore the extent of dissimilarities in residence patterns within north-west Europe which John Hajnal and Peter Laslett have identified as following one household system.[7]

The classifications of residence patterns used in the present study measure the proportions of elderly men and women who lived alone or with non-relatives only. These classifications indicate whether the most frequent co-resident of the elderly man or woman was their spouse or their child, and if there was a co-resident child whether it was more likely that their child would be married rather than unmarried.

The assumption underlying the emphasis in many studies on the proportions living alone is that these were potentially the most vulnerable of the elderly, in that they were without resident familial support should they need personal care.[8] A further assumption is that many of the elderly who were living with non-relatives only were in a comparable situation, in that unrelated persons, even when sharing a household, maintained separate budgets and enjoyed a measure of residential independence.

These assumptions need careful evaluation. In the first instance, residential isolation might not be particularly significant if assistance was regularly forthcoming from kin living nearby or from neighbours. Secondly, it could be argued that living on one's own signifies not vulnerability but its opposite: an ability to cope without the assistance of others. A third qualification is that there are important distinctions which should be drawn between various categories of non-relatives: between, for example, lodgers who contributed rent to the household budget, servants who provided care but were a drain on the household budget, and the household heads in whose households they resided.

Some of these reservations are more significant than others. In the English past, for example, custom excused neighbours from the need to provide personal care.[9] Relatives, particularly unmarried adult children and married daughters, even if resident in other households, provided a greater degree of assistance but their efforts were limited by the extent of their other commitments and, sometimes, by physical distance.[10] A more difficult issue to determine is whether those elderly who lived on their own were the most vulnerable or the most capable of those people who had reached old age. Today, migration late in life to reside near or with relatives and the preferential housing of the unmarried elderly in institutions would suggest that those elderly living on their own are seen as among the most vulnerable members of society.[11] In the past the actions of the poor law authorities in housing younger women with elderly widows might suggest a similar conclusion.[12] On the other hand, those elderly who shared their households with non-relatives were not necessarily without resident care, either from servants or from other persons placed in the household by the poor law.[13] In a more detailed study than is practical in a broad overview of the living arrangements of the elderly, the classification of living arrangements would need to be extended to take account of the wide range of non-relatives to be found in households in the past.

The information on residence patterns has been derived from the analysis of census and census-type enumerations of different populations at different dates. The earliest census used is the enumeration of the inhabitants of Ealing, in 1599 lying some seven miles outside London, and the latest is the national census of England and Wales of 1991. After 1800 the principal sources have been the surviving enumerations of various state censuses. The latest of these (1971, 1981 and 1991) have yielded anonymised random samples of the national population. Nationally representative surveys also provided some information on family and household patterns in 1945 and 1962 (see Table 7.1). For earlier periods, specific local populations have been selected to include rural and urban areas with diverse economies.[14] For the period before the state census (in Britain, 1801) or before a state census which registered the ages of the inhabitants (in Britain, 1821), the information is naturally scarcer. It has therefore been necessary to rely on a handful of apparently good quality enumerations taken for a variety of purposes (not always specified or even inferable from the surviving records) by a variety of persons (not always identifiable) and not necessarily by house-to-house enumeration.[15]

No census provides a perfect record of the population at a particular date. The degree of under-enumeration varies from census to census in ways that are difficult to measure. Both the amount and the reliability of information provided on the enumerated population also vary between one census and another. In the selection of enumerations, care has therefore been taken not to include any whose purpose (in conjunction with taxation, for example) indicated that some sections of the population had been omitted. Similarly, no enumeration was included when the level of detail suggested that some relationships might not be specified. For example, lists which made no mention of any relatives other than children or of any lodgers or other unrelated persons were deemed suspect and excluded. Even so, the occasional recording of a relative, servant or lodger can give a spurious indication of a detailed enumeration. The identification of married daughters co-residing with their parents is a particular problem in English censuses before 1851 as in the absence of the information on the relationship there is no shared surname to enable a relationship with the other household members to be inferred. Censuses from other parts of Europe where women

Table 7.1 Percentage of elderly persons living alone or with non-relatives only in England over four centuries

Date	Elderly males		Elderly females	
	Alone	Alone or non-relatives only	Alone	Alone or non-relatives only
1599–1796	2	13	16	32
1891	5	16	13	26
1901	4	15	11	21
1911	6	16	12	24
1921	6	17	11	21
1945	6	–	16	–
1962	11	13	30	33
1971	13	17	36	41
1981	17	20	42	45
1991	20	22	46	47

Note: Residents of institutions other than almshouses are excluded from this and subsequent tables (Tables 7.2–7.8).

Sources:

1599–1796	Calculated from lists of inhabitants (copies in the Cambridge Group Library) of Ealing, Middlesex (1599), Chilvers Coton, Warwickshire (1684), Wetherby, Yorkshire (1776), Wembworthy, Devon (1779), Corfe Castle, Dorset (1790), Ardleigh, Essex (1796). See Richard Wall, 'Elderly persons and members of their households in England and Wales from pre-industrial times to the present', in David I. Kertzer and Peter Laslett, eds, *Aging in the Past: Demography, Society and Old Age* (Berkeley, CA, 1995), p.88.
1891–1921	Anonymised census data supplied to the Cambridge Group by the Office of National Statistics (formerly Office of Population Censuses and Surveys) for Abergavenny, Axminster, Banbury, Bethnal Green, Bolton, Earsdon, Morland, Pinner, Saffron Walden, Stoke, Swansea, Walthamstow and York. See Wall, 'Elderly persons and members of their households', p.91.
1945 Britain	Calculated from G. Thomas, 'The employment of older persons', *The Social Survey* NS 60/2 (1947). See Richard Wall, 'Relationships between the generations in British families past and present', in Catherine Marsh and Sara Arber, eds, *Families and Households: Divisions and Change* (Basingstoke, 1992), p.66.
1962 Britain	E. Shanas *et al.*, eds, *Old People in Three Industrial Societies* (London, 1968), p.186. See Wall, 'Relationships between the generations', p.66.
1971, 1981	Calculated from the Office of Population Censuses and Surveys (OPCS) Longitudinal Study. See Richard Wall, 'Intergenerational relationships past and present', in Alan Walker, ed., *The New Generational Contract: Intergenerational Relations, Old Age and Welfare* (London, 1996), p.42.
1991	Calculated by Pau Baizan and Martina Lo Conte from the OPCS Sample of Anonymised Records. See Richard Wall, 'Comparer ménages et familles au niveau Européen. Problèmes et perspectives', *Population* 51 (1996), nos1–3, p.108.

retained their maiden name or patronymic after marriage do not suffer from this problem. Lists used in the present study where there is reason to think that some married daughters may not be correctly identified but are instead included among co-resident unrelated persons are the 1692 enumeration of Lichfield, the 1701 enumeration of Stoke and the 1821 enumeration of Chiddingly.

Living alone or with non-relatives

Trends over time in the percentage of elderly women and men living alone, or alone or with non-relatives only, in England between the seventeenth century and the present day are set out in Table 7.1. Before 1800, very few elderly men (2%) but considerably more elderly women (16%) lived on their own in rural and small town England. Adding in those elderly who lived with non-relatives only indicates that just over one in ten elderly men and one-third of elderly women in pre-industrial England had no member of their family in their household. In the 1990s, much higher proportions of elderly women and men live alone, but the phenomenon is of recent origin, with the proportions of elderly men rising between 1945 and 1962. The proportion of elderly women who lived alone showed signs of an earlier rise (between 1921 and 1945), but for women too the major period of change was between 1945 and 1962. For both elderly men and elderly women, sharing a household with non-relatives had, by 1962, become a minority residence pattern, as living alone came to replace living in lodgings.

The most significant finding to emerge from Table 7.1, however, is that even in the past the proportions of elderly women and men living apart from any other member of their family were greater than the proportions of elderly men and women whom demographers estimate had surviving children.[16] The inference may therefore be drawn that a proportion of these elderly persons had surviving children but were not living with them owing to a variety of constraining factors. Such factors would include migration patterns earlier in life by either the child or the parent, other commitments (for example to in-laws) or incompatibility of temperament. The inference only holds, however, if a number of assumptions are made: in particular that the nuptiality, fertility and mortality regimes which the demographers have used to produce their simulated populations are appropriate for the specific populations selected for this study and that the rates they have used replicate the experience of the small minority of persons who survived to pass the age of 65.

Spouse or child as principal potential carer

The issue as to whether the elderly were more likely to co-reside with a spouse or a child is considered in Table 7.2. For this purpose 'child' has been defined so that it includes all single, married and widowed offspring regardless of age. In 1991 an elderly woman was three times more likely to co-reside with her husband than with a child, while an elderly man was more than five times as likely to co-reside with his wife as with one of his children. In pre-industrial times, however, elderly men and women were also more likely to co-reside with their spouse than with a child although the proportions of elderly men and women living with a child were close to the proportions living with a spouse because of the much higher rates in the

Table 7.2 Percentage of elderly persons living with spouse or child in England over four centuries

Date	Elderly males		Elderly females	
	Co-resident spouse	Child	Co-resident spouse	Child
1599–1796	59	49	41	37
1891	57	48	30	47
1901	56	51	31	50
1911	55	52	29	52
1921	57	52	32	52
1962	70	33	34	33
1991	72	13[a]	39	13[a]

[a] Maximum estimate assuming that parent(s) never share a household with either a never-married or an ever-married child.

Sources:
Wall, 'Elderly persons and members of their households in England and Wales from pre-industrial times to the present', in David I. Kertzer and Peter Laslett, eds, *Aging in the Past: Demography, Society and Old Age* (Berkeley, CA, 1995), pp.88–9, 91, 93.
1962   Ethel Shanas, Peter Townsend, Dorothy Wedderburn, Henning Friis, Poul Mihøj and Jan Stehouwer, *Old People in Three Industrial Societies* (London, 1968), p.186. See Wall, 'Relationships between the generations in British families past and present', in Catherine Marsh and Sara Arber, eds, *Families and Households: Division and Change* (Basingstoke, 1992), pp.68–9.
1991   Calculated by Pau Baizan and Martina Lo Conte from the OPCS Sample of Anonymised Records.

past of co-residence with a child and (for men) lower rates of co-residence with a spouse.

For elderly men, the frequency of co-residence with a spouse rose only after 1921, reflecting the greater rise in female than in male life expectancy. At the same time the proportions residing with a child declined so that by 1991 only about one in ten elderly men shared a household with a child, whereas more than seven out of ten lived with a spouse. For elderly women the percentage residing with a child increased between pre-industrial times and 1891, while the percentage residing with a spouse declined. The result was that between 1891 and 1921 an elderly woman was more likely to be residing with a child than with her husband. Elderly men by contrast were, as in pre-industrial times, marginally more likely to be residing with their spouse than with a child (although the difference was smaller than it had been earlier). An additional point is that the similar proportions of elderly men and women who resided with a child between 1891 and 1921 may be misleading in that the forms of co-residence could vary considerably, for example in respect of the gender and marital status of the co-resident child, or whether the parent or the child headed the household. The first two possibilities are considered further below.

As in the case of men, there was a marked decline after 1921 in the frequency with which elderly women co-resided with a child. However, there was only a modest rise after 1921 in the proportion of elderly women residing with a spouse, and this is in marked contrast with the trend for elderly men. In 1991 the percentage of women over 65 sharing a household with their spouse was still less than in the seventeenth and eighteenth century. The contrasting trends for elderly men and women are another product of the relative shifts in male and female life expectancy.

Co-residence with married or never-married children

Since the seventeenth century it has always been more common for elderly men and women to live with their children who had not yet married than with their married children (see Table 7.3). This was particularly true of elderly men. Elderly women in all periods were more likely than were elderly men to co-reside with married children. Both elderly men and women were most likely to be co-residing with a never-married child in 1911 (four out of ten elderly men and just over one-third of elderly women). The highest recorded frequency of co-residence with a married child occurred in 1921 (one-fifth of elderly men and one-quarter of elderly women). This reflected

145

Table 7.3 Percentage of elderly persons living with never-married or ever-married child in England over four centuries

Data	Elderly males		Elderly females	
	Never-married child	Ever-married child	Never-married child	Ever-married child
1599–1796	38	12	21	17
1891	36	16	29	21
1901	38	17	31	22
1911	40	16	34	23
1921	38	20	32	25
1962	22	11	22	12
1991	10	3	8	5

Sources:
Wall, 'Elderly persons and members of their households in England and Wales from pre-industrial times to the present', in David I. Kertzer and Peter Laslett, eds, *Aging in the Past: Demography, Society and Old Age* (Berkeley, CA, 1995), pp.88–9, 91, 93.
1962   Ethel Shanas, Peter Townsend, Dorothy Wedderburn, Henning Friis, Poul Mihøj and Jan Stehouwer, *Old People in Three Industrial Societies* (London, 1968), p.186. See Wall, 'Relationships between the generations in British families past and present', in Catherine Marsh and Sara Arber, eds, *Families and Households: Division and Change* (Basingstoke, 1992), pp.68–9.
1991   Calculated by Pau Baizan and Martina Lo Conte from the OPCS Sample of Anonymised Records.

the impact of the housing crisis in the aftermath of the First World War.[17] The pattern may have been repeated at the end of the Second World War but is not represented in the surviving data in Table 7.3.[18] After 1921 the proportion of elderly women and men residing with a married child fell sharply, but so too did the proportions residing with an unmarried child. Since 1891, in fact, the ratio between the proportions of elderly women and men residing with unmarried and married children has remained remarkably constant, implying that the same set of factors were involved first in raising and then in lowering the rates of co-residence with married and never-married children. The other conclusion to be drawn from a consideration of Table 7.3 is that a significant minority of elderly men and women in the English past resided with married children even though English society in the past has been portrayed, and rightly so, as dominated by households confined to parents and their unmarried children.[19]

Residence patterns of the English elderly in comparative perspective

Having considered the evolution over time in the residence patterns of the elderly in England, the focus can now turn to a consideration of the distinctiveness of that experience within a wider European context. In the absence of national-level data on the residence patterns of the elderly, particular populations, some urban and some rural, were selected for analysis. The principles governing the selection were to ensure the inclusion of settlements from areas of continental Europe adjacent to England as well as of some communities from further field (Hungary and Corsica). Previous work on the household structure in both Hungary and Corsica indicated that households were in general considerably more complex than was usual in western Europe in the past.[20] With these criteria met, the selection was arbitrary, being determined by the availability in the Library of the Cambridge Group of well recorded enumerations of populations from the areas selected. The classification of a particular population as urban or rural is not entirely satisfactory. Towns differ widely in size and function. For the purposes of his essay, Berkhampstead and Tring have been classed as towns, and some of the smaller towns such as Wetherby and Corfe Castle included with the rural populations. The most distinctly rural of the English populations included in Table 7.4 are Ardleigh (Essex), country areas adjacent to Berkhampstead in Hertfordshire, and Ambleside in Westmoreland. Nevertheless, the proportions of elderly living alone or with non-relatives only in these highly rural areas are not that different from the proportions in the most 'urban' of the English populations – Bilston, Lichfield and Stoke – once some allowance has been made for the possible overestimation of elderly women in the latter two populations living with non-relatives (see above).

Among the rural populations, the closest similarity between English and continental European populations in the proportions of elderly women and men living alone or with non-relatives only is provided by the rural areas of West Flanders and Lissewege (also in West Flanders). Gemmenich, on the present-day border of Belgium and Germany, Ghisony in Corsica and Kölked in Hungary were clearly different, with a much reduced incidence of elderly persons living alone or without any related persons in their household.

The living arrangements of the elderly inhabitants of English towns were less distinct from those of elderly persons resident in the two continental populations included: Pontoise in northern France and Bruges in Flanders. Some of the towns had very high proportions of elderly persons living apart from other members of their family. This was particularly true of elderly

Table 7.4 Percentage of elderly persons living alone or with non-relatives only in rural and urban areas in western Europe, 17th C. to 19th C.

Area	Date	Elderly males		Elderly females		Numbers	
		Alone	Alone or non-relatives only	Alone	Alone or non-relatives only	Males	Females
Rural areas							
England							
Chilvers Coton	1684	0	8	20	30	12	10
Wetherby	1776	7	11	22	28	27	36
Corfe Castle	1790	2	15	15	35	39	40
Ardleigh	1796	0	6	0	25	16	12
Berkhampst'd region[a]	1851	9	20	7	15	90	111
Ambleside region[b]	1861	9	27	6	24	92	94
Belgium							
Gemmenich	1709	0	0	0	6	12	18
Lisswege	1739	0	8	0	28	12	14
West Flanders	1814	2	13	2	33	61	58
Corsica							
Ghisony	1770	0	0	0	0	19	13
Hungary							
Kölked	1816	0	0	0	10	8	10
Urban areas							
England							
Lichfield	1692	5	13	17	49	38	66
Stoke	1701	5	20	8	39	39	39
Berkhampstead	1851	2	11	17	21	54	68
Tring[c]	1851	2	19	3	23	59	71
Bilston[d]	1851	3	16	3	17	164	214
France							
Pontoise	1781	2	24	5	40	169	203
Belgium							
Bruges	1814	0	17	2	34	191	318

[a] Little Gaddesden, Fritsden, Northchurch, Wigginton, Aldbury, Pattenham, Long Marston, Betlow and Wilstone.

[b] Langdale, Nether and Over Stavely, Rydal and Longbrigg, Troutbeck and Undermilbeck in the sub-district of Ambleside (enumeration districts 9–15).
[c] Excluding Long Marston, Betlow and Wilstone (included in Berkhampstead region).
[d] Enumeration districts 1a–z, AA, BB, revised 2 and 3 in parishes of All Saints, St Mary, St Luke and St Leonard, Bilston.

Sources: Calculated from copies of lists of inhabitants and census enumerations in the Cambridge Group Library.
For Lichfield, see Wall, 'Elderly persons and members of their households in England and Wales from pre-industrial times to the present', in David I. Kertzer and Peter Laslett, eds, *Aging in the Past: Demography, Society and Old Age* (Berkeley, CA, 1995), p.42.
The enumerations of Berkhampstead and Tring have been published by Goose. See Nigel Goose, *Population, Economy and Society in Hertfordshire in 1851. Vol. 1: The Berkhampstead Region* (Hatfield, 1996). The list of the inhabitants of Ardleigh has been published by Erith. See F.H. Erith, *Ardleigh in 1796: Its Farms, Families and Local Government* (East Bergholt, 1978). For Pontoise, see Jacques Dupâquier, *Pontoise et les Pontoisiens en 1781* (Pontoise, 1992), and for West Flanders and Bruges, 'Vlaamse Vereniging voor Familienkunde, afdeling Brugge', *Volkstelling 1814*, Vols I, III, V and VI (Bruges, 1976–7).

women. Four in every ten elderly women resident in Pontoise in 1781 were living either alone or (and predominantly) only with people with whom they were not related. In Lichfield in 1692 almost half of the women over 65 were alone or living with non-relatives, although in this case there is reason to question whether all relationships within the household have been recorded.

Where elderly persons were living with related persons the most frequent co-residents were the spouse and children. A comparison on these lines of the living arrangements of elderly men and women in England and elsewhere in Europe is presented in Table 7.5. There was considerable variation among English rural populations in the percentage of elderly women resident with a spouse or child (from a high of 58 per cent to a low of 31 per cent with a co-resident spouse, and from a high of 57 per cent to a low of 30 per cent with a co-resident child). Such variability means that it is sometimes difficult to see clear differences between these residence patterns and those of the urban elderly or the residence patterns of elderly persons living in other parts of rural Europe. The proportions of elderly women residing with a child and the proportions of elderly men residing with a spouse or child in English towns fall within the range found for rural areas. The one major difference is the much lower proportions of elderly women residing with a spouse in the urban areas; this is probably as a result of males experiencing higher rates of mortality than rural males. The same pattern does not hold for males residing with a spouse, even though female mortality was also likely to have been higher in the towns. The impact of higher female mortality on the residence patterns of males may have been suppressed by the ease with which urban males could remarry. There were many more women

Table 7.5 Percentage of elderly persons living with spouse or child in rural and urban areas in western Europe, 17th C. to 19th C.

Area	Date	Elderly males		Elderly females	
		Spouse	Child	Spouse	Child
Rural areas					
England					
Chilvers Coton	1684	75	58	40	50
Wetherby	1776	63	37	42	30
Corfe Castle	1790	49	46	38	35
Ardleigh	1796	62	69	58	42
Berkhampstead region[a]	1851	49	54	31	57
Ambleside region[b]	1861	52	47	40	48
Belgium					
Gemmenich	1709	67	92	39	78
Lisswege	1739	58	58	50	21
West Flanders	1814	67	69	52	46
Corsica					
Ghisony	1770	58	95	69	92
Hungary					
Kölked	1816	38	100	25	90
Urban areas					
England					
Lichfield	1692	68	54	23	34
Stoke	1701	59	54	26	46
Berkhampstead	1851	59	59	22	53
Tring[c]	1851	54	52	30	45
Bilston[d]	1851	63	52	36	50
France					
Pontoise	1781	61	40	32	30
Belgium					
Bruges	1814	58	46	25	38

[a] Little Gaddesden, Fritsden, Northchurch, Wigginton, Aldbury, Pattenham, Long Marston, Betlow and Wilstone.
[b] Langdale, Nether and Over Stavely, Rydal and Longbrigg, Troutbeck and Undermilbeck in the sub-district of Ambleside (enumeration districts 9–15).
[c] Excluding Long Marston, Betlow and Wilstone (included in Berkhampstead region).
[d] Enumeration districts 1a–z, AA, BB, revised 2 and 3 in parishes of All Saints, St Mary, St Luke and St Leonard, Bilston.

Sources: Calculated from copies of lists of inhabitants, and census enumerations in the Cambridge Group Library.

For Lichfield, see Wall, 'Intergenerational relations past and present', in Alan Walker, ed., *The New Generational Contract: Intergenerational Relations, Old Age and Welfare* (London, 1996), p.42. The enumerations of Berkhampstead and Tring have been published by Goose, *Population, Economy and Society in Hertfordshire*, and the list of Ardleigh by Erith, *Ardleigh in 1796*. See Table 7.4.

For Pontoise, see Dupâquier, *Pontoise et les Pontoisiens*, and for West Flanders and Bruges, 'Vlaamse Vereniging voor Familienkunde'. See Table 7.4.

than men living in these towns (the numbers of elderly men and women in each population are included in Table 7.4).

The wider European perspective establishes Gemmenich on the German border, Ghisony in Corsica and Kölked in Hungary as distinctly different, with very much higher percentages of elderly men and women co-residing with a child. By contrast, elderly men and women in Pontoise and Bruges were relatively unlikely to be co-residing with children. In Ghisony and Kölked all but a handful of elderly persons were sharing a household with a child: rates of co-residence which the levels of childlessness and mortality in pre-industrial populations would seem to preclude.[21] Such a high incidence of co-residence with children could only have been achieved by frequent remarriage, by the census recording stepchildren and perhaps grandchildren as offspring of the household head, or possibly by the omission from the census of individuals not in families.[22] Remarriage seems an unlikely explanation. Kölked and Ghisony had lower, not higher, than average proportions of elderly men residing with a spouse. Among the continental European populations the highest rates of co-residence by elderly men were recorded for West Flanders (where there was frequent remarriage by men) and for Gemmenich, while the highest rates of co-residence of elderly women with a spouse were reached in Ghisony.[23]

Whether these elderly men and women were residing with married or never-married children is considered in Table 7.6. Variations across Europe in the frequency of co-residence with married children are largely in line with the observed variations in European household forms (higher proportions of complex households in eastern and in some parts of southern Europe.[24] In Kölked (Hungary) all the resident children were married, and high proportions of married children were present both in Ghisony and (less in conformity with Laslett's mapping of household forms) in Gemmenich too. However, not insignificant proportions of elderly men and women were residing with married children in a number of the English rural populations.[25] The rates of co-residence with married children, particularly

Table 7.6 Percentage of elderly persons living with never-married or ever-married child in rural and urban areas of western Europe, 17th C. to 19th C.

Area	Date	Elderly males		Elderly females	
		Never-married child	Ever-married child	Never-married child	Ever-married child
Rural areas					
England					
Chilvers Coton	1684	50	8	30	20
Wetherby	1776	26	7	23	17
Corfe Castle	1790	33	13	12	22
Ardleigh	1796	56	12	33	8
Berkhampstead region[a]	1851	36	20	30	27
Ambleside region[b]	1861	29	23	26	24
Belgium					
Gemmenich	1709	58	42	56	39
Lisswege	1739	42	17	14	7
West Flanders	1814	57	15	45	3
Corsica					
Ghisony	1770	58	58	69	38
Hungary					
Kölked	1816	0	100	0	90
Urban areas					
England					
Lichfield	1692	46	8	25	9
Stoke	1701	51	3	31	15
Berkhampstead	1851	42	22	35	20
Tring[c]	1851	39	19	22	24
Bilston[d]	1851	37	30	24	28
France					
Pontoise	1781	25	15	15	15
Belgium					
Bruges	1814	36	13	23	18

[a] Little Gaddesden, Fritsden, Northchurch, Wigginton, Aldbury, Pattenham, Long Marston, Betlow and Wilstone
[b] Langdale, Nether and Over Stavely, Rydal and Longbrigg, Troutbeck and Undermilbeck in the sub-district of Ambleside (enumeration districts 9–15).

c Excluding Long Marston, Betlow and Wilstone (included in Berkhampstead region).
d Enumeration districts 1a–z, AA, BB, revised 2 and 3 in parishes of All Saints, St Mary, St Luke and St Leonard, Bilston.

Sources: Calculated from copies of lists of inhabitants and census enumerations in the Cambridge Group Library.
For Lichfield, see Wall, 'Elderly persons and members of their households in England and Wales from pre-industrial times to the present', in David I. Kertzer and Peter Laslett, eds, *Aging in the Past: Demography, Society and Old Age* (Berkeley, CA, 1995), p.42.
The enumerations of Berkhampstead and Tring have been published by Goose. See Nigel Goose, *Population, Economy and Society in Hertfordshire in 1851. Vol. 1: The Berkhampstead Region* (Hatfield, 1996). The list of the inhabitants of Ardleigh has been published by Erith. See F.H. Erith, *Ardleigh in 1796: Its Farms, Families and Local Government* (East Bergholt, 1978). For Pontoise, see Jacques Dupâquier, *Pontoise et les Pontoisiens en 1781* (Pontoise, 1992), and for West Flanders and Bruges, 'Vlaamse Vereniging voor Familienkunde, afdeling Brugge', *Volkstelling 1814*, Vols I, III, V and VI (Bruges, 1976–7).

by elderly women, were very much lower in rural West Flanders than in England. Elderly men and women living in Pontoise and Bruges were also less likely than were elderly men and women living in English towns in the mid-nineteenth century to be co-residing with married children. The majority of English households in the past were small and limited to couples, lone parents and their unmarried children, but it is now apparent that in respect of the elderly, higher proportions of simpler forms of household were to be found in certain populations in adjacent areas (northern France and West Flanders) on the continent.[26]

The gender-balancing of the household

A further issue requiring examination is whether an elderly widower was more likely to live with a daughter, and an elderly widow with a son. Even though the factors promoting or hindering co-residence of the widowed with their children are likely to be complex and to be influenced by the particular circumstances of both parent and child, there is good reason to anticipate a general tendency in the direction indicated. Elderly widows needed the economic support that could come from the earnings of a son while a widower might appreciate the housekeeping services provided by a daughter. Where the existence of such patterns can be established, we may infer attempts to achieve gender balance in the household. Variation between populations in the relative rates of co-residence with a son or daughter can help to establish how the significance of the services they provided to their elderly parents might be alternatively enhanced or lessened by differences in the nature of the local economy which affected the level of wages or the availability of work.

Evidence on the relative number of elderly widowers and widows resident with at least one son or daughter is set out in Table 7.7. The rates are expressed in the form of a ratio where a ratio of 100 indicates an equal number of widowers (or widows) residing with a son as with a daughter. Ratios over 100 indicate a higher proportion residing with a son, and ratios under 100 a higher proportion residing with a daughter. In addition to the set of urban and rural populations considered in Tables 7.4 to 7.6, evidence has been added for a number of other populations including both agricultural and industrial areas in 1891 and 1921, all 13 populations for which the Cambridge Group holds anonymised data from 1891 and 1921 (see Table 7.1) and for a national sample of the population of England and Wales in 1981.

Inspection of Table 7.7 establishes that in rural England before 1891, elderly widowers were more likely to be living with a son than with a daughter. In 1891 and 1921 the pattern was reversed. In pre-industrial times, elderly widows, too, were more likely to be living with a son than a daughter, with the pattern reversing in this case between 1851 and 1891. By 1981, the only year after 1921 for which such information is currently available, the earlier pattern of both widows and widowers residing more often with a son than a daughter had re-established itself. Before 1891, relative to elderly widowers, elderly widows were more likely to be living with a daughter. After 1891, again relative to widowers, there were more elderly widows living with sons. The conclusion may be drawn, therefore, that differences in the numbers of elderly widows and widowers living with sons and daughters are not to be explained by attempts to achieve a gender balance in the household. Only in 1891 and 1921 were elderly widows resident in agricultural areas more likely than were elderly widowers to be co-residing with sons, and only in 1921 did the number of elderly widows residing with a son exceed (and then only slightly) the number who resided with a daughter. Moreover, there is no evidence of attempts to achieve a gender-balanced household in any of the rural communities on the European continent. In West Flanders, both elderly widows and widowers were more likely to reside with a daughter than with a son. By contrast, in both Kölked and Ghisony there was a marked preference for co-residence with a son.[27]

Elderly widows and widowers residing in towns in England were more likely than were widows and widowers in rural areas to reside with a daughter.[28] The two continental towns of Bruges and Pontoise also had more widows and widowers co-residing with a daughter. However, if this is a distinctive characteristic of the residence patterns of elderly widows and widowers

154

Table 7.7 Relative number of elderly widowers and widows resident with a son or daughter

Area	Date	Widowers		Widows	
		Ratio[a]	N	Ratio[a]	N
Rural areas					
England	1599–1796	108	27	108	25
England	1821–1831	222	20	178	25
Berkhampstead region	1851	109	23	84	59
Ambleside region	1861	150	20	82	31
Agricultural areas	1891	62	115	90	192
Agricultural areas	1921	52	126	107	215
Belgium					
West Flanders	1814	88	15	86	13
Corsica					
Ghisony	1770	225	13	200	6
Hungary					
Kölked	1816	400	5	700	8
Urban areas					
England					
Lichfield	1692	40	7	54	20
Stoke	1701	267	11	200	15
Berkhampstead	1851	56	14	41	24
Tring	1851	62	13	50	24
Bilston	1851	57	47	76	65
Staple industry areas	1891	59	97	77	191
Staple industry areas	1921	61	176	80	360
France					
Pontoise	1781	73	26	72	50
Belgium					
Bruges	1814	73	38	48	101
England as a whole	1891	67	337	73	782
	1921	63	601	72	1343
	1981[b]	126	367	144	1874

[a] Number of widowers (widows) resident with at least one son divided by the number of widowers (widows) resident with at least one daughter × 100. (A ratio of 100 indicates equal numbers of widowers and widows residing with sons and daughters.)
[b] Sex ratio of offspring aged 40+ resident with male or female lone parent. This measure differs in two ways from the ratios displayed in the remainder of the table: (a) through the

inclusion of some offspring of a never-married parent, and (b) through expressing the sex ratio of the resident offspring (each resident child aged 40+ is included), whereas the ratios elsewhere in the table show the number of widowers (and widows) resident with at least one son or daughter.

Sources: Calculated from copies of lists of inhabitants and census enumerations in the Cambridge Group Library.

For Lichfield, see Wall, 'Elderly persons and members of their households in England and Wales from pre-industrial times to the present', in David I. Kertzer and Peter Laslett, eds, *Aging in the Past: Demography, Society and Old Age* (Berkeley, CA, 1995), p.42.

The enumerations of Berkhampstead and Tring have been published by Goose. See Nigel Goose, *Population, Economy and Society in Hertfordshire in 1851. Vol. 1: The Berkhampstead Region* (Hatfield, 1996). The list of the inhabitants of Ardleigh has been published by Erith. See F.H. Erith, *Ardleigh in 1796: Its Farms, Families and Local Government* (East Bergholt, 1978).

For Pontoise, see Jacques Dupâquier, *Pontoise et les Pontoisiens en 1781* (Pontoise, 1992), and for West Flanders and Bruges, 'Vlaamse Vereniging voor Familiekunde, afdeling Brugge', *Volkstelling 1814*, Vols I, III, V and VI (Bruges, 1976–7).

1599–1796	Parishes of Ealing (1599), Chilvers Coton (1684), Wetherby (1776), Wembworthy (1779), Corfe Castle (1790) and Ardleigh (1796).
1821–1831	Calculated from enumerations (copies in the Cambridge Group Library) of Chiddingly, Sussex (1821), Rosthorpe, Cheshire (1821) and Whittington, Derbyshire (1831).
1851	Berkhampstead region: Little Gaddesden, Fritsden, Northchurch, Wigginton, Aldbury, Pattenham, Long Marston, Betlow and Wilstone.
1861	Ambleside region: Langdale, Nether and Over Stavely, Rydal and Longbrigg, Troutbeck and Undermilbeck in the sub-district of Ambleside (enumeration districts 9–15).
1851	Tring: excluding Long Marston, Betlow and Wilstone (included in Berkhampstead region).
1851	Bilston: enumeration districts 1a–z, AA, BB, revised 2 and 3 in parishes of All Saints, St Mary, St Luke and St Leonard, Bilston.
1891, 1921	Calculated from the anonymised data supplied by the Office of National Statistics. Thirteen areas defined as in Eilidh Garrett, 'Thinking of England and taking care: Family building strategies in England and Wales, 1891–1911', in Robert Rowland and Isabel Moll Blanes, eds, *La demografía y la historia de la familia* (Murcia, 1997), p.67. Not all the Staple Industry areas were distinctly urban; see ibid., n.13.
1981	Random sample calculated from the OPCS Longitudinal Study. See Wall, 'Comparer ménages et familles an niveau Européen. Problèmes et perspectives', *Population* 51 (1996), nos1–3, p.103.

living in urban areas, there was no common pattern in urban areas of elderly widows or elderly widowers residing preferentially with sons or daughters. Even in 1891 and 1921, when areas of heavy industry had particularly high proportions of widows relative to widowers living with a son (as did Bilston in 1851), it is impossible to interpret this as a distinctively urban family form since the same residence pattern is present in agricultural areas in 1891 and 1921. In other words, the relative frequency with which elderly widows and widowers co-reside with their sons or daughters differs within environments which share certain characteristics (being urban, for example). Meanwhile, similar residence patterns appear in other areas with different local economies.

Detailed examination of the microeconomies of the individual populations may help to elucidate the links between economic factors and family forms. An explorative foray into this issue follows using the information on the socioeconomic status of the elderly.

Socioeconomic status of the elderly and co-residence with sons and daughters

The interrelationships between socioeconomic factors and residence patterns are particularly visible at the level of the individual household. The higher the status of the household the more dependants it contained.[29] When there was land to pass on to the next generation, inheritance custom and practice could require the presence in the parental household of the heir.[30] The household's microeconomy determined its labour needs, detaining teenage children at home when their labour could be used productively, and exporting them as servants to the households of wealthier neighbours when it could not.[31] Such factors can be expected to influence also the residence patterns of the elderly, as decisions taken earlier in the lifecycle (the export of children or the transmission of a property) raised or lowered the probability of continued or renewed co-residence between the generations when the parents reached old age.

Table 7.8 measures the frequency with which elderly women and men from five broad socioeconomic groups (farmers, craftsmen, labourers, non-earners and paupers) co-resided with their sons and daughters in three rural and four urban areas. These five socioeconomic groups contained the largest number of elderly. Selection of areas was also based on the need to ensure as many elderly as possible were observed. The socioeconomic status of the elderly was inferred from their occupation, former occupation or source of income as given in the census (see note to Table 7.8). This measure was preferred over the alternative procedure of inferring the status of the elderly person from the occupation of the household head as likely to provide the more reliable indicator of the situation of the elderly person. Reliance on the occupation of the household head would have meant that the status of the elderly person would be sometimes determined by their own occupation (when they continued to head a household) and sometimes by the occupation of a younger family member or even a non-relative. However, the inferring of the status of the elderly person from their own occupation is not

Table 7.8 Percentage of elderly males and females resident with a son or daughter, by occupational status

Area	Date	Occupation	Elderly females			Elderly males		
			With son	With daughter	N	With son	With daughter	N
Rural areas								
Berkhampstead region	1851	Craft	20	40	10	40	40	15
		Labourer	29	21	28	29	6	17
		Pauper	37	37	19	29	53	38
		Unearned	14	43	14	36	41	22
Ambleside region	1861	Craft	17	17	18	18	36	11
		Farmer	62	31	13	62	38	8
		Labourer	21	25	24	13	13	15
		Unearned	17	33	12	15	40	20
West Flanders	1814	Farmer	57	57	7	67	78	9
		Labourer	52	59	29	22	22	37
Urban areas								
Berkhampstead	1851	Craft	31	38	13	25	38	8
		Labourer	23	38	13	11	22	9
		Unearned	33	33	9	20	27	15
Tring	1851	Craft	18	45	11	4	30	27
		Unearned	25	17	12	23	23	13
Pontoise	1781	Craft	28	36	36	14	27	22
		Farmer	38	21	24	25	6	16
		Labourer	24	14	21	13	10	39
		Poor	15	41	27	13	30	54
Bruges	1814	Craft	26	45	65	15	31	166
		Labourer	24	32	34	13	36	53
		Unearned	38	34	29	20	27	30

Note: Occupational status of elderly person (husband in the case of married women). The category 'unearned' includes both those whose income was derived from savings or investments (annuitants, proprietors of houses etc.) and those who were reported as retired.

Sources: Calculated from copies of lists of inhabitants and census enumerations in the Cambridge Group Library.
The enumerations of Berkhampstead and Tring have been published by Goose. See Nigel Goose, *Population, Economy and Society in Hertfordshire in 1851. Vol. 1: The Berkhampstead Region* (Hatfield, 1996).
For Pontoise, see Jacques Dupâquier, *Pontoise et les Pontoisiens en 1781* (Pontoise, 1992), and for West Flanders and Bruges, 'Vlaamse Vereniging voor Familiekunde, afdeling Brugge', *Volkstelling 1814*, Vols I, III, V and VI (Bruges, 1976–7).

without problems, as information on the socioeconomic status of a number of elderly is missing from the census. In particular, the socioeconomic status of a married woman has to be inferred from the occupation of her husband. The latter procedure creates a disjuncture between the inferred socio-economic status of married women and widows.

Despite these difficulties, some interesting interactions between socio-economic status, place and residence patterns are evident from the data set out in Table 7.8. Elderly women most likely to be co-residing with their sons belonged to the farming population. Least likely to be co-residing with sons were those elderly women whose socioeconomic status inferred from their own occupation or that of their husband was determined as 'craft' or 'labouring'. For elderly women, therefore, there is evidence that their resid-ence patterns in respect of co-residence with a son were influenced by their socioeconomic status. Consideration of the variation by place in the frequency of co-residence with a son indicates that socioeconomic status had much the same impact on the residence patterns of elderly women in most of the populations included in Table 7.8. There was, however, considerably less evidence (other than for the farming population) of the impact of socio-economic status on the frequency with which elderly men co-resided with a son. This would seem to imply that the attribute of socioeconomic status that helped to determine the frequency of co-residence with a son was the relative ability to support a dependant as opposed to transfers of resources or skills from parent to child. Had the latter attribute been of any signific-ance, there should have been at least as much variation in the rates of co-residence between sons and their fathers as between sons and their mothers.

Variations in the frequency of co-residence with daughters can be ex-amined in a similar way. In this case, the elderly women most likely to be living with a daughter came from two very different social groups: the poor and the farmers. Elderly women from the labouring population had the lowest rates of co-residence with a daughter. Again the variation by socio-economic group in the frequency of co-residence between elderly men and a daughter was less than was the case for elderly women. Men who had a craft occupation or who were poor were most likely, and labouring men least likely, to be living with a daughter, but the differences were slight (just over 10 per cent between the median frequency for labourers and the poor compared with a range of over 20 per cent for elderly women in different status groups). These patterns are not easy to interpret. Rates of co-residence sometimes vary in the same way for men and women (low rates for labourers, high rates for the poor) while others do not (crafts and farmers). Furthermore, if poverty for both elderly men and women was compatible with a relatively high rate of co-residence with a daughter, an almost equally high rate of co-residence could be anticipated for the social group immediately above them: the labourers. Yet relatively few elderly labouring men and women were co-residing with a daughter.

The data in Table 7.8 provide three further perspectives on the relationship between the socioeconomic status of elderly people and the frequency with which they co-resided with a son or daughter. The first approach considers the possibility that women from a particular socioeconomic group would be more likely than elderly men of equivalent status to be co-residing with a son or daughter (differences of ±5 per cent have been considered as indicating equal probability). Viewed in this way it appears that elderly craft and labouring women were particularly unlikely to be living with a son.

The second approach focuses on whether higher or lower average rates of co-residence by elderly women and men with a son or daughter were associated with particular socioeconomic groups. Differences in coresidence rates of ±5 per cent are again ignored. This perspective indicates that poor elderly women and elderly women in the craft sector were more likely than elderly women of other statuses to be co-residing with a daughter. On the other hand, elderly farming women were more likely than other elderly women to be living with a son. Elderly men from the farming population were also more likely than were elderly men in general to be co-residing with a son and elderly craftsmen more likely to be co-residing with a daughter. This perspective therefore identifies instances in which socioeconomic status had a similar impact on the residence patterns of elderly men and women: encouraging co-residence with a daughter in the case of the poor and craft sectors and co-residence with a son in the farming sector.

The third perspective provided by Table 7.8 is to consider the extent of the variation in frequency of co-residence with a son or daughter by elderly men and women of different socioeconomic status who lived in the same locality. On occasion, such differences were remarkably slight. Consider, for example, the frequency with which elderly male farmers and labourers from West Flanders co-resided with a son or daughter. At other times the differences were very considerable, as in the case, interestingly enough, of the frequency with which elderly women farmers and labourers in West Flanders co-resided with a son or daughter. It is possible that in some populations the residence patterns of the elderly were more homogeneous than in others despite the presence in the respective populations of apparently comparable status groups.[32] This would imply the existence in particular populations of other (presumably cultural) determinants of residence patterns which were of sufficient strength to suppress, at least temporarily, the impact of socioeconomic status. In order to test this hypothesis it would be necessary to undertake more detailed work on the social structure of these particular communities and to include a number of others.

Conclusion

It has been one of the objectives of this essay to measure the process of change in the residence patterns of elderly women in England since the seventeenth century and, having identified periods of change, to indicate why the change occurred then and not earlier or later. Comparisons with the residence patterns of elderly men illustrated the many ways in which the residence patterns of elderly women in the past, as in the 1990s, differed from those of elderly men in some respects but were similar in others. In the past, as in the present day, elderly women more often lived alone, and less often with a spouse, as a consequence of women marrying at a younger age and living longer than men. However, after 1800 similar proportions of elderly men and women resided with a child. At the same time it has been possible to introduce some new perspectives by noting the frequency with which elderly women and men co-resided with a son or daughter and the extent to which the frequency of co-residence varied depending on the socioeconomic status of the elderly person.

Before the twentieth century the residence patterns of the elderly in England were in many respects remarkably stable. The percentage of elderly women who lived on their own increased only after 1921. The percentage of elderly men living alone rose after 1945 (Table 7.1). However, the rise in the proportions of elderly men and women living on their own was for a time counter-balanced by a decline in the proportions of elderly persons sharing a household only with non-relatives arising from the disappearance of the live-in servant and the decline in lodging. It is tempting to interpret such changes as the translation of rising incomes into the creation of separate residential units. However, it is more difficult to link rising living standards with a change in residential patterns within these particular periods (rather than either earlier or later) or to explain why the numbers of women living on their own, given their lower incomes, should increase before the numbers of men. Demographic and cultural factors alternatively promoting or hindering modifications in residence patterns made possible by rising incomes appear to control the timing and form of the changes in the living arrangements of the elderly.

Even when the frequency of co-residence with a child was at its highest recorded point (between 1901 and 1921, see Table 7.2) only just over half of elderly men and women were actually living with a child. Estimates based on contemporary levels of fertility, marriage and mortality suggest that considerably greater numbers of elderly persons had surviving children.[33] These children must therefore have been living elsewhere, either in the absence of the factors that might have promoted co-residence (parental need, for example) or because constraining factors (earlier migration or other commitments) precluded co-habitation with the parents, however desirable.

At the end of the nineteenth and in the early twentieth century an elderly English woman was more likely to be living with a child than with her husband (Table 7.2). Both in pre-industrial times and in the 1990s her husband and not a child was the more usual co-resident. For elderly English men in the past as today, the most likely co-resident, and principal provider of care, was his spouse, the different residence patterns of men and women arising, as stated above, from women marrying at a younger age and living longer. The majority of English children who did co-reside with a parent, particularly if that parent was the father, had yet to marry (Table 7.3).

A further issue addressed (Tables 7.4 to 7.6) was whether the residence patterns of the English elderly in the past were distinctively different from those of elderly persons living in other parts of Europe. To some extent this analysis confirms for the elderly what has already been established for the household as a whole. Residence patterns of elderly English women and men were similar to those of the elderly living in the adjacent areas on the continent (northern France, West Flanders) but differed markedly from those of the elderly in parts of southern and central Europe. In the Corsican and Hungarian populations and in Gemmenich on the present day Belgian/ German border, far higher proportions of elderly men and women were residing with a child, particularly a married child.

The impact of socioeconomic factors on the residence patterns of the elderly was considered both indirectly on the basis of whether they were residing in a rural community or in town (Tables 7.4 to 7.7) and then more directly, from their occupation, former occupation or husband's occupation (Table 7.8). There was in fact no sign of any consistent differences between the living arrangements of rural and urban elderly women and men, with the sole exception of the lower percentage of women resident in towns who were living with a spouse (owing in all likelihood to the mortality rates for males exceeding those for females). The socioeconomic status of the elderly person had a much more obvious impact on their residence patterns. For example, elderly women who were either poor or who practised a craft (or who had a husband who did so) were more likely than were elderly women of other statuses to be co-residing with a daughter. Elderly women from the farming population were more likely to be co-residing with a son. It was also suggested that the residence patterns of the elderly in some communities were more homogeneous than in others as demographic and cultural factors diffused, at least for a time, the impact of the elderly person's socioeconomic status on their residence patterns. Economic factors might also have been expected to promote the co-residence of widows with sons (for economic support) and of widowers with daughters (for personal care and help with housekeeping) but, as Table 7.7 demonstrated, of this there was no sign.

Notes

1. Richard Wall, 'Intergenerational relationships past and present', in Alan Walker, ed., *The New Generational Contract: Intergenerational Relations, Old Age and Welfare* (London, 1996), pp.37–55.

2. Emily Grundy, 'Living arrangements and social support systems in later life', in Anthony M. Warnes, ed., *Human Ageing and Later Life: Multidisciplinary Perspectives* (London, 1989), pp.96–106.

3. Cambridge Group Library, Corfe Castle file, table 1e.

4. Peter Laslett, 'The history of aging and the aged', in Peter Laslett, *Family Life and Illicit Love in Earlier Generations* (Cambridge, 1977), pp.174–213.

5. Peter Laslett, Introduction, in Peter Laslett and Richard Wall, eds, *Household and Family in Past Time* (Cambridge, 1972), pp.1–89.

6. Alan Macfarlane, *The Origins of English Individualism* (Oxford, 1978), pp.165–88.

7. John Hajnal, 'Two kinds of pre-industrial household formation system', in Richard Wall, Jean Robin and Peter Laslett, eds, *Family Forms in Historic Europe* (Cambridge, 1983), pp.65–104; Peter Laslett, 'Family and household as work group and kin group: areas of traditional Europe compared', ibid., p.526.

8. Karl Schwarz, 'Household trends in Europe after World War II', in Nico Keilman, Anton Kuijsten and Ad Vossen, eds, *Modelling Household Formation and Dissolution* (Oxford, 1988), p.69, but cf. also p. 81; Richard Wall, 'Leaving home and living alone: an historical perspective', *Population Studies* 43 (1989), pp. 369–89.

9. The issue is explored in Richard Wall, 'Beyond the household: marriage, household formation and the role of kin and neighbours', *International Review of Social History* 44 (2000), no.1, pp.55–67.

10. Richard Wall, 'Relationships between the generations in British families past and present', in Catherine Marsh and Sara Arber, eds, *Families and Households: Divisions and Change* (Basingstoke, 1992), pp.63–85; Wall, 'Beyond the household'.

11. Emily Grundy, 'Household change and migration among the elderly in England and Wales', *Espaces, Populations, Sociétés* 1 (1987), p.118; Richard Wall, 'Residence patterns of the elderly in England and France', LS Working Paper 69, City University (1990).

12. F.H. Erith, *Ardleigh in 1796: Its Farms, Families and Local Government* (East Bergholt, 1978).

13. For an example of the latter, see Erith, *Ardleigh in 1796*, p.14.

14. For the period 1891–1921 the anonymised enumerations were made available to the Cambridge Group by the then Office of Population Censuses and Statistics.

15. Peter Laslett, 'Mean household size since the sixteenth century', in Laslett and Wall, *Household and Family in Past Time*, p.126; Cambridge Group listings collection, community listings forms.

16. Peter Laslett, 'La parenté en chiffres', *Annales: Economies, Sociétés, Civilisations* 1 (1988), pp.5–24.

17. Richard Wall, 'Elderly persons and members of their households in England and Wales from pre-industrial times to the present', in David I. Kertzer and Peter Laslett, eds, *Aging in the Past: Demography, Society and Old Age* (Berkeley, CA, 1995), p.93.

18. See the trends in the number of relatives in the household in Richard Wall, 'The household: demographic and economic change in England, 1650–1970', in Wall, Robin and Laslett, *Family Forms*, pp.497–8.

19. Nuclear family households, Laslett, 'Introduction', p.29.

20. Peter Laslett, 'Characteristics of the western family considered over time', in Laslett, *Family Life and Illicit Love*, pp.22–3; Jacques Dupâquier and Louis Jadin, 'Structure of household and family in Corsica, 1769–71', in Laslett and Wall, *Household and Family in Past Time*, pp.283–97.

21. E.A. Wrigley, 'Fertility strategies for the individual and the group', in Charles Tilly, ed., *Historical Studies of Changing Fertility* (Princeton, NJ, 1978), pp.135–54.

22. Richard Wall, 'Characteristics of European family and household systems', *Historical Social Research* 23 (1998), nos1–2, p.64, but see also Rudolf Andorka, 'Household systems and the lives of the old in eighteenth- and nineteenth-century Hungary', in Kertzer and Laslett, *Aging in the Past*, p.152, n.8 on the reliability of the low recorded incidence of never-married adults.

23. Richard Wall, 'Does owning real property influence the form of the household? An example from rural West Flanders', in Wall, Robin and Laslett, *Family forms*, pp.379–420.

24. Laslett, 'Characteristics', pp.22–3; Dupâquier and Jadin, 'Structure of household and family in Corsica, 1769–71'.

25. Around one-quarter of the elderly women and one-fifth of the elderly men in the two rural regions, one in northern England (Ambleside) and one in southern England (Berkhampstead), enumerated in the middle of the nineteenth century.

26. Peter Laslett, 'Mean household size since the sixteenth century', in Laslett and Wall, *Household and Family in Past Time*, pp.125–58.

27. Cf. Marchini 1994 for Corsica, in Antoine Marchini, 'Poverty, the life cycle of the household and female life course in eighteenth-century Corsica', in

John Henderson and Richard Wall, eds, *Poor Women and Children in the European Past* (London, 1994), pp.225–50.

28. The one major exception is provided by Stoke in 1701.

29. Laslett, 'Mean household size since the sixteenth century', p.154.

30. Beatrice Moring, 'The Finnish stem family in historical perspective: strategies for social and economic survival of the land-holding group', in Antoinette Fauve-Chamoux and Emiko Ochiai, eds, *House and Stem Family in EurAsian Perspective*, Proceedings of the C18 Session of the Twelfth International Economic History Congress, International Research Center for Japanese Studies (Kyoto, 1998), pp.114–37; Angels Torrents, 'Marriage strategies in Catalonia from the seventeenth to the nineteenth century: a case study', *Continuity and Change* 13 (1998), no.3, pp.475–96.

31. Richard Wall, 'The age at leaving home', *Journal of Family History* 3 (1978), no.2, pp.181–202.

32. Compare, for example, the residence patterns of elderly men and women in the town of Berkhampstead with those of the elderly from its near neighbour Tring.

33. Laslett, 'La parenté en chiffres', p.17.

CHAPTER EIGHT

Old and incapable? Louisa Twining and elderly women in Victorian Britain

THERESA DEANE

A long lived race

Historians have recently paid increasing attention to Louisa Twining's work as a leading example of upper-middle class philanthropy.[1] It is often stated that an encounter with a poor aged woman was the catalyst for her life's work. Her childhood nurse apparently, to Twining's distress, spent her old age living not with the wealthy family she had cared for but in one of the poorest districts of London. When one of the nurse's elderly neighbours was admitted to the workhouse, Twining visited her, and her reactions to the conditions she found set her on a career of workhouse reform and work to improve social conditions.[2] This essay looks at the experiences of the poor elderly women whom Louisa encountered in her philanthropic work, comparing them with the experiences of the wealthy old women within her family circle. It seeks to explore the lives of these women in some depth in order to bring to life the contrasting realities of the experiences of older women of different social backgrounds in the nineteenth century. This essay can then be compared with the other personal accounts of women of earlier and later periods.

Louisa was born in 1820 and was the youngest of nine children. Louisa's father Richard was one of ten children. The number of her mother Elizabeth's siblings is unknown, but she is known to have had about twenty aunts and uncles. Louisa spent many childhood holidays visiting her large extended family. Although she had little recollection of the only grandparent she met, given the size of the extended family it is unsurprising that some relatives lived into old age. One of Louisa's earliest memories was of two elderly great-aunts, said to have lived into their nineties. They were 'remarkably tall, upright, and imposing figures, . . . who never leant back in their chairs'. The great-aunts were Longcrofts, her maternal grandmother's family whom she described as 'a long-lived race'.[3] Louisa's belief in heredity may well have led her to expect to live similarly into old age, and for that old age to be largely free from infirmity.

As the likelihood of marriage became less probable, Louisa Twining may well have looked at the experience of other single women in her family circle and anticipated a similar life for herself. Ann Twining was Louisa's aunt. She was born in the eighteenth century, possibly in 1779, but she was an old woman in Victorian Britain. After the death of her mother, Ann became her father's companion and fulfilled many duties that her mother would have undertaken.[4] Her father died in 1824, and Ann's where-abouts are unknown until twenty years later when she was in her sixties. She had made her home in Bitteswell, a Leicestershire village. She had decided not to spend her old age living in London with or near her siblings. Her eldest sister, Mary, had married the vicar of Bitteswell at the end of the eighteenth century and had died aged 24 within a year of giving birth to her only surviving child. Her daughter was also named Mary, and when she was seventeen she became Louisa Twining's godmother. Louisa and her sisters often stayed in Bitteswell with their uncle, James Powell, and cousin Mary.

Ann lived in her own home in Bitteswell. Her days followed a routine of breakfasting at 8 o'clock in winter (earlier in the light summer mornings), dining at three, and having her last meal at seven in the evening. She went to bed regularly at ten. Her niece called every day and they went for walks together or spent time in their greenhouse growing plants. Mary's days were taken up by the day school for girls which she had founded. Ann contributed by teaching the pupils needlework.[5] Ann wrote in a letter that she was conscious that she looked old. Her hair was white and she had wrinkles on her face. She had 'feelings of age' and said that she was not 'strong'. Her health was deteriorating and she was finding it harder to move around. She had not left her home for several years and had no expectation of doing so again.[6]

James Powell never remarried and his daughter became his companion. After his death at almost 80 years of age, Mary completed and endowed a boys' school that her father had started. She also built and endowed almshouses. When her father died she was almost 60 and had never married. Sometime after the death of James Powell, Ann and Mary set up home together. Ann was the elder by almost a decade and a half, and as Mary's aunt, she was senior in social terms; however, Mary was the head of the household. Ann's infirmity increased and she never moved from Bitteswell. She died when she was 86. After Ann's death Mary remained in the village in which she was born and had always lived. Her health deteriorated sharply when she was in her early eighties and she contacted her cousin and goddaughter, Louisa Twining. Louisa had made a promise in childhood that she would look after Mary when she became old. The message arrived when she was about to depart for a holiday in Biarritz. Louisa cancelled the holiday and went to Bitteswell where she cared for Mary until her death a month later.

A hard and troubled life

The old ages of Ann and Mary contrast greatly with the old age of Louisa's nurse whom she remembered with great affection and described as 'one of the blessings of our lives'. There are several accounts of the servant's fate. The most recent is that of McCrone, who wrote that Louisa visited 'an old family nurse' in the parish of St Clement Dane's and then visited one of the nurse's neighbours after she had entered the workhouse.[7] Ray Strachey recorded a similar version in her history of the women's movement first published in 1928.[8] Strachey gave no citation; McCrone's citation was Twining's autobiography. However, Twining merely wrote that an old woman she visited went into the workhouse and that she went to see her there.[9] She did not say that one of the old woman's neighbours had been her nurse. A similar version suggests that Louisa went to the workhouse to visit a former servant, by implication a servant to the Twining family.[10] It is possible that Strachey, writing only a decade and a half after Twining's death, was retelling what was common knowledge in her circle, which may or may not have been accurate, and that this version has metamorphosed in McCrone's story. The myth is cast in further doubt by Twining's assertion elsewhere in her autobiography that her nurse, who had been her mother's nurse before her 'lived with us till her death at 73'.[11] While it is clear that the woman whom Louisa regarded as her nurse spent her old age with the Twining's, it is not possible to be so certain about other servants.

Visiting the poor by the wealthier women in the local community was an old tradition that reached its peak in the nineteenth century. It was often organised on a parish basis. Visitors were assigned about twenty or forty families on whom they would call, perhaps weekly, perhaps more casually and irregularly. Sometimes the local clergy would refer needy families to the visitors, or poor people themselves might pass messages through friends and neighbours inviting their visitor to call. The poor might be given practical help by way of blankets, food or coal tickets. If a member of the family was seriously ill the visitor would read passages from the Bible or lead prayers with the family.

Twining, like her sister Elizabeth, was a district visitor in central London in the poor area of the parish of St Clement Danes that was known as Clare Market.[12] In common with other middle-class and upper-class visitors, they believed that their work was an important way of bringing rich and poor together and promoting social harmony.[13] It was not unusual for district visitors to hear of poor people being admitted to the workhouse. When one old woman in whom Louisa felt 'much interest' made the difficult decision to give up her home and seek indoor relief she made no attempt to visit the 'poor lonely old woman'. It was an omission she long regretted. A month or so later she heard that the old woman 'had gone quite out of her mind and died'. Louisa noted this in her diary together with the fact that she often 'reproached herself', and she included it in the extracts which she published in 1880 and again in 1898. She excused her inaction, in part, with the not unreasonable explanation that at the time she assumed the workhouse was 'an inaccessible fortress, which could only be entered through great difficulties and dangers'.[14] When another old woman she visited entered the workhouse, Twining went to see her. What she found had so much impact that Twining had no difficulty in remembering the date: she cited 1 February 1853 several times in her writings.

Mrs Stapleton was a needlewoman and specialised in the best kind of 'flannel-work', which she sold directly to the 'best shops'. Along with her other health problems her eyesight began to fail and she found it increasingly difficult to sew. The combination of declining income and deteriorating health put her ability to maintain her home in jeopardy. After several months of struggling she told Twining that she was 'obliged', 'forced' and 'compelled' to give up her home and enter the Union, which was a 'dreaded retreat'.[15] Stapleton's only solace was that she hoped to meet up with a close friend. The old woman 'begged' Twining not to forget her when she entered the workhouse and Twining promised to go and see her there. It did not prove easy to gain admission to the workhouse as the only permitted visitors were 'certain' friends and relations, and even then visiting was allowed only on fixed days.

When Twining ventured into the workhouse she found the elderly and increasingly frail Stapleton not in a ward for the infirm but in one of the 'sheds' which had a brick floor and was furnished with benches. These were intended for the young able-bodied women who spent their time picking hair and oakum, that is unpicking old and matted ship ropes. It was a difficult task often done without the aid of tools and was exceedingly hard on bare hands. Stapleton told Twining that her fellow inmates were 'the sweepings of six parishes'. Their language was coarse, and their behaviour so frightening that she had stayed awake throughout her first night, so fearful 'she should have died' – a night which she was forced to spend in a bed shared with another woman. She lived 'some years' despite the harsh conditions of the institution. Whether she met up with her friend is unknown.[16]

Louisa Twining was evidently shocked by the treatment of pauper inmates. Many of the older people were unable to eat the soups or digest the heavy suet puddings. She described a bedridden older woman whose hands were crippled with fingers bent into her palm and which were made even more useless by her long fingernails. She declined the offer made by a lady visitor to cut her nails. The lady visitor would not have expected payment for cutting fingernails, unlike the pauper nurse. The old woman feared the reprisals once the pauper nurses realised that they had lost their fee. Unable to hold cutlery, she ate her food directly from the plate, 'like a dog gnawing at food'.[17]

Pauper nurses, as their title suggests, were paupers themselves, and they charged fellow inmates even for basic tasks such as making beds. The guardians also paid them in the form of extra rations as they were 'engaged in more arduous, or more responsible employment than the Ordinary Inmates' who picked oakum. At the Strand Union workhouse, where Mrs Stapleton was an inmate, they were given a half a pint of beer daily, with the exception of the nurse in the Receiving Ward who had one pint a day. Some nurses were recruited from outside the workhouse and therefore were not paupers but 'paid nurses'. Twining noted that of 70 paid nurses in London workhouses and 500 pauper nurses and their assistants, half were over fifty years of age, one-quarter were over sixty and some even over 80 years old. These poor women were 'worn out by ill health' themselves. She was not without sympathy for them but she recognised that a woman 'worn out by her own hard and troubled life both in body and mind' was an unsuitable person to nurse the sick. Nursing was a 'trying post', and needed 'tenderness and skill'.[18]

Some elderly inmates were not truly paupers. They had small savings but these were insufficient to pay for someone to look after them in their own home. Once inside the workhouse, Twining noted that they were treated the same as the penniless and perhaps profligate pauper. Moreover, they were expected 'to pay for the privilege'. These respectable poor, she argued, should have a ward of their own.[19] Twining believed that older people needed better treatment, more liberty, and that their last home should be a 'resting place'. Just before Christmas 1861, she set out to provide exactly that. Since the previous March she had been lady superintendent of the Workhouse Visiting Society's Industrial Home for Women in New Ormond Street, in Holborn, central London, which trained young girls from the workhouse as domestic servants. At the end of the year she had the Home's unused schoolroom converted into a six-bedded ward for old and infirm women. Their nurse was 'accommodated' in a curtained off corner of the room, which means she had her bed in the same room as her patients. The girls in the Industrial Home, most of whom were fifteen or sixteen years old, assisted the nurse in looking after the infirm women.[20]

Twining had applications from so many old women wanting to be looked after in the small ward that when the lease for the adjoining property became available it was purchased, and the old women moved out of the Industrial Home into their own Home. That building proved too small and they expanded into the property on the other side of the Industrial Home as well. There was a medical attendant and visiting chaplain who held a weekly Sunday service. The old women received visitors, sometimes as many as two dozen in a day. The lease and many of the start-up expenses such as furnishings for the Home for Incurable and Infirm Women were funded by philanthropic donations. Charges to the patients covered two-thirds of their costs and the inexorable struggle for charitable gifts made up the deficit. Some of the patients paid for themselves from savings or small pensions, and the sons and daughters of others also helped to meet the fees. Others had been servants and their previous employers helped defray the costs. Some of the earliest patients were paid for from the rates by their local board of guardians. Following the Metropolitan Poor Act 1867, many of the larger Unions built separate infirmaries for the sick poor. Once the sick were accommodated separately from the workhouse itself Twining no longer accepted this group and limited places in her Home to 'respectable and valued servants'. The Local Government Board's recommendation that the infirmaries should be staffed by 'sufficient' numbers of 'competent' experienced nurses was so imprecise that it was not always followed and paupers from the workhouses were still appointed as paid nurses.[21] Twining's Home clearly could not look after all the deserving elderly women in workhouses and she envisaged a network of similar Homes for men as well as women. Her extended Home continued to be oversubscribed and she personally undertook many of the visits to the applicants' homes to assess their suitability.

As an experienced district visitor Twining recognised that poverty was not necessarily caused by improvidence. It was self-evident in the crowded passageways and courts where the poor lived that a family of adults and children already crammed into one room did not have the space for an elderly relative. Nor could they necessarily afford the increased rent that would result if they took a larger home. Some families did manage to care for their elderly relatives and she described the instance of the family who kept a small back room for the 'aged and bed-ridden mother of the wife, who was always clean and comfortable' as an example of 'rare self-denial'.[22] Twining also realised that some work paid so badly (such as that done by needlewomen) that it could not 'even suffice for their present wants'. Theirs was a 'a bare existence in which saving is an impossibility'. Two such women were Mrs Kidger and Mrs Frewin who lived in Vere Street close to Lincoln's Inn Fields on the edge of the parish of St Clement Danes. It was a busy thoroughfare with haberdashers, butchers and grocers shops. When Twining started visiting, Frewin was about 80 and her companion in her mid-sixties; they used the title 'Mrs' but Twining was aware that they were both unmarried. They were one of five households at 31 Vere Street, where seventeen people lived above 'The Lamb', one of several public houses in the street. The two women were shoe binders who took pride in the fact that the aristocracy wore their shoes at state occasions such as royal weddings. After Maria Frewin died, Mary Kidger gave up their 'one tidy room' and went to the workhouse, where Twining saw her on her regular Sunday visits. Kidger was bedridden and too frail to go to the workhouse chapel to hear the Sunday service. Instead, the services were read to her, probably by Twining herself.

At about this time Louisa's mother died aged 86. Louisa and her un-married sister Elizabeth had lived with their mother at the family home in Bloomsbury since their father's death ten years previously. The sisters inherited the leasehold of the house but they chose not to continue living there. Elizabeth accepted their brother Richard's offer of moving to Dial House, the family's second property in Twickenham. Louisa, however, had the responsibility of the Industrial Home and its associated Home for Elderly and Infirm Women. Moreover, she had well developed plans for a third institution. Faced with the choice of relocating to a small riverside village outside London, Louisa decided to continue to meet her commitments to the existing institutions, open a new Home, and for that Home to be her own home.

Elizabeth had celebrated her sixtieth birthday the previous year and she had a large and busy philanthropic portfolio. This included running a mission house that hosted ancillary activities such as temperance meetings, prayer and Bible meetings, and a savings bank. She was also the secretary of the Lady Visitors Committee at a school, was a district visitor, a workhouse visitor and a hospital visitor.[23] Elizabeth had decided to retire from the busy life of a philanthropist. The sisters' choices reflected the fifteen-year age gap between them.

Louisa intended the new Home to accommodate only young middle-class women afflicted with epilepsy (as an alternative to expensive private homes, the loneliness of lodgings, or the insane ward of the workhouse). However, she found once again that there were more applications from older women for beds in her Home in New Ormond Street than she could provide for, so she made the decision to open the upper floor of the new institution to old women. The Home, St Luke's, was opened in spring 1866. It was conveniently situated in Queen's Square into which ran New

Ormond Street. In the census of 1871, there were 29 women resident in the two Homes, and about half of them were aged between 60 and 80. Five were over 90. There were as many widows as there were spinsters and the age distribution varied little according to their marital status. The census enumerators recorded only the former occupations of some of the old women. These included a housekeeper, domestic servants, a dressmaker and a former nurse. None are known to have had a personal connection with Twining.[24]

No holiday seasons

St Luke's was also the fulcrum for many of Twining's parish-based activities such as a mother's meeting and its associated clothing club. As Twining's sixtieth birthday approached, she settled down to write an account of her public work, which was published in 1880.[25] She found the responsibility of managing the Homes increasingly difficult to cope with and she began to reduce her commitments. The management of the Industrial Home for Girls was transferred to the philanthropic Metropolitan Association for Befriending Young Servants. A few years later she tried, but failed, to arrange for another society to take over the adjacent Home for Infirm Women. The existing committee continued to implement her policies but relieved her of any connection with it. That the lease on the Industrial Home had only four years to run, together with the fact that she still made the effort to attend its annual anniversary services, suggests that she was anxious to relinquish day-to-day control but not to sever her connections completely. At about the time she removed the Industrial Home from her portfolio she was involved in the creation of the Workhouse Nursing Association (WNA). The pressures of the post of secretary of a new and rapidly growing society conflicted with her long-standing commitments and she appointed an assistant secretary. During the late 1880s she also turned down new opportunities to further her philanthropic career. She received separate enquiries from the Holborn Board of Guardians and the newly created London School Board asking if she would stand as a candidate for election to their bodies. She declined both because the posts would be very time consuming and she felt she had enough demands on her time.

When she returned from her summer holiday in 1881 the volume of work and responsibilities overwhelmed her. This was exacerbated by the absence of some of her principal workers. She felt the responsibilities of the work generated by the WNA fell solely upon her shoulders. Uncharacteristically, she recalled the work as a 'burden', and by the end of the year she had decided to close St Luke's. In fact she had already steadily reduced the number of residents. Several years previously the Home had stopped caring for women with epilepsy, and young women studying art had taken the space they had occupied. By the end of the 1870s only two art students remained. The students would have been less demanding residents than their predecessors, but even their lesser demands were too much. By the time of the 1881 census there were only a few servants left, together with Twining herself. The following year Louisa Twining resigned from all her posts. She arranged storage for her furniture and donated many of her pictures, including those she had painted herself, to institutions such as the Working Men's College. In August she left England for a holiday which was to last twelve months. Philanthropic work, in which she noted there were 'no holiday seasons', had worn her out. She was 61 years old.[26]

Her recollection of the holiday was that the 'sudden change from over-pressure of work and occupation was [also] too great, and the re-action to a lack of interest in all such matters, left too great a blank'. The holiday was not going to plan either. She described the flooding which had closed many railway lines in Hungary and northern Italy as a 'trying fate' because it meant major changes in her itinerary. When she finally arrived in Rome for the winter the city was a disappointment as she had been there before and so the 'charm of novelty was gone'. It rained so hard that she was not able to go out and indulge in her hobby of sketching. The other hotel guests irritated her. She wrote letters to the Working Men's College in London and admonished them for not acknowledging her gift of pictures.[27] Louisa Twining was finding it difficult to relax.

By the spring she was going on 'enchanting trips' and having a 'delightful time'. She was enjoying herself once more. In September she returned to England and, having shed all her work and responsibilities for a year, she 'felt free', but she also had 'no home to go to'.[28] One possibility was living with her sister in Twickenham. Elizabeth had recently founded a cottage hospital and was actively involved in its management. She was living at Dial House with four other women, servants and a housekeeper. The housekeeper, Susan Norman was a retired mission woman. Ten years previously, when Elizabeth was in her mid-sixties, she had shared her home with three young women whom she was training for domestic service as well as two older women, one a former governess and the other an old servant. It was work similar to that of Louisa's but within her own home and on a smaller scale that she could manage alone. By the time she was in her mid-seventies she had reduced her household and her commitments and was no longer training maids. Elizabeth's home still contained five women and it is possible that a second adult, who was not a servant, would have made the house feel crowded. It would also mean that Louisa would have to defer to her sister as the head of the house.

174

Louisa Twining moved nine times in the first month after her holiday. When she finally settled in Kensington Palace Gardens, to her surprise she found she knew many of her neighbours. In two months nearly one hundred people had called on her, thus allaying any worries about being isolated in a new home without a working life. She had rejected the idea of returning to the pressures of parish work having had 'so large and unfettered a share of this in my old sphere'. In the spring she was elected as a poor law guardian for Kensington.

Twining used her status of poor law guardian to improve the provision made for the elderly inmates of the Kensington Union workhouse as well as in the infirmary. In the workhouse they were still given sheets made from linen, a material which was cold to the touch. The large cold wards made this worse and she was not surprised to hear that they removed them from their beds and slept only under blankets in winter. The workhouse master agreed to order no more after the existing stock of linen sheets was worn out.[29] The diet also was often unsuitable for the old people, some of whom were entirely toothless, and it was probably at Kensington that she arranged to have the tough meat minced for them.[30]

When the committee work of the Kensington poor law guardians was allocated as usual in the spring of 1889, Louisa Twining's name appeared but was later crossed out. As the year progressed she took part in committee work despite not having been formally appointed at the usual time. On Christmas Eve her sister Elizabeth died. The following April she gave formal notice to her colleagues that she would not be standing for re-election. Once again she closed up her home and moved, this time to Worthing on the Sussex coast, for reasons that are unclear.

The move was not successful. She had expected mild weather, but two of the coldest winters for twenty years followed. Twining occupied herself by introducing a district nursing service. She paid several visits to London, including two to attend meetings of the WNA and another to give evidence to a select committee on Metropolitan hospitals,[31] and she went to Liverpool to give a paper based on her evidence to a conference of women workers. After two years she moved from Worthing.

She decided not to live in London again. On her visits she had found its 'whirl of busy life . . . increasing in intensity', and the traffic was more and more congested. The metropolis was not suited, she concluded, to someone whose 'work is nearly done'. In 1893, Louisa moved to a town where she had spent several childhood holidays: Tunbridge Wells in Kent. When she was told that she would find nothing to do in such a quiet place because 'every branch was occupied', she replied that she was glad to hear it was so. Twining was in her early seventies and had resolved to undertake no more public commitments. She started work on a second volume of memoirs, which this time included her private life as well as her public life.[32] Four months later she had completed her autobiography, and was elected poor law guardian to the Tonbridge Board.[33] During the election the local paper published a letter from 'Diogenes' arguing that she should not be guardian but only a lady visitor, but if Twining was elected 'Diogenes' supposed 'her presence would adorn the luncheon table'.[34] There were over 20,000 guardians in England and Wales, and in 1893 only 119 were women. When Twining was elected she was the first woman guardian for the Union, which may explain 'Diogenes' opposition.[35] One of her hardest struggles as a member of the Tonbridge Board of Guardians was the introduction of visits to the workhouse girls who went into domestic service, and the ensuing debates were extensively reported in the local paper. Thomas Manwaring, a guardian and local farmer regularly opposed her. He complained that her behaviour was 'very objectionable' when she visited the girls without the authority of the Board. When it was pointed out that she had visited in her private capacity, he continued to object, saying that the practice 'was worthy of censure'. Later it was proposed to authorise Twining to visit the girls twice a year. Manwaring said, 'If an old woman came into his house and wanted to ask his wife 500 questions, she would be asked to go out and take the girls with her'.[36]

The number of inmates in the Tonbridge Union workhouse varied widely throughout the year, from around 250 to more than 500, but the usual number was about 450. As with other workhouses, the inmates' labour provided many of the services. One of these services was work in the laundry, which had to deal with between five and six thousand pieces of washing every week. In the summer of 1894 the master complained to the Board that there were only five women fit enough to wash clothes. By inference the women inmates were physically too weak from ill health or old age, or possibly both, to do the vigorous work of washing by hand. The guardians decided to buy washing machines.

Some of the old women in the workhouse were issued with a ration of snuff and others with tobacco. On one occasion the women believed the amount was too small and collectively refused their ration of snuff. Shortly after, perhaps encouraged by the dispute over snuff, an elderly woman appeared in front of the Board's fortnightly meeting to make her complaint in person. The workhouse master had stopped her tobacco and she had been moved to another ward whose inmates she described as 'infidels and washerwomen'. The master was asked to account for his actions. He said that she 'was one of the difficult cases to be met with in all unions' and that she was 'refractory' which was a phrase that he commonly used to mean that an inmate physically fought with other inmates. However, he did not want to punish her 'because of her age'. At least one guardian could not believe that she smoked but there was no record of their reaction to her 'refractory' behaviour. Her complaint, like that of the snuff ration, was received with amusement and laughter. The problem with the snuff was referred to a visiting committee and the old woman was advised to follow the master's instructions. She had been in the workhouse 36 years.[37] However, conditions in the workhouse had improved by this time to the point where elderly women were worrying about snuff and tobacco rather than about their basic needs.

As in Kensington, Louisa Twining was involved in philanthropic work, in the local community of Tunbridge Wells. She was president of the local branch of the National Union of Women Workers, which at this time provided a network for thousands of women philanthropists through conferences, journals and publications.[38] In 1893, she spoke at a public meeting of the Brabazon Scheme that was also attended by the association's founder, Lady Meath. The scheme organised the making of handicrafts in order to relieve the monotony of the institutional regime for the older inmates. The following year Twining similarly attended and spoke at a public meeting of the Tunbridge Wells District Nursing Association whose nurses were affiliated to the Queen's Institute, and whom she encouraged the Union to employ. She was not, however, involved in the day-to-day running of local philanthropic associations.

Twining found the duties of being a poor law guardian monotonous in contrast with her earlier work. This was assuaged by the relief of sharing responsibility among a team of guardians instead of having overall responsibility herself, as had often been the case with her philanthropic work. However, the work still had its moments of pressure. When the Tunbridge Wells guardian insulted Twining by calling her an 'old woman', it was with connotations of being too old for the work of guardian. She had intended to resign as guardian in 1895 but changed her mind. Vigorous campaigning resulted in the election of a second woman, Miss Ludlow, and Twining remained in post for a further year in order to support the newcomer. Another woman, Mrs Lander, then took her place as guardian. Louisa Twining had decided that the town of Tunbridge Wells 'did not agree with her' and at 76 years of age she was 'retiring of necessity from active life'. She then went to live quietly in Rochester, Kent, apparently for no reason other than it was a city that had always interested her. She settled down and wrote a third largely autobiographical book that was completed the following year.[39]

Little is yet known of how she spent the time in Rochester. She kept closely in touch with the WNA and went to London for meetings. She was well informed about current affairs and had letters published in newspapers. At the age of 78, she revisited her childhood home in London's Strand. She missed the street cries of women selling fresh milk and the Bavarian girls singing to sell their brooms. The Strand of her childhood had become an area 'usurped' by 'gigantic towering buildings'. An interviewer noted that Twining described the changes 'almost pathetically'. The following year she declined an invitation from the annual conference of poor law guardians to attend their annual meeting. Travelling to London for meetings was increasingly tiring and she was finding it harder to keep closely in touch with changes in her work. So, in 1900 she moved back to the capital and at the end of the year she attended a poor law conference where she was 'enthusiastically greeted' and her speech was received with 'laughter' and many 'cheers'.[40]

Her public status had changed from someone at the peak of their professional career to one whose lifetime contribution to public life should be acknowledged. She had already been wrongly described as the first woman poor law guardian, such was her status, and she was subsequently a subject in the series of profiles of 'veteran' workers in the yearly reports of poor law conferences.[41] On her eighty-fourth birthday, Twining was presented with an illuminated address in a silver box. There were nearly 300 names on the address including those of Princess Christian, Lady Meath and Florence Nightingale, and the occasion was reported in the local paper.[42] Earlier that year, Princess Christian had successfully proposed Twining for election as a Lady of Grace of the Order of St John of Jerusalem. The philanthropic society had a royal charter and as well as its own charitable work it admitted to its roll of members those who furthered the Order's objects. Election to different parts of the roll depended on social status, and Florence Nightingale and the wealthy philanthropist Angela Burdett Coutts were also made Ladies of Grace. Twining was elected probably for her work alleviating the suffering of the sick workhouse inmates, her work to replace pauper nurses by trained nurses and for her interest in district nursing. It was an award of which she was justly proud and she was photographed wearing the silver medal in the shape of a Maltese cross.[43] Twining was already vice-president of several philanthropic societies.

The last five years of her life were spent quietly in her home on the edge of Kensington. She had the occasional letter published in the national press, but other than that little is known about how she spent her days. The last two years of her life were a time of 'great suffering and weariness'. Even so, she continued to attend the daily church services of the Church of England, though she now had to be taken in a bath chair.[44] She struggled against bronchitis for a year but remained mentally alert enough to write to *The Times* to express her 'extreme satisfaction' at the new Local Government Board draft order. The day after the letter was published she developed acute bronchitis and died a week later.[45]

Conclusion: habits of industry

As the youngest in her family, Louisa Twining not surprisingly outlived all her siblings. Her sisters Emily and Fanny both lived into their eighties and her brother Richard died aged ninety-eight. She was proud of their longevity.[46] Emily and Fanny were both widowed in the middle of the century and never remarried. Richard outlived his second wife and retired to Bitteswell. Louisa's last home was a short walk from her niece Adelaide Morgan, and Adelaide was with her at her death. The elderly women in the Twining family used their kinship network of daughters, nieces and cousins to provide support without any loss of independence. They were able to live to the end of their lives in their own homes because of their wealth: Mary Powell, Elizabeth Twining and Louisa Twining all had resident servants. Mary and Elizabeth are an example of the 'useful, respected older woman, sharing her home with others equally or more needy' which has been noted elsewhere as representative of an earlier part of the century.[47] Elizabeth sent one of her maidservants to be trained as a nurse, and Agnes Edginton became the matron of her hospital and was with Elizabeth at her death. It is not known if any of the other women employed nurses, but they would have been able to if they so wished. Ann Twining felt lonely living alone but her move to her niece's home may have had as much to do with her increasing debility and therefore her physical wants, as with her psychological need for companionship.

Louisa's closest friend was probably her sister Elizabeth. They had provided companionship for their bereaved mother just as Mary and Ann had done for their fathers, the difference being that the two sisters were able to share the stresses and strains of caring for their elderly mother. That Louisa did not move to Dial House on her return from the year-long holiday can probably be explained by the loss of independence it would entail. It has not been possible to explain the peripatetic nature of her later years in contrast with the stability of the first sixty years of her life, and little is known about Louisa's household from the time she left St Luke's. She never married, had no children and is not known to have had a close companion in this period. The preference of these single women not to live with married relatives reflects the dominance of the nuclear family as the normal household unit rather than the extended family.[48]

Just as Ann valued the family visits of young relatives, who did not live nearby, so too did Louisa. She enjoyed the companionship of nieces on her holidays abroad. Two joined her at different times on her year-long absence. In her last years, the Reverend W.H.G. Twining would bring his sons to visit her. She would indulge them with muffins while she and their father discussed the poor law and their family's genealogy. He also provided continuity with her late friend Angela Burdett Coutts who had endowed the church of which he was the incumbent and supported some of his work in the parish. Angela had also been an important supporter of Twining's early work and paid the rent and provided furnishings for many of the institutions that Louisa founded such as the Home for Incurable and Infirm Women in New Ormond Street. When Twining read Burdett Coutts's obituary in *The Times* she was prompted to write a letter acknowledging the importance of her friend's contributions.[49]

These rich unmarried women gave each other practical support such as Mary's care of Ann. Sometimes they bequeathed each other substantial legacies, as Elizabeth did to Louisa, supplementing their large inheritances from their wealthy parents. The rich also used their money to help the elderly poor. Mary and Elizabeth restored almshouses. Mary also left several small annuities to elderly women in Bitteswell. Other gifts, such as Louisa's legacies to the Kensington District Nursing Association, would benefit the elderly who were among those cared for by the Association. These women often singled out servants as beneficiaries of their good works. The first patient of the Home for Infirm and Elderly Women was an elderly retired servant. When the lease on the property expired, the Home moved to Whetstone, a few miles to the north of London, and Twining bequeathed it five hundred pounds. Similarly, Elizabeth's hospital was for the lower paid and its patients could include older people. Louisa used the payments of the richer patients in St Luke's to offset the lower and uneconomic fee she charged their less well off counterparts. Wealthy employers paid for their retired servants in Twining's Homes. She may have felt that they had a moral duty to help their old employees, though they had no legal duty to do so.

The contrast between her own family and those of the poor was not lost on Twining. She knew that many poor people were lonely and that women such as Mrs Kidger and Mrs Frewin entered the 'last resort of the workhouse' not only because of their poverty but also because they were 'without friend or relative to care for them'. It is noteworthy that it was only when Kidger died that her companion entered the workhouse. Frewin is representative of the many poor older people, especially women, who either outlived their friends and family or had no family. They made up a large proportion of the old people in the workhouse. Twining was not the only one who noted this. Once inside the workhouse their 'prison-like' existence was reinforced on visiting days when no one came to see them and they would 'lament their loneliness'.[50] It distressed Twining at Tunbridge Wells to deal with applications for relief from women of over 90, some of whom were applying for the first time. She believed that the richer inhabitants of the town should support the poorer and that the very old should be saved from the disgrace of pauperism. One way of doing this was by payment of publicly funded pensions. Twining's support of pensions indicates that she did not believe that charity was the total solution for poverty in old age. State pensions, which were paid from 1909 onwards, were not intended to provide enough to live on but only to augment existing pensions, and would not have helped old women such as Stapleton, Kidger and Frewin. Twining was among the first to recognise that older people were a group who needed a particular type of care.[51]

Louisa Twining was well known for her energy, particularly in her work during her later years. She believed that she and her siblings inherited their 'habits of industry', like their longevity, from her parents. Louisa's mother was 'constantly occupied' even in her last year of life. When her eyesight deteriorated to the point where she could no longer read or do fine needle-work she made garden nets and coarse flannel work, which she gave to the poor. Ann Twining persevered with teaching needlework at Mary's school despite her failing eyesight. When Mrs Stapleton's eyesight failed she was unable to make flannel work and lost not only the means of making a living but her home also. Twining's references in her autobiography to old women include the retired governess who made envelopes, the nurse at a children's hospital who taught the girls from the Industrial Home nursing, and her own cook at St Luke's. The exact age of the women is unclear but the implication is that they were doing useful work at a stage in life at which it could not be taken for granted.[52]

The Brabazon Scheme, which was active in the Kensington and Tonbridge workhouses when Twining was a guardian, gave the inmates means of occupying themselves. The poor aged women inmates who were too frail for the heavy work were given sewing such as mending as their workhouse task. Once this was done they were allowed to make petticoats, macramé, bell pulls and such like under the Brabazon Scheme. The scheme's annual treat at which the objects were sold to fund the next year's work was popular with the inmates. Twining noted the 'blessing and contentment' of the old women who would otherwise have nothing to fill the monotony of the dull institutional regime. The aged inmates also cared for the garden, which was 'radiant through the summer with brilliant blossom'. There is no reason to suppose that they enjoyed growing plants any less than Ann and Mary had done. The rich and the poor alike found ways of purposefully occupying their time as they grew older.[53]

It is not known whether Louisa managed to continue with her hobby of painting in her old age. She did, however, busy herself with researching her family's genealogy, a project begun by Elizabeth in her youth. Louisa enlisted the help of the Reverend W.H.G. Twining to trace their origins in Gloucestershire and they published the results.[54] On occasions she drew attention to her age. She wrote to *The Times* in support of women's suffrage opening with the statement, 'I am not a "new woman"; on the contrary I am an old one'.[55] Her sense of humour extended to her own single state in an article for young girls in which she wrote 'Whether I am an "old maid" or a young one matters little if what I have to say is worth saying'.[56] At her first meeting of the board of guardians in Tunbridge Wells she wore a black bonnet, dress and gloves and carried a reticule, as was her usual manner of dress in old age. It gave an impression of being old fashioned.[57] In her mid-eighties she resigned the presidency of the Women in Local Government Society but was persuaded to serve a second year. In a 'rigorous speech' at the annual meeting she explained that she had been reluctant to remain their president because of her recent protests against 'the continuance in posts of old and incapable people'. The speech caused 'some amusement': her audience could see for themselves that she was an example of a woman who was old, but who was far from incapable.[58]

Acknowledgements

I would like to thank Mr S.H.G. Twining of R. Twining & Co. for assistance with the genealogy of his family. Thanks are also due to Pat Thane and Jessica Cooke for their comments on this essay.

Notes

1. Theresa Deane, 'Nineteenth century philanthropy: the case of Louisa Twining', in Anne Digby and John Stewart, eds, *Gender, Health and Welfare* (London, 1996), pp.122–42; Jane Finnis, 'Louisa Twining and the Workhouse Visiting Society', MA thesis (University of Melbourne, 1995); Patricia Hollis, *Ladies Elect: Women in English Local Government 1865–1914* (Oxford, 1987); Kathleen E. McCrone, 'Feminism and philanthropy in Victorian England: the case of Louisa Twining', Canadian Historical Association, *Historical Papers* (1976), pp.123–39; Julia Parker, *Women and Welfare: Ten Victorian Women in Public Social Service* (Basingstoke, 1989); Frank Prochaska, *Women and Philanthropy in Nineteenth Century England* (Oxford, 1980).

2. Ray Strachey, *The Cause: A Short History of the Women's Movement in Great Britain* (1928; London, 1989), pp.80–1; McCrone, 'Feminism and philanthropy', p.136. For a comprehensive examination of Louisa Twining's career see Theresa Deane, 'The professionalisation of philanthropy: the case of Louisa Twining', D.Phil thesis (University of Sussex, in progress).

3. Much of the following is drawn from Louisa Twining, *Recollections of Life and Work* (London, 1893); idem, *Thoughts on Some Social Questions Past and Present* (London, 1903), p.35.

4. See, for example, Richard Twining to Daniel Twining, 7 November 1803, British Library Additional Manuscript 39,931, f.123 (hereafter BL Add. MS).

5. Jeanne M. Petersen, *Family, Love and Work in the Lives of Victorian Gentlewomen* (Bloomington, IN, 1989), p.141.

6. Letter, Ann Twining to Mary [surname unknown], 20 November 1843, BL Add. MS 39,932, f.128–129.

7. McCrone, 'Feminism and philanthropy', p.136.

8. Strachey, *The Cause*, p.80.

9. Twining, *Life and Work*, p.111. For a second account, see Louisa Twining, *Recollections of Workhouse Visiting and Management* (London, 1880), pp.91–2.

10. Hollis gives no reference for this point. Hollis, *Ladies Elect*, p.198.

11. Twining, *Life and Work*, p.30.

12. For Elizabeth's account of her own experiences, see Elizabeth Twining, *Leaves from the Notebook of Elizabeth Twining* (London, 1877).

13. For the work of the district visitor, see Prochaska, *Women and Philanthropy*, ch. 4, pp.97–137, and Anne Summers, 'A home from home – women's philanthropic work in the nineteenth century', in S. Burman, ed., *Fit Work for Women* (London, 1979), pp.43–63.

14. Twining, *Workhouse Visiting*, p.91; idem, *Workhouses and Pauperism and Women's Work in the Administration of the Poor Law* (London, 1898), p.55.

15. Twining, 'History of workhouse reform', in Angela Burdett Coutts, *Women's Mission: A Series of Congress Papers on the Philanthropic Work of Women* (London, 1893), p.266; Twining, *Workhouse Visiting*, p.92; idem, 'A paper on the condition of workhouses', in Louisa Twining, *Workhouses and Women's Work* (London, 1858), pp.39–53; idem, *Life and Work*, p.112.

16. Twining, 'History of workhouse reform', p.266; idem, *Workhouse Visiting*, pp.6, 92; idem, 'Condition of workhouses', p.46; idem, *Life and Work*, p.112.

17. Twining, 'Condition of workhouses', pp.43–45. For other examples of the harshness of life in the workhouse, see M.A. Crowther, *The Workhouse System 1834–1929* (Cambridge, 1981), and A. Digby, *Pauper Palaces* (London, 1978).

18. There are several versions of the pamphlet. This quotes from Louisa Twining, 'Workhouses and women's work', in *Recollections of Workhouse Visiting and Management* (London, 1880), pp.138–96. She quoted the statistics from Anna Jameson, *Communion of Labour* (London, 1856), p.91.

19. Louisa Twining, 'The sick, the aged and incurable in workhouses', *Journal of the Workhouse Visiting Society* 27 (October 1863), pp.110–11.

20. Twining, *Life and Work*, p.179; untitled leaflet (1865), Nightingale Collection, HI/ST/NC18/543, London Metropolitan Archive (hereafter LMA).

21. Brian Abel-Smith, *A History of the Nursing Profession* (London, 1960), p.43.

22. Twining, *Life and Work*, p.124. For self-help, philanthropy and the poor law in general, see Alan Kidd, *State, Society and the Poor in Nineteenth Century England* (London, 1999).

23. Theresa Deane, 'Elizabeth Twining', *New Dictionary of National Biography* (Oxford, forthcoming).

24. Census, 21 New Ormond St, London, RG 10/371/37–38 (1871); Census, 20 Queen's Square, London, RG/10/369/8 (1871), Family Records Centre (hereafter FRC).

25. Twining, *Workhouse Visiting*.

26. Twining, *Life and Work*, p.240, 250–2.

27. Ibid., pp.252–3; L. Twining to the Working Men's College, 28 November [1882], box A1, 107, archive of the Working Men's College, London.

28. Twining, *Life and Work*, p.254, 257.

29. Twining, *Workhouses and Pauperism*, pp.110–11.

30. *Nursing Notes*, 25 (1 November 1912), no.229.

31. *Charity Organisation Review*, 7 (1891), no.76, p.195 and no.79, p.306; *Second Report from the Select Committee of the House of Lords on Metropolitan Hospitals* (1891).

32. Twining, *Life and Work*.

33. Ibid., pp.vii, 288–9; idem, *Workhouses and Pauperism*, p.130.

34. *The Kent and Sussex Courier*, 10 March 1893 (hereafter *Courier*).

35. The following year the property qualification for guardians was scrapped and consequently the number of women guardians rose to 875 in 1895. Hollis. *Ladies Elect*, p.241. See chapters 5 and 6 of this work for the experiences in general of women poor law guardians.

36. *Courier*, 20 October 1893 and 9 March 1894.

37. Ibid., 27 October 1893 and 1 December 1893.

38. Hollis, *Ladies Elect*, pp.25–7.

39. *Courier*, 13 September 1893, 19 January 1894, 3 April 1896, 27 May 1896, 4 October 1912; 'A talk with Miss Louisa Twining', *The Quiver* (1903), pp.463–7; Twining, *Workhouses and Pauperism*, p.x.

40. *The Quiver*, p.463; *Annual Central Poor Law Conference* (London, 1899), p.565; *South Eastern Poor Law Conference* (London, 1900), pp.142–3.

41. Obituary of William Bousfield, *Poor Law Conferences 1900–1901* (London, 1901), p.xiii; *Poor Law Conferences 1903* (London, 1903), pp.ix–xxi.

42. *The Kensington News*, 18 November 1904; *Charity Organisation Review* 16 (December 1904), no.96, p.297.

43. Photograph in the possession of Mrs Margaret Hopkinson-Woolley.

44. *Guardian*, obituary of Louisa Twining, 4 October 1912.

45. *The Times*, 17 September 1912; death certificate of Louisa Twining (September, 1912), FRC.

46. Twining, *Social Questions*, p.35.

47. Pat Thane, 'Gender, welfare and old age in Britain, 1870s–1840s', in Digby and Stewart, *Gender, Health and Welfare*, p.193.

48. José Harris, *Private Lives, Public Spirit: Britain 1870–1914* (London, 1994), p.63.

49. *The Times*, 1 January 1907. For the life and work of Burdett Coutts, see Edna Healey, *Lady Unknown, the Life of Angela Burdett Coutts* (London, 1978) and Diana Orton, *Made of Gold, a biography of Angela Burdett Coutts* (London, 1980).

50. Twining was quoting an unidentified workhouse chaplain. Twining, *Workhouses and Women's Work*, p.167; Rev. J.S. Brewer, 'Workhouse visiting', in *Lectures for Ladies on Practical Subjects* (Cambridge, 1855), p.288; Twining, *Life and Work*, pp.122–4. For the experiences of women in general, see Pat Thane, 'Women and the poor law in Victorian and Edwardian England', *History Workshop Journal* 6 (1978), pp.29–51.

51. Twining, *Out Relief and Charity* (London, n.d.), [reprinted from *A Threefold Chord*, 1 October 1892], p.6; Pat Thane, *Foundations of the Welfare State* (London, 1996), pp.18, 75–7; E.P. Hennock, 'Poverty and social reforms', in Paul Johnson, *Twentieth-century Britain: Economic, Social and Cultural Change* (London, 1994), pp.82–6.

52. Twining, *Life and Work*, pp.22–3, 83, 159, 191; letter, Ann Twining to Mary [surname unknown], 20 November 1843, BL Add. MS 39,932, f.128–129.

53. *Courier*, 4 May 1894 and 25 July 1894; Twining, *Suggestions for Women Guardians*, (London, 1887), p.12; idem, *Workhouses and Pauperism*, p.155.

54. Louisa Twining, *Supplement to 'Some Facts in the History of the Twining Family'* (Salisbury, 1893).

55. *The Times*, 12 July 1897.

56. Twining, *Order and Disorder* (Salisbury, 1885), p.1.

57. *Courier*, 5 May 1893; *Nursing Notes and Midwives Chronicle*, 25 (1 November 1912), no.229.

58. Papers of the Women in Local Government Society, WLG 27, LMA.

CHAPTER NINE

'An inheritance of fear': older women in the twentieth-century countryside

STEPHEN HUSSEY

I possess a specific memory that both disturbs and intrigues me; feelings that lie at the roots of my writing this article. The memory dates back to when I was a young man of about 18. At that time my grandmother, a widow who lived close to my family's home, would often visit on a Sunday, coming for her lunch and spending the afternoon with us before returning in the early evening. On one occasion I must have joined my father in the car as he drove her the half a dozen miles back to her bungalow. The journey was an unremarkable one, taking us from our village through the outskirts of a nearby town to her home. Our conversation was not memorable, except for one brief moment: for along the way we passed the half-hidden buildings of a small cottage-hospital. At this point, and for a few minutes after, she appeared unnerved. She turned to us and said, 'Don't ever put me in there. Don't ever put me in that place.'

All this seemed strange to me at the time. I recall being amused that this normally resolute old lady could be disturbed by the sight of this small collection of buildings. It was some years later, after my grandmother's death, that I began research into the lives of rural working-class people, people like my grandmother, who had been raised in the first half of the twentieth-century. Then her reaction came to make some sense. By using oral history, by talking to other people of her generation, I quickly found that hers was not an irrational response, but representative of an emotion that pervaded the lives of working-class people.

Put simply, all shared a common fear of institutional care, of ending their lives away from their homes, relatives and friends in a space which was governed by others and shared with strangers. What also emerged was that this fear was rooted in one particular model of institutional care. This was not that of residential homes that by the time of my research in the early 1990s had come to dominate the care of the old. Instead it was the workhouse, an institutional system that had ended formally in 1929. Looking back, I realise I had stumbled upon the condition that Peter Laslett claims is 'still rumbling on the historical horizon for the British poor': I had come across the fear of the workhouse.[1]

The word 'workhouse' elicits a set of images still current today. Many of us will think of the austerity of its buildings, the mean-spirited care provided within its walls, the desperation of its inmates and the pitiless authority of its staff.[2] These and several other of its associated images have enjoyed a longevity which is a testimony to the workhouse's enduring presence as a source of fear in the twentieth century. This essay seeks to examine the key components of this stubborn fear and how it became increasingly concentrated within the lives of older people.

The essay focuses upon older women in the period 1918 to 1950. These women feared the workhouse with an immediacy that is only now beginning to dissipate. Yet it was also these generations that saw, first, the reform of the poor law and its workhouses, and then their abolition. This essay explores this disjuncture between the formal demise of the workhouse and its informal continuance in the fears of the old. It will suggest that the roots of this disjuncture can be traced to specific features of the workhouse. Reform of the system, its recasting and replacement by public assistance institutions, private and local authority residential and care homes all failed to shift the frightening image of the workhouse and the trepidation it created. To a large extent this fear was passed to the old from past generations, particularly those of the second half of the nineteenth century. Within this process the image of the workhouse and institutional care of all types were welded together and represented, sometimes in accurate warnings, at other times as grotesque myth. Whether this inheritance of fear was justified or groundless mattered little, for it touched all, influencing the lives and emotions of older people as well as their families.

In discussing the fear prompted by the workhouse, strict gender divisions can seem clumsy or artificial. In employment, domestic labour, recreation, worship, parenting, education and so on, older women's and men's experiences differed and were defined to greater and lesser degrees by gender. But the workhouse and the emotions it elicited were broadly shared by both. The workhouse challenged the central pillars of working-class respectability, representing a threat to an individual's liberty and independence. It brought shame by exposing the limitations of the individual and their family's ability to cope. Pride in independence and shame at its loss were emotions common to women and men. In his *Memoirs of a Surrey Labourer*, the rural commentator George Sturt recalled the ignominy brought upon his friend and widower, 'Bettesworth', the subject of his book, when 'removed' to the workhouse, no longer able to cope at home:

> With all their kindness, it must be said of the labouring people that they want tact. Bettesworth's poor home had become a sort of show, in its small squalid fashion. The door stood wide open; there were half a dozen people in the living-room, where the old man of late had shut himself in with his loneliness and his independence; upstairs in bed he must have been aware of the nakedness of the place now displayed. The unswept hearth and the extinct fire were pitiful to see; yet there stood women and children, seeing them . . . I think there were two or three other women standing near Bettesworth's cottage. They were probably waiting to see Bettesworth removed, as he duly was, at mid-day.[3]

Here the humiliation felt by this single old man was one that the onlooking women must have fully comprehended.

This essay uses examples from the lives of older women whenever feasible. Indeed, it is possible to identify key areas in which women's fears of the workhouse differed from those of men. However, we should not forget that the workhouse lingered as a presence in the lives of every older working-class person, woman or man.

The research presented here emerged from a project that examined the lives, relationships and household economics of rural working-class people between the wars. Part of the research plan was to investigate the lives of older people in the countryside, but this proposal soon encountered problems. Raw demographic sources such as the census spoke of the twentieth-century countryside witnessing an unprecedented growth in the numbers of its older people, and yet accompanied this with little detail about how these people lived, still less about their relationship with the workhouse. The minute books of poor law guardians showed that some of the old lived in penury, and yet told nothing of how they coped. Qualitative sources, the personal documentation of individual lives, also proved frustrating. Autobiography, increasingly an access point into the lives of working people for modern historians, proved fruitless. The process of 'life review', reflection upon one's own life, is a central preoccupation of many people's later years. However, this is a process which seems only rarely to touch upon the present predicaments of its participants. For example, John Burnett's attempts to write working-class history through the use of the autobiography is dominated by contributions from Victorian and Edwardian men writing as veterans, looking back to their younger, more vibrant working lives. The results make for an enthralling history, but of the lives of older people, and in particular the lives of older women, we learn little.[4]

Oral histories often prove no better as a source. My research upon the working-class household was based upon sixty interviews with men and women who had lived in communities in rural Essex or rural Buckinghamshire between 1918 and 1950.[5] Each person interviewed was asked, among a series of other questions, about the older people who had lived in their community. However, beside the long and detailed explanations of topics such as women's employment, marital relations and childhood, their memories concerning the old were threadbare by comparison. This absence of insight was a symptom of time. Put simply, the people I questioned lacked the intimate, first-hand experience of being old in the first half of the twentieth-century. That generation is simply no longer with us. Nor was there a generation of oral historians present to capture their observations. All that oral history leaves are the scattered images of the old of an extinct generation remembered in the elderly memories of those who were then young.

Nevertheless, the scattered fragments of oral testimony I collected did unite on one striking theme. Throughout the interviews a single matter was raised and repeated when our conversations turned to older people. This was the way in which all held the workhouse in trepidation. Nowhere was this better illustrated then when I spoke to Alice Martins of Steeple Bumpstead in north Essex. She was aged 96 when we met. As we talked, she told me of how she had cared for her father during the last days of his life. Her story spoke for the memories of many others that I was to talk to, blending the sense of duty she felt towards a parent with the strong undercurrent of fear held by the aged towards the workhouse. Her storytelling also shared its narrative style with many others I spoke to. Most strikingly, she told me, as others were to do, of the fear of having to 'go away':

> *Mrs Martin*: He didn't want to go away and I said, 'He's not going to go if I can look after him at home.' He died, he died with me.
> *Interviewer*: Do you think that was a big fear among old people, that they didn't want to go?
> *Mrs Martin*: Yes, it was at that time of day.
> *Interviewer*: Where would they have to go?
> *Mrs Martin*: That was an old, what did they used to call it? The Union [Union Workhouse]. But they don't call it that now. They had such a dread. He did anyway.[6]

The recollections of the people interviewed attested the blend of fear and resistance which heavily underscores twentieth-century popular attitudes towards the workhouse. The oral evidence is supported by other sources which highlight the emotion as an integral part of the life of the old. For example, the Royal Commission established in 1905 to review the work done by the poor law, admitted in its report of 1909 that, wherever its investigation had taken them they had been told of older people suffering terrible neglect in their own homes rather than submitting to the institutional care offered by the workhouse, concluding that in the face of such determination boards of guardians were 'powerless to remove them to an institution against their will'.[7] From witnesses, the Commission received many graphic accounts of the resistance that older people were prepared to mount when the workhouse beckoned. From rural Suffolk came the testimony of a local relieving officer who told the Commission of the types of troublesome case presented to him whenever he was required to 'remove' an older person:

> I had a case of an old lady of ninety. Three times I went to the house to try and get her away, and I took Mrs Brown [the relieving officer's wife] with me once. She barred the windows and I could not get in. We had to get her out of the house. At last I went there the third time; she took a poker to me. I said, 'You have got to go.' I took her up and lifted her into the carriage. I got another old woman eighty years old to go with her. On the road the patient fainted, and I thought she was dead. I took her back to the post office, and the post-mistress gave her a drop of brandy, and then I took her on. She is still alive, but I should never risk a case like that again. We ought to have the power to apply to the magistrates to get the proper legal authority.[8]

From the surviving records of rural relieving officers in Essex come similar stories. Their abbreviated notes give scant detail, and yet little imagination is needed to picture the desperate struggle for independence and the deep dislike of the workhouse that underscore these accounts. From Ongar, Essex, in 1908 an officer records, 'Woman aged 85, in caravan many years, partly paralysed, refused to enter [workhouse] Infirmary, found dead.' Two years later at Billericay the officer accords a little more detail to a similar case: 'Brentwood, old couple, wife Pensioner, declined to enter Infirmary, "Would rather die than leave the house", which medical Officer of Health then had cleaned; they crouched around a fire, in great need of a wash themselves. Within a fortnight both found dead.' A further example of a woman at Great Burstead in 1932 offers a still more graphic instance: 'Pensioner, fifteen shillings a week in all, friendless, had seen far better days, urged by the Rural District Council to enter House; living in four-ton motor lorry alone, "I would do anything rather than go inside." September, again urged: "I would sooner go to a dog's home." '[9]

So pervasive was the fear of the workhouse that by the early twentieth century it became a commonplace of narratives concerning the older rural working class. If the old were not imparting nuggets of rustic wisdom, writers and commentators had them living in fear of the 'house'. In 1895, when Charles Benham, an Essex newspaper proprietor and amateur poet, sought to define and capture in verse an image of old age in the countryside about him, he used the fictional narrative of 'The Death of Mike'. For Benham, Mike's experience of death was designed to typify those of the class of which he was part. The poem describes this old labourer and his wife during the man's last moments. Their feelings are those of relief, relief that he will have ended his life outside the workhouse:

> Howd me up a little, Martha, so I can look around;
> Lor, I feel that cowd an' weak, jes' wrap my showders in your gownd.
> I'm a dyin', ent I, Martha? I don't scarcely recollec'
> Who I be or where I bin to – I'm a dyin I expec'.
>
> Guess I bin dreamin', Martha, what I min I thought jes now
> I were in the Warkus, wond'rin when I got here an' how.
> Oo, that wor a laonesome feelin', wonnerful good news that seem
> When I knaow tha's all onreal – that were nahthin but a dream.
>
> Howd me up a minute, Martha, open that ere winder there.
> Op' it wider, ah, that's better, so I git a breath o'air,
> So I see the fiel's an' that, an' knaow I ent a dreamin' still,
> So I know that ent the Warkus, where I be a lyin' ill.

The poem is followed by a short prayer, in which Mike's only hope is that his wife might also be spared the workhouse:

> Lord, I dew believe in him who died upon the cross for we,
> Which I thank'm God A'mighty; tell him so, I pray from me,
> I carn say n'more, I fare to feel as pow'rless as a mouse,
> But look arter poor owd Martha, don't she'll goo 'ithin the House.[10]

Although writing some fifty years after Benham, another notable Essex author, Samuel Levy Bensusan, uses identical imagery in what was to be the last of his many 'country books', published in 1945. Here Bensusan recalls visiting an aged farmworker who had acted as his part-time gardener during the man's 'retirement'. Upon discovering that the old man lay dying in his cottage bedroom, Bensusan records their last conversation:

I expressed the usual conventional hope that I'd see him in my garden when the spring came round. He shook his head.
"I'll be under nex' year's daisies," he said, "but there that don't sin'ify. I've had me harvest supper, and took me harvest money, an' th' owd overseer won't be able to turn me outer house an' home."[11]

In other words he was happy because he would not be sent to the Union to die. It was not death that older people feared, it was the stigma of the workhouse.

Images like these, snapshots from the memories of individuals, the notes of a relieving officer, the thoughts of a poet or the observation of a writer, all are valuable for the historian. They allow an impression of the experience of growing old in the past. Nevertheless, such insights need to be tempered with caution. It is too easy to take from them a belief that the degree of fear engendered in older people by the workhouse is an accurate measure of its actual presence. Ronald Blythe's work *The View in Winter* offers a good example of the seductive nature of this image. In one distinctive passage Blythe maps out a maxim, seemingly applicable to working-class communities of the countryside in the 1920s and 1930s, in which old age sets in train an inevitable downward spiral towards poverty, destitution and, finally, the workhouse:

> Illiterate, economically embarrassing to the self-supporting parish, the fate of the common labourer and his wife in old age was to be punished by society for daring to grow old. The visiting officer called and they left for the workhouse, sometimes in a cart, often walking, their eyes averted. They had transgressed. They had gone on living when they were beyond value. There they were parted, often after half a century of marriage, and were only to see each other now and then by application to the Master who, estimating if they had a bit of go left in them, set them to tasks. And so they'd scrub and peel and chop their paths to the grave, via the infirmary. All the people in the 1930s countryside had witnessed this. It was commonplace up until the last war.[12]

Portrayals such as this represent a misreading of the available evidence. They take the pervasive fear felt towards the workhouse as a signal that the numbers of older people for whom life in the workhouse was a reality ran to frightening proportions, that it was the normal end to the lives of working people. In fact, at the time of which Blythe is writing, very few elderly women and men resided in workhouses. Their numbers, too, were falling, and had been since the beginning of the century (see Table 9.1).

For elderly women, in particular, the threat of the workhouse was minuscule. Table 9.1 records that in 1931 less than one in every 100 women aged 65 to 74 were resident in public assistance institutions (as the workhouses were now to be known). Even in extreme old age the numbers do not make terrifying reading, with the proportions rising to just over three in every 100 women aged 75 and above. For men the numbers are higher, but only slightly, at between two and three and then just above four in every 100 for the same age categories. There is little here to suggest that incarceration of

Table 9.1 Percentage of the aged population of England and Wales in poor law institutions, 1901–31

Date	Age groups			
	Male		Female	
	65–74	75+	65–74	75+
1901	5.82	9.25	2.81	5.62
1911	6.04	7.39	2.30	4.37
1921	3.17	4.75	1.43	3.32
1931	2.44	4.05	0.96	2.71

Source: David Thomson, 'Workhouse to nursing home: residential care of elderly people in England since 1840', *Ageing and Society* 3 (1983), p.49. Reproduced with permission of Cambridge University Press.

the old was occurring on a significant scale. As the 1909 Royal Commission strove to make clear, it was now no longer 'the normal or the inevitable fate of the aged to be forced to apply for Poor Law relief. Still less is it true that the working-man will probably end his days in the workhouse.'[13] Yet the fear of the workhouse continued.

The number of older people entering the workhouse was falling owing to a series of well documented welfare reforms. The introduction of state pension provision in 1908 was the most obvious step in a process that edged many towards positions of modest financial security in old age. Provision was extended in 1911 with the ending of pauper disqualification, which had denied pension payments to those that had been in receipt of poor relief since 1 January 1908.[14] Accompanying this, direct attempts at reducing the numbers of elderly workhouse residents were made by the local government board (from 1871 the co-ordinating body for poor law administration in England and Wales).[15] In a series of circulars, the Board (LGB) recommended that individual poor law unions should soften their treatment of older paupers by providing, wherever possible, relief outside the workhouse and maintaining them in their own homes.[16] There were also to be ongoing reforms to the workhouse, designed to soften its image in the public perception. From the late nineteenth century onwards, again under the auspices of the LGB, poor law unions were encouraged to modify the treatment of their older residents. It was intended that the workhouse should not deter those old persons who might seek the help of the relieving officer, but instead assume the role of a resting place for those who could no longer care or be cared for in their own community. The workhouse was to be seen as the last, rather than the first in a set of provisions for the support of the old. If an older person had to enter a workhouse it was the hope of the LGB that they would find a system that sought not to punish them but instead welcomed them as 'indulgently treated guests in comfortable quarters specially designed for their accommodation'.[17] Although these wishes were never to be fully realised, the workhouse of the interwar years was a different institution from its nineteenth-century counterpart. As early as 1895, a report to government on the position of older people had found that, where they entered the workhouse, they were treated in what was deemed generally to be a satisfactory manner. In particular, the report went to lengths to dismiss the popular notions of workhouses as being ' "barbarous tests", worse than prisons, places which the poor would rather starve than enter . . .'. It went on to conclude that attempts to improve conditions were being made whenever possible:

> The facts unquestionably show that the physical conditions of life in the workhouse are superior on the whole to those enjoyed by some of the independent poor, that the provision for their mental and moral wants has received and continues to receive in increasing proportion the earnest attention of Boards of Guardians.[18]

Statements like this conceal the great variations in workhouse conditions which remained in the twentieth century. In many of the provincial poor law unions improvements were slow and came piecemeal, held back by the disruption created by the First World War and then by the depression years of the 1920s and 1930s.[19] However, the rural workhouse was undergoing change. Taking the rural poor law unions of Essex as our example, we find gradual improvements being made from the late nineteenth century onwards. Cumulatively they slowly softened the worst aspects of workhouse care for older women. The regimentation of workhouse lifestyles and the loss of personal liberty were one central area of reform addressed by rural guardians. In 1895, both Billericay and Maldon workhouses granted older inmates permission to wander freely about the grounds during the day, a move that was followed at Chelmsford in 1907. Attempts were made to make the accommodation more comfortable. At Maldon in 1900, a sitting room was provided that was separate from the sleeping quarters; it was furnished a year later with twelve Windsor chairs. Lockers were added next to beds as a place where personal possessions might be kept. At Great Dunmow in 1907, Windsor chairs were also provided, this time replacing the bare forms which had previously offered little comfort. Here, too, guardians agreed to supply 'a table or two, heating in the small day-room, better lavatory accommodation, and more towels and combs', although improvements did not go unfettered, as 'flannel underclothing and extra suits were refused'. The workhouse diet, often the source of popular condemnation for its poor quantity and quality, received gradual attention. When medical officers from the local board of health visited the Chelmsford workhouse in the early years of the twentieth-century they found older inhabitants enjoying 'more milk than they could drink, and four meat dinners per week'. Again, many of the improvements were modest, but the small concessions such as the granting of extra tea and sugar for female inmates aged over 70 at Billericay in 1895, or the issue of enamel plates replacing wooden ones and the addition of a weekly fish dish around the turn of the century at Braintree, meant that by the interwar years the workhouse diet surpassed that of the majority of those that remained in their own homes.[20]

The complaints of the chairman of the Billericay board of guardians that the LGB was now 'constantly urging them to make their workhouses like palaces' were extravagant. Nonetheless, his words hint at wider changes in attitude towards older inmates encouraged by poor law authorities.[21] The late nineteenth century had put in motion a set of improvements which meant that by the interwar years boredom was a more likely complaint in the rural workhouse than cruelty. Condemnation and punishment had been replaced by a degree of care and provision. Yet this did nothing to displace the fear of the workhouse in the minds of the elderly. Instead, the twentieth century merely saw a growing gap between popular perceptions of the scale of the workhouse's threat and its actuality.

In 1913 came cosmetic attempts at reform through the official abandonment of the term 'workhouse' and its replacement with the unwieldy, yet seemingly more respectable title of public assistance institution. In 1929, the poor law system formally came to an end and public assistance institutions were transferred to local authority control. Finally, in 1948 the public assistance institutions were taken over by the newly formed National Health Service. Throughout, fear continued in the public consciousness, as did the old terminology of 'workhouse', 'master' and 'inmate'. Conducting research in the late 1950s, the sociologist Peter Townsend found that the workhouse, now long disbanded, still held deep resonance in the working-class communities he studied. As a vivid and typical example of the attitudes and terminology of the older people he spoke to, his fieldnotes record for one elderly woman, 'Mrs C has a terror of going into an institution. "The old workhouses, I mean. They call 'em differently now, but a lot of them are the same. I wouldn't want to go in any place like that, I'd rather be in me own 'ome than be looked after a bit better in one of those places." '[22] The workhouse remains today as the model for which many older women and men often reach when they contemplate institutional care, and is still the one which social services have to struggle to overcome.[23]

What gave the workhouse such a fearsome stature? What ensured that it continued to generate a threat in the minds of the aged that so comprehensively outpaced its reality? The answers to both questions lie with a set of concerns present within working-class communities, including a loss of liberty, the ending of self-reliance, removal from lifelong partners, family and community, anxiety about treatment once inside, and trepidation at the physical architecture of the workhouse building. Answers can also be sought in the shifting demographic make-up of the workhouse and the welfare institutions which followed it, and furthermore in the process of the transmission of stories, myths and precepts between generations that so ingrained a hatred of institutional care into successive generations of older people.

However much the workhouse was reformed, it remained in the popular conscience as the ultimate menace to an individual's liberty. The 1895 Royal Commission reported the popular view that workhouses were seen as something akin to prisons, the Commissioners knowing enough to link the dislike of the workhouse with what they termed an 'exaggerated fear of the discipline and the interference with absolute freedom which are imperative in such establishments'.[24] For rural working-class women, the values of thriftiness, of being seen to cope on little without outside intervention or assistance, were enshrined as positive attributes, just as sobriety and hard work were for men. The workhouse signalled an end to this state of independence, and a submission to the hands of others. With it went the self-reliance that represented the bedrock of working-class culture. And despite the concessions to individual liberty slowly emerging in the early twentieth century, the workhouse still stood for a regime in which the workings of the institution held precedence over the desires of the individual.

Workhouses represented an archetype of the kinds of 'total' institution that were to preoccupy postwar sociologists such as Erving Goffman.[25] Uniform clothing and bedding, the homogeneity of wards, furniture, cutlery and utensils, the minimal number of personal effects that an individual was permitted to bring in, all spoke of institutional order above individual liberty and self-identity. Nowhere was this more clearly demonstrated than in relation to workhouse attitudes to time and its control. In this respect workhouses were managed assiduously by the resident master and matron. Times were given for rising in the morning, for going to bed, for visits from friends and relations, for visiting the master, and for meals. Indeed, there were few activities not regulated by the clock. Visiting the Orsett workhouse in Essex on Christmas Day in 1911, a local journalist noted approvingly the 'sumptuous dinner' set before residents which included 'roast beef (from cattle fed on his Majesty's farm at Balmoral), mashed and baked potatoes, plum pudding, and beer and mineral waters, according to choice.' Yet even on this day there was no escaping the rigid timetable which residents were forced to follow, the journalist reporting that the elderly were woken at 5.30am as usual. However, in order to mark the day, the staff sang carols. Breakfast was then served at 8am, followed by lunch at 12.30pm, before tea at 5.30pm and bed at 8pm.[26]

It was a common criticism of the workhouse that it took older people from their communities and from their families.[27] On one basic level this removal entailed isolation and loneliness brought about by the physical distances between an individual and their home. But there was another real sense in which they were removed, and it was here that the workhouse offered a threat which did differentiate between women and men. Writing about the experiences of older women entering residential care in postwar Britain, Fennell, Phillipson and Evers have identified the ways in which older women came to be known in their own communities by a rich set of 'social identities' within which the stigmatising and negative image of oldness is simply one among many other more positive ones. In the villages of the early twentieth century this was certainly true. Older women fulfilled an intricate set of social roles. Many continued to be workers, taking on paid employment such as washing or needlework in their home or going out to char, or even working in the fields if their constitution allowed it. Other women were caregivers to the wider community, acting as unofficial midwife or 'handywoman' as they were known. Often these same women would lay out the dead. Many old women were also carers within their own families, taking on childminding responsibilities for a son or a daughter's young family. Even if they were none of these things, older women were carers for surviving husbands or keepers of their own household. To continue in these diverse social roles gave them independence, pride and status in their own eyes and those of the wider community. The workhouse threatened to take elderly women from these contexts in which respect and social standing were secure, and place them within another in which their central defining characteristics were that they were old and now dependent. As Fennell *et al.* conclude, 'For older women who arrive unknown and unknowing, in a new environment, "oldness" becomes a "master status", the main determinant of ascribed identity among strangers.'[28] It was the varied and rich components of their own self-being that elderly women so prized and which the workhouse must have threatened.

For elderly men, the identity that came with a well defined, full-time occupation such as ploughman, stockman, carpenter, wheelwright, was a stronger, less ambiguous one to carry into old age and into an unknowing institution than that of unpaid housewife, part-time charwoman or occasional handywoman. The workhouse, even if not welcomed, offered men a degree of continuity in other ways. In particular there was the sense that men looked to others to care for them, that domestic tasks such as cooking, cleaning and washing were the responsibility of others. At home these roles were filled by their wives or, if the man was alone, then frequently by a daughter or daughter-in-law. The workhouse, at the very least, provided a continuation of this type of role, with meals provided and the washing done. For women, in contrast, the workhouse cut directly across the types of work that formed a central strand to their self-identity. Managing a household, cleaning it, doing the washing, shopping, cooking, looking after others, all offered a crucial structure to their days. Recent gerontological work by Evers has shown the positive link to be made between the high morale of some older women and their ability to 'structure their lives in relation to their own domestic order'. For many women these domestic routines may have been established over forty or fifty years of adult life and represented a central continuity upon which to sustain themselves in old age as their health began to fail, as they lost a spouse and saw friends die.[29] The workhouse seemed to threaten to take even this comfort from them.

In other ways, fear of the workhouse was generated by factors that crossed gender boundaries, troubling elderly women and men. Certain aspects of the workhouse regime had, by the beginning of the twentieth century, seeped deep into the public mind. Some contained elements of truth, but others had little evidential basis. When, in 1913, the rural writer George Sturt came to visit his local workhouse in Surrey, he was impressed by the surroundings and the levels of care he found:

> From the vestibule, along the airy corridors, and through the large, cheerful wards to the comfortable day-rooms, the building seemed almost unnecessarily sumptuous; and all that I could see and hear showed that the attendance of nurses and doctors and officials in general was worthy of its scene. So far as efforts went to make the machinery successful, I was convinced that as a ratepayer I was getting my money's worth.[30]

Yet Sturt was still able to note another, more disturbing side to the workhouse:

> the quietness of them [the residents] seemed unnatural. Something like fear, not so much of any person or thing, as of invisible regulations, dumb forces, pervaded the atmosphere. Not prisoners in the legal sense, these people were practically imprisoned; human beings in a cowering state, afraid to be themselves.[31]

The line between actuality and myth possessed little meaning, as stories built up the workhouse's terrifying reputation. Among these, death became linked inextricably in the public mind with the institution. A very small proportion of all old people died in the workhouse, but a high proportion of those who entered at late ages, when they could no longer cope, did so, as might be expected. In consequence it became 'one of the most enduring of memories from the Poor Law era'.[32] It was not only the fear of a lonely death in the workhouse which was spun into public mythology, but also a deep strand of apprehension regarding the fate that might befall any workhouse corpse. Ruth Richardson, in her brilliant study of the Anatomy Act 1832, remembers how in her own north London childhood during the 1950s, local lore had it that the hospital close to her school, once a workhouse infirmary, 'belched the smoke of human fuel', and that in the playground 'small children nodded knowingly, and told each other that those who went in there never came out'.[33]

Richardson's work highlights a further layer to the fear of the work-house. The Anatomy Act, that from 1832 gave permission to poor law authorities to supply the dissection classes of the surgical schools of Britain with unclaimed pauper corpses, remained in place into the twentieth century (and indeed remains today). One of its repercussions was to strengthen the popular link between the workhouse and, not simply death, but an inability even then to rest unmolested. It was perhaps for this reason that so many of the rural poor, like their urban counterparts, were wholehearted subscribers to the burial clubs and other insurance schemes which prospered in the nineteenth and early twentieth century, offering some peace of mind against this terrifying and undignified end.[34]

Workhouses also impressed themselves upon the popular consciousness by their very scale and structures. They dominated the skyline of many provincial market towns, representing, with town and shire halls and the bigger schools, the most imposing buildings. Workhouse architecture was forbidding. Many followed a common design, with grounds walled or fenced, buildings several stories tall, with high windows and little external embel-lishment. Often the buildings had design and layout features similar to those of other feared institutions: the prison, the asylum and the orphanage. For a rural population unaccustomed to regular contact with such large institu-tions, the very presence of these imposing buildings helped to embed the workhouse further into community mythology. These edifices loomed as an intentional symbol of the repercussions of any failure to remain self-reliant in old age.[35] This fear has remained, clinging to its buildings, proving resist-ant to organisational and name changes. While workhouse buildings have remained in use as residential homes for the elderly, they have also con-tinued to carry some of their old symbolism as places of lost hope, abandon-ment and destitution. No matter what new facilities they were given, and however much attention was paid to brightening their decor, as long as workhouse buildings have remained their historical background continues to accompany them, shaping the fears of generations of older people through the collective memories they inspire.[36]

Loss of independence, sacrifice of self-reliance, an enduring reputation for mistreatment, a close association with death and a fear of the buildings themselves, all explain this preoccupation with the workhouse by the aged. There are, however, two final elements to explore if we are fully to explain why fear of the workhouse has remained so constant. Both involve alterations to the policy of the poor law in the late nineteenth century. The first created a distinct change in the demographic structure of the workhouse, creating an institution dominated by the old. The second left the older generations of the interwar period, in particular, with childhood memories of the workhouse that instilled a heightened sense of threat taken by them into their later lives.

From the late nineteenth century the workhouse population underwent a partial demographic shift. Popular and governmental distaste had slowly grown for mixed institutions, in which the old and the young, the sick and the healthy, the honourable and the feckless, the moral and the immoral could mingle. Answers to the varied social, physical and spiritual needs of this combined population were increasingly sought in separate institutions. In particular, the deterrent aspect of the workhouse was dropped for the able-bodied poor. From the mid-1890s, in theory, this group were to be maintained, wherever possible, in their own homes: a decision underlined by the introduction of National Insurance from 1911. It was also hoped that other workhouse 'cases' could be provided for by a burgeoning number of specialised institutions and solutions. The introduction of non-contributory old age pensions in 1908 was designed to remove the older able-bodied from outdoor relief. Single mothers were to reside in maternity homes and, after the Children's Act 1908, orphaned or abandoned children were to be boarded-out in children's homes or with foster parents. But progress on all these fronts was slow and varied greatly from place to place, as boards of guardians proved either reluctant or unable to push through reform. By 1929, 60 per cent of workhouse inmates were still under the care of the old type of unspecialised, mixed workhouse.[37]

Nevertheless, workhouse populations in rural Essex, as elsewhere in England, were undergoing change. At Maldon, relief lists show older people coming to dominate the workhouse population in both absolute and percentage terms. In 1870, Maldon contained a highly diverse range of inmates: a six-month period ending in March of that year shows that the workhouse admitted 306 people, 81 (around 27 per cent) of whom were aged 60 and above. By the same six-month period in 1930 the sum of older people at Maldon represented 143 from a total of 257, a growth in percentage terms of 29 per cent (to 56 per cent). Compare this with the numbers of children admitted to the workhouse over the same periods and one sees a shrinkage in numbers from 94 to 13, a fall from 31 per cent of all admissions to just 5 per cent. The Maldon workhouse, like many other small rural workhouses, remained in the interwar years a mixed institution, but one in which older people now accounted for the majority of its residents.

It should be added that it was not merely the elderly as an undifferentiated group that had come to dominate the workhouse. State pensions, introduced in 1908 at 5s. per week, permitted a minimal defence against extreme poverty. By the interwar years it was not simply the old but the very old and the aged who were chronically sick who made up an increasing proportion of workhouse residents. Few older women now entered the workhouse simply because poverty impelled them. Most came instead owing to a combination of factors which might include failing health, disability, partial dementia, extreme age, and the absence of familial support. Writing in the early 1930s, soon after the formal ending of the poor law, George Cuttle, historian of the rural boards of guardians, reviewed the last decades of the workhouse:

> In 1897–8 aged people were admitted, not merely because of age, but also because they were past work; they were not usually Infirmary patients, and much less hospital cases. In 1927–8 most of this type were receiving Pensions and being cared for medically in their own homes; some having no relatives to receive them, and unable to care for themselves, came in as 'debility' cases.[38]

The changing workhouse population was noted and soon became a central concern of local boards of guardians. At Chelmsford in 1913, the workhouse population was described as 'poor and decrepit', with the accompanying remark that 'only helpless old people come now', it being noted that the average age of six admissions in September stood at 87 years. At Braintree in March 1912, the guardians bemoaned the fact that whereas once up to 20 able-bodied women might be set upon the needlework tasks of the workhouse, repairing clothes and bedding, 'now not one was to be found either for this or for laundry work; so help was hired.'[39] Equivalent evidence from other rural areas was placed before the 1909 Royal Commission on the poor laws, much of it bemoaning the absence of the younger women upon whom so much of the day-to-day functioning of the workhouse had once depended. From one chairman of a rural board of guardians came the grumble that the 'house' possessed 'hardly more than one able-bodied', explaining that, 'we wish we could have one or two more. We have a large laundry, and they are able to do a good deal of work which otherwise we could not get done at all.'[40]

This shift in the institution's population may have helped to embed further the workhouse as the place for the older poor in the minds of the wider working-class population. By the 1920s, if any one in a village community had cause to visit a workhouse they would have witnessed an institution in which the aged dominated in terms of their numbers. Furthermore, the growing numbers of very old and the very sick within their wards served to strengthen the conceptual links between the workhouse as a place of extreme destitution and of death.

One further and final factor might shed light on the close association of the workhouse and fear which has continued through the twentieth century. If, by the 1920s, older people viewed the workhouse as an institution whose specific purpose was to detain them if their own personal, familial and community mechanisms of support were to fail, it was also these generations of working-class women and men, growing old in the 1920s, 1930s and 1940s, who carried with them a particularly powerful memory of the workhouse from childhood. The fear of the workhouse has, as we have seen, been transported across generations of working-class people through a set of associated images and characteristics involving loss of freedom, physical separation from loved ones, the association with death and bodily desecration, and the spectre of its imposing buildings. Yet the urgency with which older people of the early and mid-twentieth century felt these threats might be linked, tentatively, with changes to poor law provision during the nineteenth century.

A good deal of scholarly attention has been paid to the operation of the nineteenth-century poor law and its workhouses. Detailed research has highlighted a distinct shift in provision from the mid-1860s lasting for a period of around 20–30 years.[41] During this brief interlude, local poor law authorities were urged by their central controlling body, the poor law board (later to become the LGB) to attempt meaningful restrictions on expenditure. A central target in this process was the expenditure given in outrelief or doles to older people. The adoption of these policy changes was by no means universal in geographical terms, nor did they signal a complete cessation of all payments to the elderly poor. However, they did have the overall effect of curbing outrelief to the old. The result of this was twofold. Much of the financial aid once given to older people through the poor law now became the responsibility of their family. At a time when working-class living standards were showing gradual improvements, many families may have been able to help, care and even house an older relative. For other old men and women, either without family or with family unable or reluctant to help, a withdrawal or reduction in outrelief threatened their independence, and, as Peter Wood has shown, this period was one in which the number of older people entering workhouses in Victorian Britain did increase markedly.[42]

During this short period it seems likely that some older women who had once been supported in their own community by relief, were compelled to enter the workhouse. Throughout, the threat was never large. In 1901 just 5 per cent of the English and Welsh population aged over 65 were resident in poor law institutions, an increase from the 3.6 per cent recorded in 1871.[43] However, people growing old between 1918 and 1950 would have been children during this period of poor law austerity. It is possible that they acquired an added dimension to the loathing with which earlier generations had held the workhouse. They, like generations of old people before and after, shared the feelings of fear at the potential loss of freedom and independence, the division from community and family, the spectre of death and the foreboding of the buildings. But if any generations of the poor had experienced at first-hand the sight of older people being taken by the visiting officer, their eyes averted, to paraphrase Ronald Blythe, it was probably the children of the late nineteenth century.[44] If any generation were likely to have visited grandparents or elderly family friends in the workhouse, it was this generation. Even if direct contact with the workhouse remained an exceptional experience, village homes, pubs and workplaces during the 1860s, 1870s and 1880s would have heard talk of those that had seen an elderly acquaintance having to go to the 'house'. Perhaps above all else, this generation could recall the trepidation with which the workhouse was held at this time by their grandparents and elderly neighbours. It was this fear, embedded in popular working-class memory and inherited from the elderly of another generation, which was to stay with them, to be rekindled when they themselves faced old age and the uncertainties that it brought.

Acknowledgements

I would like to thank Essex County Council for their generous support of the research presented here.

Notes

1. Peter Laslett, *A Fresh Map of Life: The Emergence of the Third Age*, 2nd edn (Basingstoke, 1996), p.23.

2. See Deane in this volume.

3. George Sturt, *Memoirs of a Surrey Labourer* (London, 1907), p.253.

4. John Burnett, *Useful Toil: Autobiographies of Working People from the 1820s to the 1920s* (London, 1974). Joanna Bourke, *Working-Class Cultures in Britain 1890–*

1960: Gender, Class and Ethnicity (London, 1994) makes a similar use of auto-biography, but once more the experiences of later life are largely absent. See also Kugler in this volume.

5. Stephen Hussey, *Work, Gender and the Rural Household, 1918–1950* (Harlow, forthcoming).

6. Interview with Mrs Martins, born 1896, interviewed 1992.

7. Helen Bosanquet, *The Poor Law Report of 1909* (London, 1909), p.59.

8. *Report of Royal Commission on the Poor Laws and Relief of Distress, 1910*, Vol. VII, Cmd 5035, p.276.

9. George Cuttle, *The Legacy of the Rural Guardians* (Cambridge, 1934), appendix 8.

10. Charles Edward Benham, *Essex Ballads* (Colchester, 1895).

11. S.L. Bensusan, *Back of Beyond: A Countryman's Pre-war Commonplace Book* (London, 1945), p.38.

12. Ronald Blythe, *The View in Winter* (London, 1979), p.52.

13. Bosanquet, *The Poor Law*, p.44.

14. Pat Thane, 'Non-contributory versus insurance pensions 1878–1908', in Pat Thane, ed., *The Origins of British Social Policy* (London, 1978), pp.103–4; *Statement with Regard to Persons in Receipt of Poor Law Relief on 31st December, 1910, Who Received Old Age Pensions and Ceased to be Chargeable to Guardians during the Four Weeks ended 28th January, 1911*, Cmd 5612, lxix, p.2. See Deane, this volume, for a discussion of the older women and the workhouse.

15. M.A. Crowther, *The Workhouse System, 1834–1929* (London, 1981), pp.73–4; Pat Thane, *Foundations of the Welfare State*, 2nd edn (London, 1996), pp.33–4.

16. Sidney and Beatrice Webb, *English Local Government. Vol. 8: English Poor Law History, Part II: The Last Hundred Years* (London, 1929), p.357; Peter Wood, *Poverty and the Workhouse in Victorian Britain* (Stroud, 1991), p.157.

17. Webb, *English Local Government*, p.350.

18. *Royal Commission on the Aged Poor* (1895), Cmd 7684, xiv, pp.xxxi–xxxii.

19. Crowther, *The Workhouse*, pp.89–90.

20. Cuttle, *Legacy*, pp.40–51.

21. Ibid., p.52.

22. Peter Townsend Collection, *The Family Life of Old People*, Box 35, ESRC Qualitative Data Archive Resource Centre, QUALIDATA, University of Essex. My thanks to Paul Mason for drawing my attention to this and other information in the Townsend Collection.

23. Dianne Willcocks, Sheila Peace and Leonie Kellaher, *Private Lives in Public Places* (London, 1986), pp.17–18.

24. *Royal Commission* (1895), p.xxxi.

25. Erving Goffman, *Asylums: Essays on the Social Situation of Mental Patients and Other Inmates* (New York, 1961).

26. 'Christmas at Orsett Workhouse', 30 December 1911, unnamed newspaper press-cutting, Essex Record Office, T/Z 43/2.

27. See, for example, *Royal Commission* (1895), pp.348–9.

28. Graham Fennell, Chris Phillipson and Helen Evers, *The Sociology of Old Age* (Milton Keynes, 1988), p.105.

29. Ibid., p.106. See also Helen Evers, 'The frail elderly woman: emergent questions in ageing and women's health', in E. Lewin and V. Olesen, eds, *Women, Health and Healing: Towards a New Perspective* (London, 1985), pp.90–5.

30. George Sturt, *Lucy Bettesworth* (London, 1913), p.112.

31. Ibid., p.113.

32. David Thomson, 'Workhouse to nursing home: residential care of elderly people in England since 1840', *Ageing and Society* 3 (1983), p.49.

33. Ruth Richardson, *Death, Dissection and the Destitute* (London, 1987), p.xvi.

34. Ibid., pp.275, 279.

35. For the ways in which buildings can shape collective community memories, see Judith Modell and John Hinshaw, 'Male work and mill work', in Selma Leydesdorff, Louisa Passerini and Paul Thompson, eds, *Gender and Memory* (Oxford, 1996), pp.133–49.

36. Robin Means, 'Social services for elderly people: from Beveridge to Thatcher', in Julia Johnson and Robert Slater, eds, *Ageing and Later Life* (London, 1993), p.312; Charles Webster, 'The elderly and the early National Health Service', in Margaret Pelling and Richard M. Smith, eds, *Life, Death and the Elderly: Historical Perspectives* (London, 1991), p.167; Willcocks *et al.*, *Private Lives*, p.19.

37. Crowther, *The Workhouse*, p.89. Thane, *Foundations*, pp.35–6, 176.

38. Cuttle, *Legacy*, p.162.

39. Ibid., p.58.

40. *Royal Commission* (1910), p.278.

41. See David Thomson, 'Workhouse', p.50; Crowther, *The Workhouse*, p.58; M.E. Rose, 'The crisis of poor relief in England, 1860–1890', in W.J. Mommsen, ed., *The Emergence of the Welfare State in Britain and Germany 1850–1950* (London,

1981), pp.52–3; Mary MacKinnon, 'English poor law policy and the crusade against outrelief', *Journal of Economic History* 47 (1987), pp.603–4.

42. Wood, *Poverty*, p.156.

43. Karel Williams, *From Pauperism to Poverty* (London, 1981), p.205.

44. Blythe, *The View*, p.52.

CHAPTER TEN

Old women in twentieth-century Britain

PAT THANE

In twentieth-century Britain, for the first time in history, it became normal to grow old. Although, as we have seen, survival to old age was more common in past centuries than is sometimes thought, it was not until the 1930s, in Britain, that the overwhelming majority of every age cohort lived from birth to old age. This was due to the rapid decline, from the later nineteenth century, in infant mortality rates, and in deaths among adults in middle life. As Tables 10.1 and 10.2 show, expectation of life at birth almost doubled from 39 years for men, and 42 years for women in 1841 to 76 years for men and almost 81 years for women in 1991. Also, the tables show that throughout the twentieth century most old people in Britain were female. This had been so since compulsory registration of births and deaths was introduced in 1837 and probably for very much longer.[1]

The low life expectancies of the mid-nineteenth century were strongly influenced by high infant death rates. These figures do not mean, as is often thought, that most people who survived to adulthood died in early middle age. People who survived early childhood had a good chance of surviving at least to their fifties or sixties, if not beyond.

Not only death rates but also birth rates fell to historically low levels over the twentieth century. One consequence was that, in Britain as in most developed and many less developed countries, the proportion of older people in the population rose to historically high levels (Table 10.3).

This ageing of the population caused gloomy, though often ill-informed, speculation about the ill-effects likely to result, especially upon the economy, owing to the growing costs to the working population of medical and social security services for older people, who were assumed to be dependent and a burden. These concerns were first voiced from the 1930s to the 1950s,[2] then again in the 1980s and 1990s.[3] Much of the concern was rooted in

Table 10.1 Expectation of life at birth for generations born 1841 to 1991, United Kingdom

Year of birth	Males	Females	Year of birth	Males	Females
1841	39	42	1921	61	68
1851	40	43	1931	66	72
1861	42	45	1941	69.6	75.4
1871	44	49	1951	72.7	78.3
1881	47	52	1961	73.6	79.1
1891	48	54	1971	74.6	79.7
1901	51	58	1981	75.5	80.4
1911	56	63	1991	76	80.8

Sources: *National Population Projections 1989 Based*, Series PP2, No.17, OPCS (London 1991, table 2, p.5); P. Johnson and J. Falkingham, *Ageing and Economic Welfare* (London, 1992), p.23. Reproduced with permission of Sage Publications.

Table 10.2 Ratio of females to males in elderly population, Great Britain, 1881–1981

Year	F/M (60/65+)	F/M (85+)
1881	1.97	1.64
1901	2.05	1.74
1921	2.04	2.07
1941	2.03	2.20
1961	2.26	2.32
1981	2.02	3.26

Sources: Selected census volumes, 1881–1981; P. Johnson and J. Falkingham, *Ageing and Economic Welfare* (London, 1992), p.27. Reproduced with permission of Sage Publications.

negative stereotyping of older people and their capabilities. The predicted heavy social and economic costs did not eventuate in the middle of the century, and many were sceptical about their probability at the end of the century.[4] A paradox of twentieth century culture was that the lengthening of life, which for centuries had been dreamed of and which was a product

Table 10.3 Percentage of population aged 65 and over, Great Britain, 1851–1991

Census year	%
1851	4.6
1881	4.6
1911	5.2
1931	7.4
1951	10.9
1971	13.2
1981	15.1
1991	15.7

Sources: Censuses of Population; Pat Thane, 'Old age: burden or benefit', in H. Joshi, ed., *The Changing Population of Britain* (Oxford, 1989), p.57. Reproduced with permission of Blackwell Publishers.

of greatly improved living standards, was greeted with such pessimism when finally it came about.

But how old was old in the twentieth century? Was age 60 any more satisfactory a marker of the onset of old age in the twentieth than in the seventeenth century?[5] As in earlier centuries, old age was defined in a plurality of ways, shaped by a variety of influences including the imperatives of government bureaucracy and of statistical measurement, the images disseminated by a proliferating range of communications media (magazines, newspapers, advertisements, novels, film, television, the Internet, scholarly publications), by subjective experience and by each individual's perception of the experience of others as they aged. No definition of old age exists in isolation, rather it is embedded in a mesh of intersecting influences. For example, the introduction of state pensions at the beginning of the century produced a media image of the 'old age pensioner', a categorisation and homogenisation of a large age group which many older people, and scholars studying old age, came increasingly to resist. Definitions and images of old age differed according to gender, social condition and race, the latter becoming increasingly important as Britain became increasingly multicultural over the century. 'Old age' plays a variety of roles in modern culture, and many identities are available, serially and simultaneously, to older people, as they are to younger people. Let us look at these definitions, images and roles more closely.

How old is old?

When state pensions were introduced in Britain in 1908 they were payable at age 70. This was the first time in modern history that the British state had defined old age as such.[6] The poor law authorities had strenuously refused to establish an age at which 'old age' was a sufficient qualification in itself for receipt of poor relief; rather, relief was paid at whatever age an individual became too old to be self-supporting (provided that he or she lacked other resources sufficient for survival).[7] The state paid pensions to its own civil servants, from 1857. These were paid initially at the age at which the individual was judged past efficient work and on condition of retirement. From 1910 they were not paid below the age of 60, and retirement with a pension became compulsory at age 65. At the beginning of the twentieth century, very poor old women officially became old later in life than much better off, overwhelmingly male, civil servants.

Even in 1908 the age of 70 was widely regarded as an upper boundary for the onset of old age. In the thirty-year public discussion which preceded the Old Age Pensions Act 1908, there was much resistance, especially among working-class people (the expected targets of the pension), to a fixed pension age. It was argued that both men and women varied widely in the ages at which they became incapable of earning a regular income and that the pension should be paid at the age of incapacity for regular work rather than at a single universal age. The government resisted this potentially costly proposal. When supporters of pensions proposed a fixed age, it was normally 60, or 65, sometimes – with workers in heavy manual trades such as mining in mind – as low as 55. The age of 70 was chosen for a pension funded wholly from government revenue because it was less costly than payment at an earlier age.[8] The choice was immediately criticised as allowing too many people who were visibly 'old' to die in poverty before reaching the pensionable age.

The majority of recipients of the first pensions were female. The pension was means-tested and targeted very poor old people, the great majority of whom in the twentieth century, as in earlier centuries, were women. The pension age was reduced in 1925 to 65, which by that time was popularly accepted as the threshold of old age. Pensions for 65–70 year olds were payable only to regular contributors to the National Insurance scheme, most of whom were male, and to their wives.[9]

There followed, from 1935, a campaign by women, who formed the National Spinsters' Pensions Association, to fight for a lower pensionable age for unmarried women. Unmarried women were as independent-minded in the twentieth century as in the seventeenth and eighteenth, as described by Amy Froide in this volume. The spinsters, as unmarried women were routinely named at this time, argued that unmarried women in their fifties and beyond were discriminated against by employers. The campaigners claimed that male employers preferred to employ younger women whom they regarded as more decorative; though the men often preferred to argue that women declined in competence in their fifties. The spinsters argued that for these reasons women were often forced into retirement in their fifties and so needed a pension at age 55.

A government investigation in 1938 found that it was indeed harder for all women from age 45, but more seriously from 55, to hold or find employment than for men of the same ages or for younger women. The causes were less clear. The report found, as did much other research at this time, that although women outlived men, women had poorer health from earlier ages. However, the report concluded:

> It is impossible to say in a general way that women, married or unmarried, are or are not fit or unfit for work at 55. The answer must depend on the type of work and the physical condition of the woman . . . we feel sure that many are unfit at that age because the conditions of their life have been too hard. In some occupations women are less fit to continue after the age of 55 than others.[10]

The government committee did not investigate charges of discrimination on grounds of appearance or assumptions about the competence of post-menopausal women. It concluded, however, that all women merited a pension at an earlier age than men: married women because, on average, they were five years younger than their husbands and a pension paid at age 60 would enable the couple to receive their pension at much the same age; and it would clearly have been anomalous to exclude unmarried women. The pensionable age for women was reduced to 60 in 1940. In this curious episode – it is still not fully understood why the government acted as it did – the 'old age' of most women was defined in relation to that of men. The 'spinster' campaign suggested that some older women experienced discrimination at this time. It is less clear whether this was greater than before or simply more visible. By the 1930s, more women were employed in a wider range of occupations than before, especially in the 'white blouse' service sector, and were more exposed to possible discrimination.

Pensionable ages remained unchanged after the Second World War, when, from 1946, the right to a pension was extended to the whole population and no longer confined to manual workers. Change was again imposed in 1990 by a European Union ruling that gender differences in pension ages was discriminatory. The British government committed itself in 1993 to equalising the pension age at 65 by 2010.

These changes through the century suggest that the pensionable age was, at best, a malleable definition of when old age was thought to begin, and one which was shaped by political and financial as well as cultural influences. The introduction of state pensions led to the creation of the 'old age pensioner' as a stock description of an old person. Receipt of the very small pension introduced in 1908 did not require the relinquishing of paid employment, though such employment would have had to have been very poorly paid to enable an individual to qualify for a pension under the maximum means limit of £31.50 per year. Similarly, the poor relief system had supplemented very low wages. From 1946, retirement was a condition of receiving the state pension, and increasingly retirement from paid employment at around age 65 became the norm. In consequence a new cultural barrier was erected between older and younger people. In previous centuries, retirement of older people from regular work had been common enough among those who could afford to make the choice. It was an option rarely available to the very poor.[11] It became possible after the Second World War owing to the certainty of pensions at this age and, possibly, by the greater capacity of families to provide help to retired relatives in the greater prosperity of the postwar period. Pensions provided little more than bare subsistence; indeed, it has been argued that they were hardly more generous, relatively, than poor law payments in the 1840s.[12] However, the great difference was that everyone could be sure to receive them on a permanent basis from the age of 60 or 65, whereas poor relief had always been restrictive, uncertain and confined to a minority of the aged poor.[13]

This certainty of a pension affected the lives of older women more directly than retirement. In the late 1940s, most older women were not in paid employment, although their numbers increased steadily over the remainder of the century. For those not working for pay, work, in the form of domestic responsibilities, continued unchanged across the life-course. Even women who retired had normally long carried the double burden of work in and outside the home, and continuing responsibility for domestic work after 'retirement' provided continuity in their everyday lives. For many men, the coming of retirement, sometimes involuntary and unanticipated, created a disruption, a sudden confrontation with old age, which many found shocking and for which they were unprepared, especially among the first generations of manual workers to experience it. More generally, the fact that most older people were no longer active in paid work created a barrier between the lives of older and younger people. Chronological age became more important than functional age in determining access to paid employment and the social status associated with it. More positively, the availability of a period of leisure between working life and physical decline created new possibilities in the later lives of women and men. Faced with rising expectations and greater general affluence in the second half of the twentieth century, more people than ever before could enjoy new possibilities for active retirement. Successive age cohorts were able to imagine and plan for this phase of life as the first generation of retirees of the 1940s and 1950s had not.

The cultural changes in the lives of older people in the mid-twentieth century were dramatic. Not everyone experienced them as gains. Although old people were the age group most likely to be stereotyped as possessing unitary characteristics, in fact social, economic and physical differentiation was greatest at later ages: in terms of age, in a group comprising people from their sixties to past 100; in terms of physical condition, from the very fit to the extremely frail; and in terms of income, since some of the richest and the very poorest were in older age groups; and in terms of image and power. Notwithstanding a commonplace representation of people past their sixties as dependent and fragile, influential older people, in high-status occupations did not retire and relinquish power unless they wished to do so, and they were not necessarily publicly perceived as old. Margaret Thatcher was not defined as weak and decrepit when she remained prime minister past the age of 60, and she remained formidable after her involuntary retirement; nor was Queen Elizabeth II, in her seventies at the end of the century; nor indeed was her great-great grandmother, Queen Victoria, who occupied the throne, aged 81, when the century opened.

In the first seventy years of the twentieth century, society became more clearly stratified by chronological age, signified by fixed ages for leaving school and receiving the state pension. By the end of the century the age boundaries seemed less certain. For many women and men, pensionable age and retirement increasingly diverged. In the 1980s and 1990s, economic pressure, in particular unemployment and business 'downsizing', enabled or forced increasing numbers of people in Britain and elsewhere to retire at an earlier age, from age 50 upwards.[14]

In consequence, the age of retirement from work increasingly diverged from that of physical decline and also from functional and chronological old age as they were scientifically and popularly defined. Improvements in living standards, including diet, and consequently in health, for most of the population had the result that by the 1980s medical opinion placed the onset of serious debility associated with old age at around age 76. Those who were fit and active in the mid-sixties were likely to remain so for at least another decade, though with some weakening, for many people, from the later sixties. At the same time as women and men became physically 'old' later in life, their formal social and economic roles during the years of added vigour appeared to be diminishing. Popular generalisations about the onset of old age in the 1990s placed it later in life than had been the norm earlier in the century. This accorded with real change and was echoed in accounts of personal experience. A refrain of older people, socialised to feel 'old' at a certain age, having reached that age, was: 'I don't feel old'.[15]

Strategies of survival in old age

Old age continued to be popularly associated with poverty throughout the twentieth century, but as in all centuries, by no means were all old people poor. Old women were more likely to be poor than old men. We have already seen that women were more likely than men to qualify for the rigorously means-tested old age pension introduced in 1908. A survey for the Joseph Rowntree Foundation published in 1994 found that the oldest women were still the poorest group in society.[16] The poverty of the 1990s was less horrific than that of the 1900s. B. Seebohm Rowntree succinctly described the life of one of the many poor old women who appeared in his classic study of poverty in York in 1899:

> Widow. Age sixty-three. Two rooms. Takes in washing; most industrious and hard-working. Will not give up work though suffering from a tumour, which should be operated on, would she consent . . . Will not apply to Guardians for help while she can work. This house shares one [water] closet with two other houses and one water-tap with six others.[17]

Improved living standards for older people over the course of the twentieth century were relative to the still faster rise in general levels of affluence, but the causes of poverty among old women described in other essays in this volume for earlier centuries changed little. In the twentieth century, women still outlived men. Some still acquired prosperity and independence as a result of widowhood, but many more lived in poverty having never married (more common in the first half of the century), having been left as widows by poor men, or, an increasing experience in the later twentieth century, following divorce.[18] Women still had fewer opportunities than men to accumulate assets to protect them in later life owing, above all, to more limited opportunities for employment and to lower earnings.

Throughout the century poor old women and men continued to live, as in earlier times, in an 'economy of makeshifts'.[19] Twentieth-century economists gave this struggle for survival a new, if less picturesque, name: 'income packaging'. The main components of the 'package' have remained unchanged through the centuries: paid work, public welfare, savings, family support, charity. We have seen that paid work was a diminishing resource for older people in the second half of the century, and welfare, in the form of pensions, an increasingly secure one. But work had always brought only

Table 10.4 Percentage of elderly men and women reported as living alone, United Kingdom, 1684–1985

Year	Males %	Females %	All %
1684–1769	6	14	10
1891	10	16	13
1901	7	13	10
1911	8	9	9
1921	10	18	14
1951	8	16	13
1962[a]	11	30	22
1980[a]	14	38	28
1985	20	47	36

Source: P. Johnson and J. Falkingham, *Ageing and Economic Welfare* (London, 1992), p.33. Reproduced with permission of Sage Publications.
[a] Those aged over 60.

a limited and inadequate income for the very poor, and pensions have never provided full subsistence. Even in 1951, just a few years after the introduction of the improved postwar pension scheme based on Beveridge's proposals, 767,000 pensioners required a means-tested supplement to the basic pension to ensure their survival.[20] The proportion of old people requiring such a supplement remained more-or-less stable into the 1990s.[21]

It was widely assumed in popular and political discourse and among some scholars, that families were not important providers for the support of older people in modern, highly mobile societies. This was reinforced by the conviction of economists that welfare states 'crowded out' family support and that altruism and reciprocity were redundant in modern market-based societies. This seemed to be supported by statistics of the steadily growing number of old people, especially women, who lived alone (Table 10.4).

These statistics could be, and often were, interpreted as evidence of the increasing isolation of old people from their families. Yet there was also consistent evidence, especially in the second half of the century, that many old people lived alone not because they were neglected, but as a positive choice. At last, growing numbers possessed the resources to exercise the preference for independent living that older people had expressed for centuries.[22] Some, sadly, as at all times were isolated and neglected, sometimes because they had no surviving close family. Nevertheless, the fact that older people lived alone did not necessarily mean that they lacked frequent and close contact with family and friends, who indeed gave support when it was needed, just as old people themselves gave support to others. No more than in earlier centuries could old people be stereotyped as undifferentiated dependants. They gave as well as took: in the case of older women, often in the form of care for grandchildren or sick or disabled friends or relatives. A survey in 1947 found that:

> contact with old people in their homes immediately brings to light the fact that the family is of fundamental importance. This is best seen by the extent to which old people who are ostensibly living alone . . . are in actual fact by no means living alone, but are in close and regular contact with their children.[23]

Moreover,

> the old people had relatives living so close that the limitations imposed by architecture were resolved by family affection – in times of ease each household more or less going its own way, in time of stress functioning together as one unit.[24]

A succession of surveys, up to the end of the century, made the same discovery. The speed and ease of late twentieth-century communications compensated for the effects of greater spatial mobility.[25] Of course, 'family care can be among the very best and the very worst experiences that human beings can devise for one another', which was why many old people preferred to preserve their independence.[26] Furthermore, not all old people possessed surviving close relatives, but in the twentieth century as in earlier centuries[27] women in such a situation often formed networks of friendship which provided the same supportive role as did blood relatives.[28]

The experience of old age

The greater affluence of old people at all levels, the availability of a new and wider range of consumer goods, plus the effects of medical and technological advances profoundly influenced the experience of old age in the twentieth century. New technologies generated new and widely disseminated, images of older people in magazines, advertisements, films and television. Individuals could manipulate their own image with the use of a growing range of items of make-up, hair dyes and cosmetic surgery, together with increasingly widespread attention in the later part of the century to the very long established age-retardants of diet and exercise.[29] All of these techniques, however, were most easily available to the affluent. The use of cosmetics was more acceptable earlier in the century for women, conspicuous adornment having been socially unacceptable for men since the early nineteenth century, though increasingly in the later twentieth century it became acceptable for younger men and discreetly practised by older men.

Disguising the visible signs of age by older women was condemned by some as obeisance to a cult of youth, encouraged by the media, and was said to demonstrate refusal to accept the realities of ageing and to 'grow old gracefully' and 'naturally'. As described in earlier essays, 'natural' ageing, unassisted by adornment or medical intervention, could be far from 'graceful'.[30] The assumption that at a certain age women should cease practices that had been a part of their everyday experience since their teens, or that 60 year olds should not wear certain types of clothes, smacked of another kind of stereotyping, which was generally underpinned by a belief that in earlier times older people had presented themselves 'fittingly', adopting a dress code suited to their years. Like many of the assumptions about change over time which pervade the discourse of ageing, this was incorrect. In 1754, Lady Jane Coke wrote disapprovingly of current fashion trends at court:

> One thing is new, which is there is not such a thing as a decent old woman left, everybody curls their hair, shows their neck, and wears pink, but your humble servant. People who have covered their heads for 40 years now leave off their caps and think it becomes them.[31]

She was neither the first nor the last to criticise older women for refusing to 'be their age', as others saw it.

It was unclear, in the twentieth century as in the eighteenth, who had the right to decree what was a fitting appearance for people at all ages for the sixties to past 100, and why it was 'unnatural' to grow old *dis*gracefully, as some older women preferred. Some commentators, of all ages, still expected a uniformity of behaviour from 'old people' against which a number of old people, perhaps more than in past ages, protested. Rather, they welcomed the increased flexibility of codes of appearance which characterised Britain at the end of the twentieth century.

Medical advances such as hip replacements and heart by-passes improved the quality of life for many older people, despite the neglect of research into the effects upon old people of some of the diseases most likely to kill them, in particular cancer and heart disease.[32] Also, the last days and months of some old people were made miserable by the capacity of modern medical technology to sustain life past the point at which it was worth living.

The menopause was more extensively discussed as a medical problem in the twentieth century, as indeed were many conditions in which scientific medicine made unprecedented advances, and remedies, such as hormone replacement therapy, were introduced to counter the ill-effects experienced by some women due to menopause. However, it remained quite unclear whether the menopause caused women more discomfort than in earlier periods and, if so, to what proportion of women and why. Menopause was less obviously than in previous centuries a visible marker of the onset of old age owing to the proliferation of means to disguise it.[33]

Old age and subjectivity

How old women perceived themselves and how they were perceived by others in the twentieth century can be glimpsed in a variety of personal documents. Many diaries, letters and other private sources exist for the recent past and they can only briefly be sampled here. To take just one example, the energetic, committed, well-to-do social reformer Beatrice Webb reflected in her diary on her own ageing and that of her husband, the Labour Party politician Sidney Webb. She had unusual opportunities to discover how her ageing was perceived by others. On her seventy-fifth birthday in 1933 she recorded:

'Mrs Webb retains to a remarkable degree her mental vigour and industry' observes the *Evening Standard*. Telegrams, greetings, newspapers ringing me up for interviews which I refuse. I don't feel mentally vigorous and industrious, but relative to the senility usual at that age I suppose I am so. And Sidney certainly is so.[34]

She oscillated between commentary on her failing powers and relief at the degree of activity of which she was still capable. She observed the variety of experiences of ageing among her friends and relatives. In 1934 she described a friend:

As a woman verging on seventy, she seems as charming to me as she was as a young one thirty years ago. She used to be good to look at – so she is at present, as a somewhat withered flower; if the form is crippled and movements infirm, there is the same charm of expression.

Beatrice's youngest sister, Rosy, who as a young woman had been a highly problematic anorexic, was now, at close to 70, enjoying greater independence than ever. She was here for a week, between her voyage to the Arctic regions round about Spitsbergen and returning to Majorca for the winter . . . at seventy Rosy is happier and healthier than I have ever known her during her youth and prime of life . . . she has become a globe-trotter with a purpose – the enjoyment and picturing of nature and architecture . . . her husband and children are more or less dependent upon her for subsidies and she certainly is generous with her limited income – travelling third class or cheap tourist, staying at cheap lodging . . . the secret of her happiness is her art, her freedom to go and do as she likes and make casual friends by the way . . .

But an 84 year old friend had slipped into miserable old-old age:

Louise is hopelessly crippled and creeps about the house. Her mind is clear and old age and helplessness have softened her outlook on the world . . . but she is desperately lonely and bored with existence . . . The plain truth is that the aged feel what their children and some of their friends are thinking about: 'If you are not enjoying life, why don't you die and be done with it'. And the old person may feel that there is no answer, except that he does not want to die or does not see any comfortable way of doing it.

Beatrice Webb died, aged 85, in 1943. Her diary conveys an explicit struggle against a stereotype of helpless dependency, initially triumphant, but less successful as time went on. She was an unusual woman in her fame and influence.

Fifty years after Beatrice Webb's death a group of women who were not public figures recorded their own experience of ageing and how they experienced it in others. The Mass Observation archive invited its regular panel of respondents to write about their observations on growing older.[35] Mass Observation was formed in 1937 as a forum for the anthropological study of everyday life in Britain. It went into decline after the Second World War, but was reborn in 1981, amassing observations now by inviting a regular, renewable, panel of 600 people to respond in writing to two annual directives on a variety of topics. Mass Observers were not 'representative' of the British population in any strict, social scientific sense, but nor were they seriously unrepresentative. Naturally they were literate, but so were the great majority of the twentieth-century British population. They were, on the whole, middle class, though many were lower middle class, with some working-class respondents. None appears to be very wealthy, nor did they have serious financial difficulties. Overwhelmingly they appear to be white. They can be said to come from backgrounds comparable to those of a very high proportion on the British population at the end of the twentieth century. They were scattered through the country. Mass Observation provides a unique opportunity to read the opinions, expressed at length and in their own words, of people whose views are rarely recorded. What follows is based on analysis of a sample of the written responses from women to a directive issued in 1992 on the subject of growing older.[36]

A dominant theme of the responses was the relativity of the process of ageing. A 65 year old retired local government officer in Sussex summed up a widespread feeling that: 'it's this habit of wanting to treat all people of a certain age group in the same way that seems wrong, whatever that age group is. People are no longer allowed to be individuals'.[37] A retired library assistant from Rotherham (Yorkshire) commented:

> Now that I am 67 I must consider myself to be 'elderly'. General outlook and attitude seem to be the deciding factor in placing people in age categories. The old saying 'you're as old as you feel' has some truth in it and we all know people who are old at 40 and some who are much older but have an interest in life and an awareness of all about them, who give an impression of comparative youthfulness in spite of the lines and wrinkles.[38]

A 67 year old housewife from Kent wrote:

> These days you aren't classed as old until you are 80. I don't feel old, with fashions very flexible you can look fashionable up to any age. My mother is 95 and she wears fashionable clothes.[39]

A 59 year old retired radiographer also felt 'quite put out when the media describe anyone under 80 as "old". My 100 year old mother has only just agreed to being called "old" '.[40] The 'flexibility' of modern fashion, the disappearance of age-related dress codes was often mentioned as central to the blurring of age boundaries that were widely perceived.[41]

A 74 year old retired barmaid, from Harrogate in Yorkshire wrote:

> Titles of age, young, middle age etc. really don't mean much, do they? I know young people of 25 who are 90 in their head and 90 year olds who are young and outgoing. I decide how to age people by their behaviour . . . I think a lot of age is in your head . . . unless you are unfortunate to have ill-health, even then keeping your mind lively helps.[42]

Such relativism cannot simply be ascribed to self-deception among old women, seeking to deny the unpleasant reality of ageing, for it was shared by some younger women. A shop supervisor from Plymouth in Devon who was approaching the age of 40 discussed in some detail the varieties of ageing she saw among women around her:

I remember my mother saying 'I may be a wrinkled 57 on the outside, but I'm 17 inside', when I caught her playing hopscotch out on the pavement with my daughter. I'm beginning to understand what she meant . . . some people are born 'middle aged' while some old folk sparkle, are open-minded and have a zest for life.

I find it very difficult to estimate people's ages. Indeed age doesn't seem a very important consideration in view of improved housing, nutrition and medicine . . . with extended life expectancy, I believe you can be considered young until late 40s, then be at a peak until 55–66 years (perhaps retirement age is one of life's landmarks) then enjoy a further rewarding and active phase (perhaps this is middle age) until the physical deterioration which eventually comes with advancing years forces you to slow down into 'old age', which can still be a rewarding experience if you have your faculties and a decent standard of living. Of course, there are many factors other than chronological age which determine whether you are perceived to be young, middle-aged or old. Good health . . . social and economic status . . . doing a job one enjoys.

As a volunteer worker for social services, I have supported women I've regarded as being a generation older than myself and suddenly realized that they are ten years younger than me. They have a poor self-image, are worn down by marital and financial problems, are in poor shape physically . . .

On the other hand as a member of a keep-fit association, I am often amazed when fellow-members reveal their ages. Women in their 70s with trim, supple bodies glow with vitality and enthusiasm for life and look twenty years younger.

She compared her parents, mother aged 67, father 70, with her mother-in-law aged 68. Her parents:

dress well and keep abreast of change. Mum is interested in trends in fashion and make-up and adapts them to suit her – they are active, alert and open-minded. They feel they are valued members of society who have 'earned' their retirement . . . [though] everything takes a bit longer now and there are a few twinges.

On the other hand my mother-in-law's whole life has been tied up in the domestic issues of her family. She has no hobbies or special interests, doesn't have strong views on anything and just potters through life. She's perfectly content and a lovely lady but I can't believe she's only a year older than my mother. Her hair turned white years ago. She never wears make-up or colourful, adventurous clothes and has a very diffident manner. To an outsider she must look an 'old lady' whereas my mother is still attractive and a force to be reckoned with![43]

Another woman who was not yet old by any definition, a 47 year old civil servant in Kent, commented:

Old is definitely not for oneself. My mother says 'These old people' . . . not including herself at 80, but she means doddery, decrepit, won't do for themselves, some of them are younger than her.[44]

A 63 year old sales assistant, also from Kent, offered her own 'ages of men' and women, adopting a trope that was centuries old:[45]

at 60 retirement becomes imminent and needs thought
at 70 enjoy what you have, throw caution to the wind
at 80 impart your knowledge of life to others
at 90 sit back and enjoy everything.[46]

Similarly, a 44 year old receptionist described the 'ages of woman', in rather more pessimistic terms:

By 50 the grey hairs might be showing slightly and there might be menopausal problems, but notwithstanding she is still living life to the full. By 60 she might be slowing down, but can still keep up looking after the grandchildren and taking exercise. By 70 and 80 though there is a big difference, with not being as active and having a lined face.[47]

The respondents were divided as to whether women aged faster than men, though most emphasised the negative impact of retirement on men and the benefit to women of the continuity of their working lives at later ages and of the acceptability of the use of cosmetics for women. The receptionist quoted above thought that 'women show their age more than men no matter how careful you are'. The Rotherham respondent thought:

It appears that women are more resilient and are tougher than men in some ways, but I think they age at about the same rate although old men look more decrepit than old women particularly if they have no-one to care for them.[48]

Another retired library assistant, aged 69, from London, wrote:

Men dislike old age more than women because of loss of physical strength. Some women seem to *look* old and so act as frail etc. Men seem to be more vocal over aches and pains.[49]

A 78 year old widow from Winchester (Hampshire) believed:

Men would seem to stay younger until they retire when often they settle down to old age, whereas women have a slow decline . . . Women look younger and stay younger because they take more pride in their appearance. They enjoy looking nice, buying clothes, using cosmetics, having their hair done, all this makes for ageing for women to be superficially slower than men.[50]

The Kent housewife wrote that, 'a woman doesn't seem to age as quickly as a man as she can always find something to do and go out shopping and therefore speaks to other people'.[51] A retired social worker commented that, 'in my experience men deteriorate *mentally* more than women'.[52]

A 39 year old voluntary social worker in 'an award winning day centre for the so-called elderly' observed:

There are some cases where men seem to age rapidly on retirement and seem to feel their lives are over, whilst women if they survive the transition from mother to 'mother-whose-children-have-left-home' often seem to gain a new lease on life. But 'one cannot generalize'.[53]

Relatively few mentioned the menopause, and those who did so had mixed views.[54] A 58 year old clerk in London wrote:

Women are worst affected by ageing, because often they think when they lose their physical attractiveness they are done for. I don't think men care about that quite so much. Then too there is the age barrier of the menopause for women, some women think that once past that, they are indeed 'past it' and there is no equivalent barrier for men, nothing so sudden and drastic.[55]

A 61 year old retired civil servant in Middlesex was more optimistic about the lives of older women: 'Hopefully they will sail through menopause, perhaps with medical help and feel in better health than they have had for years'.[56] A 64 year old secretary/administrator from Hove (Sussex) 'had a very nasty "change of life", but was rescued by HRT which is *the* greatest invention since cut bread'.[57] The relative absence of reference to it suggests that many women experienced menopause in a less negative fashion than commentators have suggested.

A stronger theme was the need and capacity of older people for independence. Inability to sustain independent living emerged as the most important marker of the onset of old age, for women and men. A 60 year old midwife from Grimsby in Lincolnshire stated that ' "old" is when you can no longer do what you want'.[58] The retired library assistant from Rotherham confessed:

Now we come to my fear. I would hate to think that I could not continue to live an independent life in my own home. Having to rely on other people must be dreadful, but how much worse if one is in a Home.[59]

The widow from Winchester wrote:

> I regard anyone under 40 as young. From 45–65 as middle aged. Elderly under 75 and old as 75 plus. *But* although I am aged 78 I do not think of myself as old but elderly. Perhaps because I am fairly independent and can look after myself.[60]

Another woman was willing to:

> give up my own home if disabled, not otherwise. I would *not* expect any of my family to care for me in their own homes.[61]

The retired civil servant from Middlesex wrote:

> I would rather stay in my own home when I am widowed, with my family not too far away or perhaps move to a sheltered flat, or even a home, dependent on my state of mind. I would never make my family feel guilty if they could not care for me. I would not expect them to.[62]

Several respondents expressed fears that when they ceased to live independently they would be stereotyped and patronised. The writer from Rotherham described how an 'old lady' in a residential home:

> was infuriated by the patronizing tone adopted by many of the staff when talking to old people, as though they were half-witted or, at any rate, small children. I used to notice this on my book trolley round on geriatric wards.[63]

This dislike of stereotyping of older people went further; it was seen as undeservedly constraining the lives of older people.[64] A 66 year old retired social worker living in rural Wales commented:

> The need to look young [for men and women] is much more to do with careers and getting jobs. And this is, I think, the crucial point about ageing, how it gets in the way when job hunting or seeking promotion, and in other aspects of social life. Ageism is not seen as a problem like racism or sexism yet it is as damaging and as widespread.[65]

A writer and counsellor living in London expressed her response to conventional stereotypes:

> Yesterday I was 60. There – I have come out and said it. How does it feel? Well a whole lot better than I thought. Never, but never have I so dreaded a birthday. But why should this be such a milestone? We are indoctrinated, that's why. I got my travel pass this morning and hoped I would not bump

into anyone I knew at the office. So I am a Senior Citizen and an old age pensioner? This is ludicrous because I feel 25 going on 18. The years I suppose have been kind to me but no-one stays the same. Still I know my personality is as eccentric and adventurous as it ever was . . . is it my imagination or are people stepping outside the age categories as it becomes increasingly difficult to tell how old they are . . . even if they almost kill themselves with aerobics etc. ultimately it is what is in the mind that is going to make the difference . . . I know a very chic lady, not thin, looks about 65 or so, who has just had her 80th . . . good personality, sharp, attractive . . . Another local lady died before Christmas at 89 years . . . again, good personality and she kept her own house to the end . . . But I cannot say I would wish to be another age or that there was a favourite time. NOW! That's it. Never have I been so happy, secure, had a job I love with such satisfying hobbies and interests.[66]

This optimistic woman had a good marriage to a younger man, following an earlier disastrous marriage. The ageing of their husbands influenced the outlook of many women on their own ageing. A 67 year old retired clerk wrote:

I feel considerably older than I did even five years ago, probably because I have a husband who has Parkinson's disease and I am unable to leave him to himself for more than a week . . . I am not enjoying getting old and I don't believe if everyone was honest they would not agree with me.[67]

Individual personality and other aspects of their environment affected the women's outlooks on ageing. A 54 year old information assistant from the Isle of Wight wrote:

I have lived too long. I am not decrepit but I no longer think the world such a wonderful place. I live in an insular community where progress is slow.

The writers had divided views about whether older people were respected in British society, a question they were asked to respond to by the directive owing, no doubt, to a widespread view in late twentieth-century society that old people were less respected than in 'the past'. In general they took a relativistic view. The Harrogate ex-barmaid wrote: 'Respect, what on earth is that? Lots of people today have no respect for themselves, never mind old people'.[68] The London clerk wrote:

No. I don't think we respect elderly people. I think the general feeling is 'they've had their life, why don't they just die and make room for younger people'. Respect in this country at this time seems to be tied very much to money and earning capacity. We respect rich people, and a rich old person is respected for his wealth, not his age.[69]

A 52 year old Shropshire school secretary reflected:

> I am beginning to be aware of a lack of respect for age and experience . . .
> haven't all older people felt that the younger generation have little respect
> for them. I doubt today's younger people are any different to previous
> generations.[70]

The retired social worker in Wales felt that she had 'lost status by retiring,
no one asks my opinion any more'.[71] On the other hand, an 'almost 65' year
old housewife from Lancashire thought:

> Yes, I think most people respect the elderly. In fact some elderly don't respect
> the younger ones today.[72]

Others were unwilling to generalise.[73] A 48 year old carer commented:

> No, I don't think as a society we respect older people en masse, but I cer-
> tainly respect my older friends in Oldham.[74]

A part-Chinese civil servant aged 47 commented:

> We were brought up to respect our grandparents and that attitude continues
> in this family (the Chinese influence) but this means that grandparents are
> remote. They get their own way and people running round after them but
> they are not their grandchildren's friends.[75]

Several writers discussed the changing experience of old people over the
century by making comparisons between their own ageing and that of their
parents and grandparents. A retired social worker from South London recalled:

> my grandparents did not *do* very much outside their homes whereas my
> elderly and old friends attend day classes (university extra-mural) and visit
> family and friends in this country and abroad.[76]

Or they recalled memories of their own attitudes earlier in life. A 44 year
old receptionist from Preston, Lancashire, wrote:

> When I was 20 or 30 then 50 seemed quite old to me. In the 1980s 50s can
> be seen as attractive, interesting, experienced and valuable. This wasn't the
> case in the 1960s when I was in my teens as the Twiggy thin-as-rake look was
> in and everything seemed to revolve around teenagers . . . I don't think of 60
> year olds as doddery any more but only as middle-aged.[77]

Conclusion

The Mass Observation respondents quoted here provide valuable expressions of how individual women perceived and experienced the major changes in the lives of older people over the twentieth century. Above all, survival to old age became an almost universal experience and it acquired new characteristics: by the second half of the century most people retired from paid employment while they were still physically fit, with a secure, if not necessarily large, income; more people remained active to a late age while having access to a greater range of activities. These experiences were shared by men and women, though not always in identical ways: women were less likely than men to experience retirement from paid employment as a seriously disruptive break in the life-course, partly because their places in the labour market were less secure than those of men; in consequence women were more likely than men to suffer poverty in old age. But this had long been so.

The Mass Observation respondents also point to long-term continuities between the experiences of the late twentieth century and the earlier centuries discussed in other essays of this volume. Still women outlived men, but often not in better health, owing largely to their greater poverty. Still there was immense variety in the living conditions of old people, from the very rich to the very poor, struggling in the 'economy of makeshifts', from the very active to the sadly decrepit. We also see continuing through the centuries a resistance to simple chronological definitions of old age and awareness of difference in individual experiences of ageing; also the persistence of stereotypes of appropriate behaviour for old women, and of resistance to those stereotypes, combined with strong feelings about the importance of independence and assertion of the capacity of very many (but sadly not all) people at late ages to control their own life and to play a role in their family and their community.

Notes

1. E.A. Wrigley and R. Scholfield, *The Population History of England, 1541–1871* (Cambridge, 1989).

2. Pat Thane, 'The debate on the declining birth-rate in Britain: the "menace" of an ageing population, 1920s–1950s', *Continuity and Change* 5 (1990), no.2 pp.283–304.

3. World Bank, *Averting the Old Age Crisis* (Washington, D.C., 1994).

4. Lincoln Day, *The Future of Low Birth-rate Populations* (London, 1992); P. Johnson and J. Falkingham, *Ageing and Economic Welfare* (London, 1992); P. Thane, 'Old age: burden or benefit?', in H. Joshi, ed., *The Changing Population of Britain* (Oxford, 1989), pp.56–71.

5. See Botelho in this volume.

6. Although it had, long before, defined ages (normally 60 or 70) at which people were deemed too old for certain tasks, such as army or jury service. Botelho, this volume, p.47.

7. See Botelho, this volume, p.49.

8. Pat Thane, 'Contributory versus non-contributory old age pensions, 1878–1908', in Pat Thane, *The Origins of British Social Policy* (London, 1978), pp.84–106.

9. For details, see P. Thane, *The Foundations of the Welfare State*, 2nd edn (London, 1996), pp.184–7.

10. *Report of the Committee on Pensions for Unmarried Women*, Parliamentary Papers, 1938–39, Vol. 14.

11. L. Hannah, *Inventing Retirement* (Cambridge, 1986).

12. D. Thomson, 'The decline of social welfare: falling state support for the elderly since Victorian times', *Ageing and Society* 4 (1984), pp.451–82.

13. E.H. Hunt, 'Paupers and pensioners: past and present', *Ageing and Society* 9 (1989), p.451.

14. Martin Kohli, Martin Rein, Anne-Marie Guillemard and Herman van Gunsteren, *Time for Retirement: Comparative Studies of Early Exit from the Labor Force* (New York, 1991).

15. Paul Thompson, Catherine Itzin and Michelle Abendstern, *I Don't Feel Old* (Oxford, 1990).

16. Joseph Rowntree Foundation, *Inquiry into Income and Wealth*, Joseph Rowntree Foundation (York, 1995).

17. B. Seebohm Rowntree, *Poverty: A Study of Town Life* (London, 1902), p.63.

18. See Schen, this volume.

19. Ibid.

20. Rodney Lowe, *The Welfare State in Britain since 1945* (London, 1993), p.144.

21. Johnson and Falkingham, *Ageing*, p.54.

22. See Froide, this volume.

23. J.H. Sheldon, *The Social Medicine of Old Age* (Oxford, 1949).

24. Ibid., p.152.

25.   P. Townsend, *The Family Lives of Old People* (London, 1960); idem, 'Surveys of old age in Great Britain, 1945–1958', *Bulletin of the World Health Organization* No. 21 (Geneva, 1959); P. Townsend and D. Wedderburn, *The Aged in the Welfare State* (London, 1965); Raymond First, Jane Hubert and Anthony Forge, *Families and their Relatives: Kinship in a Middle-class Sector of London* (London, 1969); H. Qureshi and A. Walker, 'Caring for elderly people; the family and the state', in C. Phillipson and A. Walker, eds, *Ageing and Social Policy: A Critical Assessment* (Aldershot, 1986), pp.109–27; G. Claire Wenger, *The Supportive Network: Coping with Old Age* (London, 1984); Janet Finch, *Family Obligations and Social Change* (Cambridge, 1989); M. Rein and H. Salzman, 'Social integration, participation and exchange in five industrial countries', in Scott A. Bass, ed., *Older and Active* (New Haven, CN, 1995), pp.237–62.

26.   Qureshi and Walker, 'Caring for elderly people', p.117.

27.   See Froide, this volume.

28.   Claire Jarvis, 'Family and friends in old age and the implications for informal support', Working paper No. 6, Institute of Gerontology, King's College, London, 1993.

29.   Pat Thane, 'Geriatrics', in W.F. Bynum and Roy Porter, eds, *Companion Encyclopaedia of the History of Medicine*, Vol. 2 (London, 1993), pp.1092–118.

30.   See Botelho, this volume.

31.   Quoted in Anne Buck, *Dress in Eighteenth Century England* (New York, 1979), p.3405. I am indebted to Lynn Botelho for this reference.

32.   Medical Research Council, 1994.

33.   See Botelho, this volume.

34.   This and the following three extracts from Beatrice Webb's diary are taken from N. and J. MacKenzie, *The Diaries of Beatrice Webb*, Vol. 4 (London, 1986).

35.   These materials are housed in the library of the University of Sussex.

36.   The sample consists of about 10 per cent (56) of the female responses to this directive.

37.   Mass Observation, *Growing Older*, file C 2091. (Hereafter cited as file number only.)

38.   B 60.

39.   B 1665.

40.   B 2154. On old age starting at 80, see also B 2611; C 1786; C 2142; C 1878, aged 72, chose 85 as the age at which old age started.

41.   B 2258.

42. B 736. See also B 122; B 1281; B 1521; B 1665; B 2134; B 1386; B 2197; B 2258; B 2605; B 2670; C 1624; C 1405; C 1713; C 1786; C 1878; C 1883; c 2053; C 2079; C 2091; C 2295; C 2142.

43. B 1215.

44. C 1990.

45. The directive invited respondents to 'try setting out your thoughts on a man or woman of 20, 30, 40, 50, 60, 70, 80, 90'.

46. B 1521.

47. C 1715.

48. B 60; see also B 2170.

49. B 86.

50. B 2646; see also B 2671.

51. B 1424; see also C 1878 and C 2142.

52. C 1405.

53. B 2197, C 2070.

54. Other surveys showed that, contrary to stereotype, most women experienced little difficulty with menopause and did not view its effects on their lives negatively. J. Harrison, 'Women and ageing: experience and implications', *Ageing and Society* 3 (1983), no.2, pp.209–35, and Sara Arber and Jay Ginn, *Gender and Later Life* (London, 1991), pp.460–7.

55. B 1665; see also B 1553; B 2066; and B 1386.

56. B 2605.

57. B 2671.

58. B 2605.

59. See also C 602; C 1990. See also Hussey, this volume, and the residual fear of life in the workhouse.

60. B 2645.

61. C 1624.

62. B 2605.

63. B 60.

64. C 2087.

65. B 1553.

66. B 1120.

67. A 1223.

68. B 736.

69. B 1665; B 2258.

70. B 1386.

71. B 1533; see also B 1521 and C 1786.

72. B 1661.

73. B 2611.

74. C 2078; see also C 2091.

75. C 1990.

76. C 1405.

77. C 1713; C 2142.

Older women in Britain since 1500

LYNN BOTELHO AND PAT THANE

Older women have existed in all societies, at all times. Yet their arrival in the historiography of England, of women, and of old age itself, has been relatively recent and their presence remains relatively scarce. Most of what we know of the lives of elderly women in the past has been garnered as academic by-product, the peripheral facts generated by research with other aims. Consequently, any bibliography of older women in England will include items whose main focus lies elsewhere.

Unlike the history of ageing in the United States, there is no general survey as yet published for Great Britain, although Pat Thane's *Old Age in English History* (Oxford, 2000) will do much to correct this imbalance. Keith Thomas's 'Age and authority in early modern England', *Proceedings of the British Academy* 62 (1976), pp.3–46, despite its age, is still a standard reference for early modern England. Joel Rosenthal's *Old Age in Late Medieval England* (Philadelphia, 1996) surveys aspects of old age for the medieval period. Both largely overlook women, as does G. Minois' *History of Old Age: From Antiquity to the Renaissance* (Cambridge, 1989), which includes among its many sweeping and unreliable generalisations the assertion that few women lived to be old due to death in childbirth. S. Shahar's largely English-based *Growing Old in the Middle Ages* (Tel-Aviv, 1995, trans. London, 1997) pays more attention to women.

One contested area of research is the question of what point marks the onset of old age. The pioneering study is J. Roebuck, 'When does old age begin? The evolution of the English definition', *Journal of Social History* 12 (1979), pp.416–29, which is concerned primarily with nineteenth- and twentieth-century England. Shahar has addressed this issue for the medieval and early modern periods in 'Who were the old in the middle ages?', *Social History of Medicine* 6 (1993), pp.313–42 and in her *Growing Old in the Middle*

Ages. Rosenthal, in *Old Age in Late Medieval England*, for his part, argues against trying to pin down precise ages and for the use of 'rough assessments' and 'approximate numbers' when considering this issue (p.32).

While not suitable for determining the exact ages that delineate the different stages of life, the 'ages of man' literature is extremely useful for insights into the cultural, physical and spiritual aspects of ageing in the pre-modern world. Historical writing on this subject is extensive, and only the most useful are included here. The classic study is J.A. Burrow's *The Ages of Man: A Study in Medieval Writing and Thought* (Oxford, 1998). Elizabeth L. Sear's *The Ages of Man: Medieval Interpretations of the Life Cycle* (Princeton, NJ, 1986) also offers insights, though it has been criticised for not engaging with the spiritual aspects of this literary device. Other useful contributions include: R.S. Guyot, 'A new theory about the ages of man' and T.R. Cole's response, 'Comments on Roland S. Guyot's "A new theory about the ages of man" ', *International Journal of Aging and Human Development* 36 (1992/93), pp.91–8, 98–101; and W.W. Jones, 'Observations on the origin of the division of man's life into stages', *Archaelogia* 35 (1853), pp.167–98. The only analysis dedicated to the life of women is M. Dove's *The Perfect Age of a Man's Life*, chapter 3, 'The ages of woman's life'. Dove concludes that the ages of man either subsumed women under the rubric of 'man' or did not discuss them at all.

This same emphasis has been true of the writing of the history of old age. Here, too, the female experience has tended to be ignored. J. Roebuck's 'Grandma as revolutionary: elderly women and some modern patterns of social change', *International Journal of Aging and Human Development* 17 (1983), pp.249–66, and C. Russell's 'Ageing as a feminist issue', *Women's Studies International Forum* 10 (1987) pp.125–32, are important counter-developments at the general level. At present, there is no dedicated survey of older women in Britain. T.L. Premo's *Winter Friends: Women Growing Old in the New Republic, 1785–1835* (Urbana, IL, 1990) provides a useful framework, despite its concentration on the early United States. Similarly, Peter Stearns' 'Old Women: some historical observations', *Journal of Family History* 5 (1980), pp.44–57, is fundamentally concerned with France, but he extends a number of his conclusions to northern Europe in general. A wide and sweeping survey that includes England's Queen Elizabeth I, among many others, is L.W. Banner's, *In Full Flower: Aging Women, Power, and Sexuality: A History* (New York, 1992).

One of the first areas of research to place older women in an historical setting was the study of household formations. An excellent introduction to the subject is D. Kertzer's 'Toward a historical demography of aging', in D. Kertzer and P. Laslett, eds, *Aging in the Past: Demography, Society, and Old Age* (Berkeley, CA, 1995), pp.363–83. For English-specific interpretations, see P. Laslett, 'The traditional English family and the aged in our society', in David Van Tassel, ed., *Aging, Death and the Completion of Being* (Philadelphia, 1979), pp.97–113, and R. Wall, 'Elderly persons and members of their households in England and Wales from preindustrial times to the present', in Kertzer and Laslett, *Aging*, pp.81–106, and his 'Women alone in English society', *Annales de Demographie Historique* 17 (1981). On patriarchalism in English households and the importance for the elderly of maintaining household headship, see H.C. Johansen, 'Growing old in an urban environment', *Continuity and Change* 2 (1987), pp.297–305; P. Laslett, 'The history of population and social structure', *International Social Science Journal* 17 (1965), pp.582–93, and G.J. Schochet, 'Patriarchalism, politics and mass attitudes in Stuart England', *The Historical Journal* 12 (1969), pp.413–14.

The construction of households of older people has also been explored in the light of the 'modernisation theory', which assumes the loss of status among the elderly as a result of industrialisation. In support of this theory, see D.S. Smith's 'Modernization and the family structure of the elderly', *Zeitschrift für Gerontologie* 17 (1984), pp.251–69. J. Quadagno is deeply critical, however, of this thesis in her *Aging and Early Industrial Society: Work, Family and Social Policy in Nineteenth-century England* (London, 1982).

A type of household common among older spinsters and widows was the 'clustering' of older women living together in one house for companionship and economic relief. See Olwen Hufton's 'Women without men: widows and spinsters in Britain and France in the eighteenth century', *Journal of Family History* 9 (1984), pp.355–74, and M. Anderson, *Family Structure in Nineteenth-century Lancashire* (Cambridge, 1971) and his 'The social position of spinsters in mid-Victorian Britain', *Journal of Family History* 9 (1984), pp.377–93.

For recent studies of single women in pre-modern England, including aspects of ageing, see: Pamela Sharpe, 'Literally spinsters: a new interpretation of local economy and demography in Colyton in the seventeenth and eighteenth centuries', *Economic History Review* 44 (1991), pp.46–65, and Judith M. Bennett and Amy M. Froide, eds, *Single Women in the European Past* (Philadelphia, 1998). For information on single women in modern Europe, including England, see: Martha Vicinus, *Independent Women: Work and Community for Single Women 1850–1920* (Chicago, 1985); the special issue on spinsters in *Journal of Family History* 15 (1990); and Maura Palazzi, 'Female solitude and patrilineage: unmarried women and widows during the eighteenth and nineteenth centuries', *Journal of Family History* 15 (1990), pp.443–59.

While the clustering of widows has only recently begun to be studied, there is a large and extensive literature on widows more generally. However, exploration of the conjunction of old age and widowhood is less fully explored. See: R.E. Archer, 'Rich old ladies: the problem of late medieval dowagers', in A.J. Pollard, ed., *Property and Politics* (Gloucester, 1984), pp.15–35; Lynn Botelho, ' "The old woman's wish": widows by the family fire?. Widows' old age provisions in rural England', *Journal of Family History* (special edition, forthcoming); S.J. Wright, 'The elderly and the bereaved in eighteenth-century Ludlow', in Margaret Pelling and Richard M. Smith, eds, *Life, Death and the the Elderly: Historical Perspectives* (London, 1991), pp.102–33; and James E. Smith, 'Widowhood and ageing in traditional English society', *Ageing and Society* 4 (1984), pp.429–49. Finally, the early modern stereotype of the aged widow has been compared to reality in C. Carlton's 'The widow's tale: male myths and female reality in sixteenth and seventeenth century England', *Albion* 10 (1978), pp.130–51, and in Barbara Todd's, 'The remarrying widow: a stereotype reconsidered', in Mary Prior, ed., *Women in English Society 1500–1800* (New York, 1985), pp.55–81.

The stereotype of old women, especially in pre-industrial England, has received a great deal of scholarly interest, particularly that of old women as witches and 'ignorant midwives'. See: E. Bever, 'Old age and witchcraft in early modern Europe', in P. Stearns, ed., *Old Age in Preindustrial Society* (New York, 1982), pp.150–90; D. Harley, 'Historians as demonologists: the myth of the midwife-witch', *Social History of Medicine* 3 (1990), pp.1–26; D. Harley, 'Ignorant midwives – a persistent stereotype', *Bulletin of the Society for the Social History of Medicine* 28 (1981), pp.6–9; A. Summers, 'The mysterious demise of Sarah Gamp: the domiciliary nurse and her detractors, c.1830–1860', *Victorian Studies* 32 (1989), pp.365–86; and A. Wilson, 'Ignorant midwives – a rejoinder', *Bulletin of the Society for the Social History of Medicine* 32 (1983), pp.46–9. Margaret Pelling's 'Thoroughly resented? Older women and the medical role in early modern London', in L. Hunter and S. Hutton, eds, *Women, Science and Medicine 1500–1700* (Stroud, 1997), pp.63–88, explores the facts behind the stereotype. Janet Roebuck and colleagues have explored stereotypes in nineteenth- and twentieth-century Britain, stressing the co-existence of positive and negative representations even of poor old women: J. Roebuck and J. Slaughter, 'Ladies and pensioners: stereotypes and public policy affecting old women in England, 1880–1940', *Journal of Social History* 13 (1979), pp.105–16.

The representation of old age projected by scholars tends to reflect a full range of stereotypes about the elderly; however, historians of the United States and Europe differ as to which view of old age they favour, as David Troyansky explains in his historiographical essay on old age: 'Historical research into ageing, old age and older people', in Anne Jamieson, Sarah Harper and Christina Victor, eds, *Critical Approaches to Ageing and Later Life* (Buckingham, 1997), pp.49–61. According to Troyansky, scholars of the United States tend to cast old age as a negative experience, while those writing of Europe have represented old age as widely varied over time and place. Pat Thane's 'Aging in the West', in T. Cole, ed., *Handbook of the Humanities and Aging*, 2nd edn (New York, 1999) contrasts approaches to the history of old age in the 'old world' of western Europe, and in the 'new' worlds of North America, Australia and New Zealand, as well as the different experiences of old age in each country. She also points out in her 'The cultural history of old age', *Australian Cultural History* 14 (1995), pp.23–39, that understandings of old age are culturally constructed and that many historians present old age in an excessively simple master narrative, one that reflects above all their own culturally constructed hopes and fears. See, too, her article on perceptions and self-perceptions of nineteenth- and twentieth-century older women, in the *Journal of Family History* 25, 2 (April 2000), pp.235–47.

As discussed in the Introduction of this book and in Thane's essay, the twentieth century has witnessed the emergence of a large, healthy and physically active group of retired older people experiencing the 'Third Age'. Peter Laslett's *A Fresh Map of Life: The Emergence of the Third Age* (London, 1989) is vital reading in this regard. See also L. Bonfield's 'Was there a "Third Age" in the pre-industrial past? Some evidence from the law', in J. Eekelaar and D. Pearl, eds, *An Aging World: Dilemmas and Challenges for Law and Social Policy* (Oxford, 1989), pp.37–53.

Pat Thane's, 'The debate on the declining birth rate in Britain: the "menace" of an ageing population, 1920s–1950s', *Continuity and Change* 5 (1990), pp.283–305, examines the alarmist reaction to awareness of the growing numbers of older people in the mid twentieth-century population. The shift in the age structure of Britain contributed to a number of significant social and economic changes, including the 'invention' of retirement from paid work as a norm for people aged 60–65. See: S. Harper and P.M. Thane, 'The consolidation of "old age" as a phase of life, 1945–1965', in M. Jefferys, ed., *Growing Old in the Twentieth Century* (London, 1989), pp.43–61; Paul Johnson, 'The employment and retirement of older men in England and Wales, 1881–1981', *Economic History Review* 47 (1994), no.1, pp.106–28; and A. Walker, 'The social division of early retirement', in Jefferys, ed., *Growing Old in the Twentieth Century*, pp.73–90. Paul Johnson's arguments are unconvincingly challenged by John Macnicol's *The Politics of Retirement in Britain, 1878–1948* (Cambridge, 1998). Macnicol, like some other social scientists, interprets the spreading of retirement, state old age pensions, geriatric medicine and other services for old people as outcomes of their deliberate marginalisation and a deepening of their dependency due to the influence of economically powerful groups, such as employers, in twentieth-century Britain. Such ahistorical arguments overestimate the independence of poorer old people in earlier centuries. See too: P. Townsend, 'The structured dependency of the elderly: creation of social policy in the twentieth century', *Ageing and Society* 1 (1981), pp.5–29. But, see the challenge by P. Johnson, 'The structured dependency of the elderly: a critical note', in Jefferys, ed., *Growing Old in the Twentieth Century*, pp.62–72.

The question of who cares for the elderly, particularly the elderly poor, is often discussed in relation to the 'nuclear–hardship' hypothesis, which postulates that the collectivity, in essence the parish and community, rather than adult children and immediate family supported the aged when they could no longer work to support themselves. For a full explanation of this theory, see: P. Laslett, 'Family, kinship and collectivity as systems of support in preindustrial Europe: a consideration of the "nuclear–hardship" hypothesis', *Continuity and Change* 3 (1988), pp.153–76. See also: D. Thomson, 'The decline of social welfare: falling state support for the elderly since early Victorian times', *Ageing and Society* 4 (1984), pp.451–82, and his 'The welfare of the elderly in the past: a family or community responsibility?', in M. Pelling and R.M. Smith, *Life, Death and the Elderly*, pp.194–221; E.H. Hunt's challenge in 'Paupers and pensioners: past and present', *Ageing and Society* 9 (1989), pp.407–30; and R.M. Smith, 'The structured dependence of the elderly: a twentieth-century creation?', *Bulletin of the Society for the Social History of Medicine* 34 (1984), pp.35–41. A challenge to this thesis is also offered by M. Anderson in his *Family Structure in Nineteenth-century Lancashire* and Marguerite Dupree in *Family Structure in the Staffordshire Potteries, 1840–1888* (London, 1995). The role of adult children and the immediate family in the care of older people is debated. For example, see: M. Evandrou, S. Arber, A. Dale and G.N. Gilbert, 'Who cares for the elderly? Family care provision and receipt of statutory service', in C. Phillipson, M. Bernard, and P. Strang, eds, *Dependency and Interdependency in Old Age* (London, 1986); J. Robin, 'The role of offspring in the care of the elderly: a comparison over time, 1851–1881', *Ageing and Society* 4 (1984), pp.505–16; D. Thomson, ' "I am not my father's keeper": families and the elderly in nineteenth-century England', *Law and History Review* 2 (1984), pp.265–86, and his 'The welfare of the elderly in the past: a family or community responsibility', in Pelling and Smith's *Life, Death and the Elderly*, pp.194–222. These tend to play down family support for older people, but see: Pat Thane, 'Old people and their families in the English past', in Martin Daunton, ed., *Charity, Self-interest and Welfare in the English Past* (New York, 1996), pp.113–38, and Pat Thane, 'The family lives of old people', in Paul Johnson and Pat Thane, eds, *Old Age from Antiquity to Post-modernity* (1998), pp.180–210, and Paul Johnson's introduction to the same volume, 'Historical readings of old age and ageing', pp.1–18.

The women who typically provide this care in the modern world, as well as the older women who receive it, is addressed by K.R. Allen, *Single Women? Family Ties: Life Histories of Older Women* (Newbury Park, CA, 1989) and

J. Lewis and B. Meredith, *Daughters Who Care: Daughters Caring for Mothers at Home* (London, 1989).

The historiography of poverty in England is extensive, and much of it addresses the age-old conjunction of old age and financial destitution, but there is little scholarship specifically tuned to the aged, female poor though it is often pointed out that older women have always suffered a higher risk of poverty than older men. The following is a limited sample of some of the most relevant items: M. Barker-Read, 'The treatment of the aged poor in five selected West Kent parishes from Settlement to Speenhamland (1662–1797)', unpublished PhD thesis (Open University, 1988); Lynn Botelho, 'Aged and impotent: parish relief of the aged poor in early modern Suffolk', in Daunton, ed., *Charity, Self-interest and Welfare*, pp.91–112; Margaret Pelling, 'Old age, poverty and disability in early modern Norwich: work, remarriage and other expedients', in M. Pelling, *The Common Lot: Sickness, Medical Occupations and the Urban Poor in Early Modern England* (London, 1998), pp.134–54; her 'Older women: household, caring and other occupations in the late sixteenth-century town', in Pelling, *The Common Lot*, pp.155–75; her 'Old age and poverty in early modern town', *Bulletin of the Society for the Social History of Medicine* 34 (1984), pp.42–7; and her 'Old age, poverty, and disability in early modern Norwich: work, remarriage and other expedients', in *Life, Death and the Elderly*, pp.74–102; as well as T. Wales, 'Poverty, poor relief and the life-cycle: some evidence from seventeenth-century Norfolk', in Smith, ed., *Land, Kinship and Life-cycle* (Cambridge, 1984), pp.351–404.

Finally, there exist four useful historiographical essays on old age. Margaret Pelling's and Richard M. Smith's Introduction to their *Life, Death and the Elderly*, pp.1–39 is an extremely comprehensive presentation, through to 1991, of the published literature on ageing, primarily in western Europe. David Troyansky's piece, 'Historical research into ageing, old age and older people', cited above, is a useful large-scale overview of the research trends in both the United States and Europe; while Pat Thane's 'Aging in the West' is an impressive encapsulation of the current state of the field. Of particular relevance to the history of old women is Marjorie C. Feinson's 'Where are women in the history of aging', *Social Science History* 9 (1985), pp.429–52.

INDEX

advice books, 6, 53
age, 15, 31–2
  assignment, 32
  authority, 25, 69–70, 101, 102
  calculation, 91
  chronological, 4, 14, 15, 44, 46, 212,
    213
  cultural, 4, 43, 44, 46, 48–52, 53,
    60
  discrimination, 211
  distribution, 49
  exaggeration, 15
  functional, 4, 14–15, 17, 44, 46, 47,
    49, 212, 213
  recording, 15, 32, 91, 112
  respect, 225–6
  self-respect, 225
  wisdom, 101
ageing, 60, 67, 236
  gendered, 60, 67
  historiography, 67
  male, 51
  marriage, 68
  medical intervention, 217
  mental abilities, 79
  physical signs, 6, 54–6, 61fn, 67,
    79–80
  perceived, 225, 226–7
  preoccupation, 67
  process, 43, 45, 47, 49, 54, 66, 67, 70,
    213, 220, 222
  self-perception, 70, 71
  stages, 69
  stereotypes, 72
Ages of Man, 45, 46, 47, 51, 91, 232–3
Ages of Woman, 46, 222–3
Allen, K.R., 237
almshouse, 114, 142, 167
  see also charity
Anatomy Act (1832), 199

Anderson, M., 234, 237
anorexia, 218
Appleby, Andy, 58
Arber, S., 237
Archer, R.E., 234
Aristotle, 45, 51
assistance, mutual, 35
astrology, 46
autobiography, 188

Banner, L.W., 233
barber surgeons, 20
barbers, 37
Barker-Read, Mary, 238
bastardy, 21–2, 25, 26,
Beauvoir, Simone de, 54
Bedlam Hospital, 23
Bennett, Judith M., 234
bereavement, 103
Bever, E., 235
Bible, 69, 75, 168
Blythe, Ronald, 203
board of guardians, 190, 194, 195, 200,
  201
Bonfield, L., 236
Botelho, Lynn, 4, 8, 235, 238
Boulton, Jeremy, 33
Brabazon Scheme, 177, 181
burial registers, 14, 15
Burnett, John, 188
Burrow, J.A., 233

capitalism, 5, 9
Carlton, C., 235
celibacy, 72
Census of the Poor (Norwich, 1570), 8,
  31–3, 36, 38
  census, 141
  data collection, 32, 36
  percentage elderly, 34

census-type documents, 112, 141
charity, 7, 49, 78, 101, 172, 180–1
  alms, 7, 37
  almshouse, 167
  blankets, 168
  coal, 168
  clothing, 15
  education, 167
  food, 16, 19–20, 168
  friends, 35
  funeral, 15–16, 19, 20
  kin, 35
  private, 17
  reform, 13, 22, 25, 26
  religious, 13, 18–19
  rent, 15, 20, 21
  wills, 25
childbirth, 90, 92
childrearing, 66, 90
  see also motherhood
Children's Act (1908), 200
Christ's Hosptial, 24, 78
churchwardens, 23, 24, 58
  accounts, 4, 14
climacteric, 53
  see also menopause
Cole, T.R., 233
collectivity, 16–18, 26, 102–3
  see also provisions for the elderly
College of Surgeons, 21
commonplace books, 53, 67
confraternities, 17
co-residence, 24, 112–16, 121, 126–30,
    137, 151, 157, 160–1
  care, 121
  children, 144–6, 149–50, 151–7,
    161–2
  employment, 154, 156, 157, 159, 160
  Europe, 151, 158, 162
  gendered, 144–5, 160
  inheritance customs, 157
  married child, 145–6
  men, 159–60
  moral support, 121
  never-married child, 145–6, 179
  non-kin, 140, 161, 174
  poor, 114, 116, 159, 160
  rural, 162
  spouse, 144–5, 149–50, 191
  status, 157–60, 161, 162
  urban, 162
  widow, 153, 154

  widower, 153, 154
  women, 125–6, 159–60
  see also household structure
cosmetics, elderly, 216–17, 222
Cowper, Lady Sarah, 55, 56
crime, 26
Crusader Kingdoms, 48

Dale, A., 237
Deane, Theresa, 9
death, 6, 8, 58, 66, 69, 71, 76, 79, 84,
    103, 172, 186, 190, 191, 198,
    199, 202
  burial clubs, 199
demography, 2, 9, 34, 67, 90–2, 112
  birth rates, 207
  determinism, 32
  historical, 32, 44, 125
  mortality rates, 31, 207
  nuptiality, 143
  structure, 4
  see also fertility; microsimulaiton;
    mortality; population modelling
diaries, 4, 47, 66, 68, 78, 79, 83, 112,
    218
  form, 67
  legal record, 76–7
  methodology, 66–7
diet, 51, 54, 56, 57–8, 59, 213
  the poor, 58, 60
  see also workhouse
disability, 34, 37, 51, 93, 216, 224
disorder, 21, 22, 38
District Nursing Association, 180
District Visitor, 169–70, 171, 172
Dobson, Mary, 59
Dove, M., 233
Dupree, Marguerite, 237

economy, 112
  determinism, 32
  informal ('black'), 36
  see also employment
'economy of makeshifts', 8, 13, 18,
    214–15
  see also survival stratagies
elderly
  economic power, 3
  percentage of population, 31–2, 34,
    91–2, 207, 209
  physically fit, 227
  political power, 3

elderly (*continued*)
  sexual activity, 72
  see also ageing; old age
employment, 31–2, 36, 51, 97–100, 166,
    197, 211–12, 224, 227
  age discrimination, 224
  availability, 36
  by-employment, 36
  farmer, 191
  female, 15–16, 20–1, 36–9, 58, 87,
    212
  femme sole, 97
  gendered, 36–9, 187
  housekeeper, 173
  knitting, 37, 98
  laws, 48
  male, 20
  marital status, 211
  medical, 16, 20–1, 37–8, 235
  midwife, 20
  moral overseers, 21–2, 25
  never-married women, 98, 211
  nurse, 16, 20, 21, 37–8, 54, 93, 104,
    168, 173, 179, 225
  odd jobs, 16
  parish, 16, 17, 20–1
  poor, 20, 36–9
  psychological benefit, 99–100
  servant, 22, 46, 58, 98, 173
  spinning, 37, 58
  status, 36, 212
  traders, 98
  washing, 16
  'white blouse', 211
  widows, 20, 22
  see also occupational identity
epilepsy, 172, 174
  see also sickness
European Union, 211
Evandrou, M., 237
Evers, Helen, 196, 198

family reconstitution, 14, 48–9
family structure
  extended, 139
  multiple, 139
  nuclear, 122, 134–5, 139
  see also co-residence; household heads;
    household structure
famine, 58
fashion, 217, 220–3
  see also cosmetics

Feinson, Marjorie, 238
femme covert, 97
Fennell, Graham, 197
fertility, 43, 59, 72, 112, 125, 143
  see also demography
filial duties, 16–17, 70, 75, 77, 81, 121,
    122, 131
  see also intergenerational relations
fraternities, religious, 25
friendly societies, 26
  see also provisions for the elderly
friends, 16–17, 35, 59, 70, 104, 109,
    180
  never-married women, 104
Froide, Amy M., 7, 9, 234
funerals, 19–20, 26

Gentilcore, David, 53
gerontocracy, 59
Gilbert, G.N., 237
godmother, 167
Goffman, Erving, 196
grandchildren, 77, 103, 125, 151, 216
grandparents, 126, 166–7, 186, 203,
    226
greensickness, 107
Guyot, R.S., 233

Hajnal, John, 140
Harley, D., 235
Harper, S., 236
Harrison, William, 21, 53
Hazan, Haim, 5, 60
health, 8, 31, 32, 58, 71
  declining, 79
  ill, 59, 90, 93, 94, 167, 176, 213, 214
  medical theory, 93
  see also sickness
Hill, Bridget, 32
Hippocrates, 51–2
history, 188, 189
  cultural, 2
  oral, 9
  micro, 48
  social, 32
  women, 2
Home for Incurable and Infirm Women,
    170–4, 180
Home for Infirm and Elderly Women,
    172–3, 180
hospital visitor, 172
hospitals, 114, 175, 180, 199

hot flushes, 54
household heads, 116–19
  elderly, 111–15
  gendered, 117–18
  never-married women, 102
  occupation, 157
  status, 119
  women, 94–6, 116–19, 124, 174
  see also family structure
household listings, 4, 112–13, 116–20,
    122
  form, 117
  methodology, 112
household structure, 4–5, 10, 31–2,
    111–31
  alone, 143–4
  controlled by vestry, 22, 25, 115
  dependence, 9–10, 124
  elderly, 3, 22, 38, 85fn, 112, 122
  'empty nest', 124, 136
  Europe, 10, 139, 147–51
  extended, 18, 23, 119
  gender balancing, 153–7
  gendered, 125, 161
  historiography, 140, 233–4
  independent, 9–10, 190
  London, 18
  methodology, 126–30, 141–3
  never-married women, 94–7
  non-kin, 143–4
  poor, 34
  rural, 147–8, 149–50, 154
  status, 139
  urban, 147–8, 149–50, 154–7
  see also co-residence; family structure;
    spinster clustering
housewifery, 53
Hufton, Olwen, 8, 234
humoural theory, 46, 53
Hunt, E.H., 237
Hussey, Steve, 9

images, old age, 5–6, 11, 209
'income packaging', 214
Industrial Home for Girls, 173
Industrial Revolution, 9
industrialisation, 5
inflation, 17
intergenerational relations, 69, 75, 77,
    81, 86, 103, 111, 121–2,
    125–6, 212
inter vivos transfer, 114

Johansen, H.C., 234
Johnson, Paul, 236, 237
jointure, 76
Jones, W.W., 233
Joseph Rowntree Foundation, 214
Josselin, Ralph, 47

Kertzer, David, 22, 23, 234
kin
  historiography, 112–13
  never-married women, 102–3, 104
  see also co-residence; networks;
    provisions for the elderly
King, Peter, 115
Kugler, Anne, 6, 9

labour market, 38
labourers, 36
Laslett, Peter, 16–17, 22, 112–13, 139,
    140, 151, 187, 233–4, 236, 237
letters, 4
life expectancy, 91, 207–8, 221
  increasing, 207–9
  see also demography; longevity
lifecycle, 2, 45, 47, 58, 73, 78, 90–1,
    119, 157, 227
  employment, 36
  female, 46
  gendered, 212
  rural, 56
living standards, improved, 209, 213,
    214
lodgers, 18, 22–3, 34, 95, 96, 124, 126,
    141
  prohibited, 22
  see also survival strategies
The London and Middlesex Chantry
    Certificate (1548), 15
longevity, 92, 93, 161, 179, 211, 214,
    227
  marital status, 92–3
  see also life expectancy

Macfarlane, A., 139
Macnicol, J., 236
Maimonides, 43, 61
marital status, 31, 32, 89, 90, 104
marriage, 8, 32–5, 38, 48, 67, 77, 90,
    94, 120, 179, 192, 225
  age, 112
  elderly, 34, 72
  European, 35

marriage (*continued*)
  female agency, 32–5
  motives, 32–5
  mutual comfort, 72
  never-married women, 167
  poverty, 35
  procreation, 72
  sex ratios, 34
  stereotypes, 34
  timing, 32
  unequal, 8, 34–9
Mass Observation, 10, 219, 227
matriarchy, 4, 61fn
medicine, 20
  care, 13
  funding, 207–8
memoirs, 47
menopause, 5, 36, 43, 48, 52–9, 60,
    63fn, 72, 78, 92, 96, 104
  age, 52
  exercise, 58
  historiography, 52–3
  marital status, 92, 108
  medical understanding, 53, 90, 91, 93,
    217–19
  physical changes, 51–2, 53, 59, 92
  symptoms, 54
  visual changes, 54–9
  see also climacteric
Metropolitan Poor Act (1867), 171
microsimulation, 125
  see also demography; population
    modelling
migration, 34, 38, 125
  elderly, 140
Minois, G., 4, 232
'modernisation theory', 234
moneylending, 97
mortality, 14, 32, 104, 112, 125, 143,
    149
  see also demography
motherhood, 68
  see also childrearing
Muir, Edward, 6

National Spinsters' Pensions Association,
    210
  see also never-married women;
    pensions
National Union of Women Workers, 177
neighbourhood, 16–17
  never-married women, 102–3

neighbours, 16–17, 59, 126, 175
  see also networks
neolocalism, 113
networks
  female, 17
  friend, 13
  kin, 13, 17, 179
  neighbours, 13
  see also friends; kin; neighbours
never-married women, 35–7, 90, 95,
    214, 234
  discrimination, 211
  elderly, 100–1
  historiography, 89–90
  independence, 96
  non-conformity, 100–1
  parish rate, 102
  patriarchy, 95–6
  pensions, 210–11
  percentage of population, 90
  politics, 101
  see also spinster
'nuclear–hardship' hypothesis, 16, 237
'nuclear reincorporation system', 22–3

occupational identity, 36, 37, 99, 119,
    172, 178, 197–8
  see also employment
old age, 75, 84, 88
  age-appropriate behaviour, 72–4,
    227
  authority, 75, 80, 81, 89–90
  concealment, 216–18
  defined, 1, 3, 4–5, 14–17, 48, 91
  dependence, 83, 196, 223
  depression, 89, 103
  de-sexed, 73–4
  diversity, 3, 5, 45, 60, 67, 90, 201,
    213, 221
  family duties, 69, 77, 79
  gendered, 43, 48, 104
  'green', 5, 43, 49, 51, 60
  historiography, 1–4, 31–2, 44–8, 104,
    118–19, 232–8
  independent, 5, 7, 9, 11, 89–90, 94,
    97, 100, 104, 113–14, 131, 179,
    181, 187, 191, 193, 215, 218–19,
    223–4
  legal exemptions, 47–8
  mental capability, 83, 100, 223
  methodology, 43, 49
  models, 66, 73, 80

old age (*continued*)
nature, 79, 89–90, 104, 106, 216–18
the old-old, 5, 7, 49, 71, 219
onset, 43–4, 46, 49, 51, 59, 60, 92, 132fn, 139, 209–14, 218, 220–3, 226, 232–3
physical appearance, 44, 51, 52, 73, 74, 79, 108, 167, 217, 220, 221, 222
physical decline, 45, 66, 81, 82, 83, 169, 181, 212, 214, 218–19
prescriptive literature, 78
religion, 3
respect, 1, 75, 77, 90
self-fashioning, 6, 68, 84
self-images, 11, 47, 66, 182
sex, 89, 93, 96
stages, 3, 5, 46, 47, 51, 60, 67, 71, 73, 116, 221
status, 43, 104, 166
social isolation, 48, 70, 74, 89
wisdom, 74, 96
young-old, 5, 43,129
see also ageing
Old Age Pensions Act (1908), 210
osteoporosis, 55–6, 8
see also ageing; elderly
Ottaway, Susannah, 10
overseers of the poor, 24, 59, 115

Palazzi, Maura, 234
parish reconstitution, 48–9
Parkinson's disease, 225
Parliament, 7, 18, 21, 26, 68
patriarchy, 7, 34, 38
patronage, 75
pauper nurses, 170, 178
Pelling, Margaret, 8, 22, 235, 238
pensionable age, 210, 211, 213
pensions, 11, 44, 181, 200, 210–11, 215
means-tested, 210, 214
state, 193, 201, 209, 210, 212
see also poor relief
personal materials, 47, 66, 188
pew seating, 24–5
Phillipson, Chris, 196
poor, the, 7, 14, 24, 25, 43, 49, 51, 187
diet, 58
sex ratios, 35–6
types, 13, 21, 24
unworthy, 19, 21

worthy, 13, 19, 24, 170
see also poverty
poor law, 32, 33, 115, 120–1, 121, 140, 187, 190, 193, 198, 210
Poor Law Guardian, 175–8, 188
Poor Law Unions, 193–4
poor relief, 13, 17, 20, 21–2, 31, 49, 59, 115, 180, 202, 212
age-preferencing, 116
age qualification, 210
discriminatory, 13, 17, 19, 25
pension, 8, 17, 24, 25, 59
reform, 13, 17, 22, 26
religious, 14, 18–19
Protestant, 14, 17, 19
Roman Catholic, 13, 18–20
rent, 20, 21, 115
see also poverty
population, 14, 17–18, 44, 139
see also demography
population modelling, 43, 45, 143
see also microsimulation
poverty, 8, 13, 14, 17, 33, 55–6, 59, 89, 171, 188, 192, 237
causes, 17, 171, 214
death, 210
diet, 56
fear, 5, 8–9, 75–6
gendered, 31–9
old age, 5, 8, 17, 168, 181, 190, 214, 227
rural, 56, 60
see also poor relief
prayers for the dead, 7, 13, 18, 20
Premo, T.L., 233
prescriptive literature, 8, 67, 68
prostitution, 38
provisions for the elderly, 13, 18, 22, 25, 75–7, 140, 237
annuities, 92, 97
community ('collectivity'), 18, 23, 126, 193, 202–3
friends, 35, 140, 216
investments, 97
kin, 9–10, 17, 18, 25, 35, 38, 94–6, 98, 103, 104, 111–12, 114, 120–2, 127, 131, 168, 171–2, 168, 179–80, 212, 215, 216
residential homes, 187, 224
servants, 96, 104, 140–1
spouse, 120
wills, 25, 92

provisions for the elderly (*continued*)
  workhouse, 168, 186, 190, 193, 194,
    202
  see also collectivity; friendly society
public assistance institutions, 192, 195
purgatory, 7, 18, 25

Quadagno, Jill, 234

reading, 69, 71, 83, 168
religion, 3, 5–7, 66, 74–5, 79, 80, 82,
    84, 87fn, 94, 101, 178
  never-married women, 100, 102, 104
  non-conformity, 93,
  Protestant Reformation, 13, 19, 20,
    25
  Roman Catholicism, 13, 19
remarriage, 17, 31, 33, 38, 39, 72, 77,
    120, 149, 151, 161
removal, 188, 192, 198
reproduction, 51, 52, 53, 72
  see also demography
reputation, 23, 74
residence, 23, 127
residential independence, 113, 114, 115,
    116, 119, 140, 224, 225
  see also household structure
residential isolation, 112, 117, 140, 142,
    143, 161, 215–16
  see also household structure
residential security, 127–30
retirement, 7–8, 11, 44, 45, 51, 67, 70,
    70–1, 71, 74, 78, 89, 100, 102,
    114, 191, 210, 212, 213, 223,
    227
Richardson, Ruth, 199
Robin, J., 237
Roebuck, J., 232, 233, 235
Rosenthal, Joel, 4, 5, 232, 233
Rowntree, B. Seebohm, 214
Russell, C., 233

Schen, Claire S., 4, 6–7, 8
Schofield, Roger, 31, 44
Schwartz, Robert, 8
Sear, Elizabeth I., 233
Second Wave Feminists, 2, 3
self-image, old age, 218–19, 220–1, 224,
    225
self-sufficiency, 16, 25, 196
servant, 126, 141, 168, 171, 173
  see also employment

Shahar, Shulamith, 46, 47–8, 49–50,
    232
Sharpe, Pamela, 234
sickness, 13, 17, 18–19, 22, 34, 37, 58,
    59, 71, 80, 83, 126, 178, 201,
    216
  see also epilepsy
Smith, Daniel Scott, 234
Smith, J.E., 235
Smith, Richard M., 14, 235, 237, 238
social status, 32, 67, 157–60, 178
sociology, 9, 127, 195–6
Sokoll, Tom, 119
spinster clustering, 96, 234
  see also household structure
spinsters, 33, 35, 99, 173, 105fn, 211
  see also never-married women
spouse desertion, 120
standard of living, 8, 9
Stearns, Peter, 14, 233, 235
stereotypes, 9, 113, 114, 120–1, 122
  female morality, 95
  marriage, 34
  never-married women, 89, 102, 105
  old age, 1, 3, 8, 10, 68, 72, 74, 80, 81,
    83–4, 89, 94, 101, 103, 207,
    208, 213, 224–5, 227, 255–6
  old men, 33
  sexuality, 95
  workhouse, 187, 189, 193–5, 198, 199
Strachey, Ray, 168
sugar, 56
suicide, 68
Summers, A., 235
sumptuary laws, 53
survival strategies, 8, 214–16

tax listings, 91
taxes, never-married women, 101–2
Thane, Pat, 2, 4, 7, 10, 232, 236, 237,
    238
Thatcher, Margaret, 213
theft, 99
Thomas, Keith, 232
Thomson, David, 121, 237
titles
  derogatory, 89
  'father', 49, 60
  gendered, 51
  'goodwife', 15, 16
  honorific, 49, 50, 51, 52, 60
  'master', 49

titles (*continued*)
  'mistress', 15, 16, 49, 70
  'mother', 15–16, 17, 27, 49, 60
  'Mrs', 172
  'old', 49, 60
  'old maid', 89, 91
  'sir', 49
  status, 49
  'widow', 15–17
Todd, Barbara, 32, 33, 113, 235
towns, 38
  feminisation, 33–4
Townsend, Peter, 195, 236
Troyansky, D., 235, 238

unemployment, 36–7, 213

vestry, 14, 23
Vicinus, Martha, 234
visiting, 70, 75
  the poor, 168–71

Wales, T., 238
Wall, Richard, 10, 112–13, 234
Webb
  Beatrice, 218–19
  Sidney, 218
Whigs, 68, 75
widow, 15, 17, 23, 32, 33, 35, 38, 46,
    48, 75, 76, 78, 81, 97, 102–4,
    162, 173, 214, 224, 234–5
  loneliness, 89
  poor, 19, 33
widower, 34, 188
widowhood, 9, 17, 66, 67, 76, 81, 90,
    111, 120, 214
  household duties, 77
  independence, 33, 68, 79
  provisions for, 75–7
  see also provisions for the elderly

wills, 4, 14
Wilson, A., 235
wisdom, 73, 74, 81
witches, 54, 235
womb, wandering, 53
women
  historiography, 2–4, 89–90, 232
  golden age, 2
workhouse, 9, 92, 114, 115, 117, 166,
    171, 133fn
  abolition, 187
  age-related privileges, 176, 194, 195
  architecture, 199
  causes of entry, 201
  conditions, 169–70, 175, 176–7, 181,
    194, 196–7, 197, 198
  death, 198–9
  demographics, 170, 196, 200–1, 201–2
  diet, 170, 176, 194–5, 196–7, 198
  fear, 5, 186, 187, 189, 190–1, 192,
    195–9, 200, 202, 203
  health care, 170, 195
  historiography, 202
  illness, 178
  mental illness, 172
  old age, 5, 169, 193, 194
  percentage elderly, 192–4, 203
  reform, 166, 187, 193, 195, 196
  rural, 194
  tobacco, 176–7
  visitors, 170, 172
Workhouse Nursing Association,
    173–4, 175, 177
Working Men's College, 174
Wrigley, E.A., 31, 44
World Wars, 146, 212, 219
Wright, S.J., 235

youth, 46, 52, 74, 95
  cult of, 73, 217